A HUMAN RIGHTS APPROACH TO DEVELOPMENT

BY

Julia Häusermann
LLB, LLM, Barrister-at-Law
President
Rights and Humanity

A Discussion Paper Commissioned by
The Department for International Development
of the UK Government
in preparation of the Government White Paper on International
Development

RIGHTS AND HUMANITY
London

Rights and Humanity, 65A Swinton Street, London WC1X 9NT

ISBN 1 874680 02 7

First published 1998

Commissioned by the Department for International Development (DFID), 94 Victoria Street, London SW1E 5JL

Typesetting, layout and design by Kate Herbert 0181 211 8943
Printed in Great Britain for Rights and Humanity, 65A Swinton Street, London WC1X 9NT by The KPC Group, South Willesborough, Ashford, Kent TN24 0BP

Photo Credits

The Author and Rights and Humanity would like to acknowledge and thank all those who contributed photgraphs this publication:

Front Cover Photo	"Dignity in the Face of Human Suffering"	Julia Häusermann, Rights and Humanity
Opposite Chapter 1	Young Girl Selling Garlands, Bangladesh, 1992	Shafiqul Alam/Drik/DFID
Opposite Chapter 2	Fled the Civil War in Liberia in 1993, now aged 93	Mary Dunawoogy Amnesty International
Opposite Chapter 3	Bhutanese refugee living in Eastern Napal Camp	Mala Guring/ Amnesty International
Opposite Chapter 4	Nedara 10 years old, Gaza	Dave Clark/DFID
Opposite Chapter 5	Al-Amal Village Society for homeless Boys	Lorraine Chittock/DFID
Opposite Chapter 6	Mother and Child, hospital in Teresina, Brazil	Sarah Errington/DFID
Opposite Chapter 7	Young girl, Jamaica	DFID
Opposite Chapter 8	Female Student learning to steer sheep	Lorraine Chittock/DFID
Opposite Chapter 9	Elderly Woman, Former Yugoslavia, SE Europe	Morgan Langham/DFID

In Memory of my Father
Claude Kingsley Rudkin Jones

And Dedicated to
All People Living in Poverty and Social Isolation

The Rt. Hon. Clare Short MP
Secretary of State for International
Development

FOREWARD BY THE SECRETARY OF STATE
FOR INTERNATIONAL DEVELOPMENT

The British Government has declared its intention to place human rights at the centre of its international development and foreign policies.

Most people identify "human rights" with liberty and physical security. Too often, people are unaware that "human rights" include the economic and social rights necessary for dignified living – the right to adequate health, food, water, education and work. Both sets of rights are given equal priority in the Universal Declaration on Human Rights, the fiftieth anniversary of which we celebrate this year.

The entire work of my Department which we have defined in the White Paper as "eliminating poverty" through sustainable development, is work for the realisation of human rights.

It is not true as some would argue that the alternatives are full bellies or human rights. The right to food, work, healthcare and the expression of views and needs are all human rights. These describe the fundamental rights of every human being on the planet. Nowhere are they fully realised.

I welcome the publication of this paper by Rights and Humanity as a useful reference for those wishing to enhance their understanding of the link between the realisation of human rights and the elimination of poverty.

The Rt. Hon. Clare Short MP

Mrs Julia Häusermann
LLB, LLM, Barrister-at-Law
President
Rights and Humanity

ABOUT THE AUTHOR

The Author is an international human rights lawyer and development worker. Her formal studies were first in Law, and then in Politics, Philosophy and Economics. Her doctoral research at St. Anthony's College, Oxford University, was in International Relations under the title "The International Response to Refugee Crises". It focused on the question of whether assistance to refugees should be strictly relief aid or have development objectives. Her field research was in the Horn of Africa and the Occupied Territories of the Middle East.

She has been working in the field of humanitarian relief and development for twenty years, and has combined this work with research and lecturing in Law, Human Rights and Refugee Studies. As a result of her experiences in Africa during the 1982/3 famine, she began to articulate and work for the implementation of a human rights approach as a tool to prevent and relieve the suffering of people living in poverty and social isolation.

She is the founder and President of Rights and Humanity, the International Movement for the Promotion and Realisation of Human Rights. Rights and Humanity was established in 1986 to tackle the plight of people living in poverty and social isolation, of whom women form the majority.

The Author is much involved in helping to develop UN and governmental policies in the field of human rights and development, and frequently acts as a consultant in this field for UN and other international bodies. In this capacity, she has been a pioneer in promoting a human rights approach to development, and in developing strategies for the inclusion of respect for human rights in public policy.

The Author has served on a number of UK Government delegations to international conferences. These have included the World Conference on Human Rights in Vienna in 1993, and the Fourth World Conference on Women in 1995.

At Beijing, she negotiated between the Islamic states and the Vatican, on the one hand, and the European Union and other Western countries, on the other, promoting agreement on a number of controversial paragraphs of the Beijing Declaration and Platform for Action relating to health and human rights.

As a member of the World Health Organisation's delegation to the World Summit for Social Development in Copenhagen in 1995, Mrs. Häusermann was responsible for drafting the references to health and human rights in the Declaration and Programme of Action, and for ensuring that respect for human rights was recognised as a basis for social development.

In the same year, she was invited to address the South African Constitutional

Assembly and to advise on the incorporation of economic and social rights into the section containing the Bill of Rights in the new Constitution.

Mrs. Häusermann is a member of two influential bodies established by the World Health Organisation – the Task Force on Health in Development and the Global Commission on Women's Health. As a result of her work, both bodies have adopted a human rights approach. This is now reflected in WHO's 9th General Programme of Work, and a human rights approach to health has been recommended in the Renewed Health for All Strategy. In December 1997, the Author chaired a World Health Organisation Informal Consultation on Health and Human Rights, which was the first time that WHO had brought together international experts in the fields of human rights, international law and public health, to examine health and human rights.

In 1992, as a visiting lecturer at Essex University in the UK, the Author established and taught the first master's degree course on economic, social and cultural rights, and was also instrumental in the establishment of the Jagiellonian University Centre for Human Rights in Cracow, Poland. In the same year she established the Human Rights and Development Forum to promote dialogue between human rights NGOs, development groups and governmental agencies.

Mrs. Häusermann is known for her efforts to promote a multi-faith and multi-cultural consensus on human rights and responsibilities and her work in strengthening commitment to the universality of human rights. She writes and lectures widely on human rights, focusing on human rights and development, health and human rights, the rights of refugees, economic, social and cultural rights, and the human rights implications of the HIV/AIDS pandemic.

CONTENTS

ABBREVIATIONS

AIDS	Acquired Immune Deficiency Syndrome	ILO	International Labour Organisation
ART	Article (of an international instrument, such as the Universal Declaration)	NGO	Non-governmental organisation
		OAS	Organisation of American States
CAT	Convention Against Torture and Other Forms of Cruel, Inhuman, or Degrading Treatment or Punishment (1984)	ODA	Overseas Development Administration (now DFID); or used to denote official development assistance
CEDAW	Convention on the Elimination of all Forms of Discrimination Against Women (1979)	OECD/DAC	Organisation of Economic Co-operation and Development /Development Assistance Committee
CERD	Convention on the Elimination of Racial Discrimination (1965)	PLWA	People living with AIDS
CRC	Convention on the Rights of the Child (1989)	RT. HON.	The Right Honourable, a British title of respect for a Member of Parliament
DFID	Department for International Development (UK)	SDD	Social Development Division of the UK Department for International Development
EU	European Union		
FAO	Food and Agriculture Organisation	STD	Sexually transmitted disease
FCO	Foreign and Commonwealth Office (UK)	UNICEF	United Nations International Children's Emergency Fund
GNP	Gross National Product	UNHCR	United Nations High Commissioner for Refugees
HIV	Human Immuno-deficiency Virus	UDHR	Universal Declaration of Human Rights (1948)
HRH	His/Her Royal Highness	UN	United Nations
ICCPR	International Covenant on Civil and Political Rights (1966)	UNDP	United Nations Development Programme
ICESCR	International Covenant on Economic, Social, and Cultural Rights (1966)	UNESCO	United Nations Educational, Scientific and Cultural Organisation
IFIs	International Financial Institutions (i.e. the International Monetary Fund or World Bank)	WHO	World Health Organisation
		WTO	World Trade Organisation

PREFACE

This Discussion Paper was commissioned by the Department for International Development in preparation of the Government's White Paper on International Development, published in the Autumn of 1997. It is intended to help articulate a human rights approach to development and to explain some of the issues involved.

The Paper was written during a few weeks in July 1997. Time constraints did not permit new research or reading, rather I was requested to draw on my own experience. The Paper therefore reflects and builds on both my own experience and that of Rights and Humanity.

Rights and Humanity adopts an approach based both on internationally recognised human **rights**, and on the principles of **humanity** which act as a common bond between peoples – compassion, tolerance, mutual respect, and solidarity. Its multi-faith and multi-cultural composition has been particularly helpful in strengthening commitment to the principle of the universality of human rights, and in promoting the realisation of women's rights in Islamic countries. For further information about Rights and Humanity please see Annex 5.

This Paper approaches human rights from a different slant to that normally found in human rights text books, in order to draw out the most relevant features in the context of development. In many ways it breaks new ground. It reflects my understanding of existing international human rights law as well as my own interpretation of how this should apply in the context of development. The approach promoted in this paper is one that Rights and Humanity has been using throughout its first decade. This pro-active approach to promoting human rights as a basis for health and human development is gaining increasing support from governments, UN agencies and representatives of civil society throughout the world, and is reflected in the UN Secretary General's call for human rights to be mainstreamed across the work of the Organisation.

This Paper is offered by Rights and Humanity as a contribution towards the thinking in this field. At the request of the Department for International Development (DFID), this version of the Paper includes answers to some of the questions most frequently raised concerning a human rights approach to development (see Annex 1). The opportunity has also been taken to add a new chapter on the wider relationship between human rights and foreign policy (Chapter 4), and an introduction setting the human rights approach to development in the context of the current global situation and proposals to mainstream human rights throughout the work of the United Nations system.

I am most grateful for the support and encouragement of Dr Rosalind Eyben and Isobel Doig in the Social Development Division of DFID, and to the many people who have commented on an earlier draft, including Annabel Grant, Sarah Hovell, Monica Vincent and Roger Wilson of DFID, David Campbell, of the Human Rights Policy Department of the Foreign and Commonwealth Office and Wendy Thomas, Director of Population Concern and a UK Trustee of Rights and Humanity. I should also like to thank Polly Vizard for discussing with me Amartya Sen's entitlements theory, and Catherine Mulholland and Isobel Monreal, of WHO, for their insights in relation to the sections on health. Finally, I owe a great debt of gratitude to my colleagues at Rights and Humanity, who have worked so hard to bring this paper to publication. My thanks go to Christine Fougére, Eugenia Sidereas, Sian Lazar, Ben James, Kate Herbert, Spencer Blundell and Christine Neale. I am also grateful to Sofia Iqbal, George Pulikuythil and Kate Dron for holding the fort at Rights and Humanity whilst this publication took priority.

All errors and omissions naturally remain my own.

Julia Häusermann
London, March 1998.

I should appreciate receiving any comments on this Paper, at the following address:

Rights and Humanity
65A Swinton Street
London WC1X 9NT
United Kingdom
e-mail: rights.humanity@pop3.poptel.org.uk

EXECUTIVE SUMMARY

" Human rights are for everyone: as much for people living in poverty and social isolation, as for the visible and articulate."

HUMAN NEED

More than one quarter of the world's population lives in poverty as measured by UNDP's human poverty index - denied the vital rights to adequate food, shelter and access to health care. A large proportion, the majority of whom are women, have very limited access to income and resources. Racism, intolerance, social prejudice and discrimination in all their forms cause untold misery. These people are excluded from the benefits of the rapid progress which is the hallmark of our time.

In the last decade, the economic and social conditions of the most disadvantaged members of our human family have deteriorated alarmingly, whilst at the same time, one quarter of the world's population has benefited from dramatic improvement in the quality of life. Although much progress has been made in the last few decades, the gap between rich and poor has doubled, with the poorest fifth of the world's population receiving 1.4% of the global income, whilst the richest fifth receives 85%. The impact of these disparities, both within and between countries, is dramatic, and is a cause of immense human suffering. It is also a cause of instability and potential conflict. Eliminating poverty therefore requires a commitment to overcoming the inequalities and inequities that are its foundation. This is a fundamental function of human rights protection.

Human rights are for everyone, as much for people living in poverty and social isolation as for the visible and articulate. The human rights framework therefore provides an important basis for poverty elimination.

The Secretary of State for International Development has called for a human rights approach to human development. In her speech on 30 June 1997 at the University of Manchester, the Rt. Hon. Clare Short stated:

> "We need a human rights based approach which ensures that our development effort will serve the needs and the rights of poor people. Human rights are central to development and to our objective of poverty elimination. However, our idea of human rights may need some adjustment."

RELATIONSHIP BETWEEN HUMAN RIGHTS AND DEVELOPMENT

The relationship between human rights and development is at once both simple and complex. The negative relationship between them is self-evident. The very definition of poverty used by UNDP - poverty means the denial of choices and opportunities for a tolerable life – is a statement of denial of the human rights and freedoms necessary to enjoy a quality of life commensurate with human dignity. In situations of conflict, violence, and other mass violations of human rights, the opportunities for development are remote. Even the provision of emergency humanitarian relief may be impeded.

Poverty is a violation of human rights

Poverty is itself a violation of human rights. In addition, it causes vulnerability to a denial of a wide range of other human rights. Conversely, discrimination, inequalities and other violations exacerbate poverty. The relationship between human rights, poverty and development is thus circular. Breaking this circle by securing the enjoyment of human rights by people living in poverty and social isolation is an effective tool in overcoming poverty and in promoting human development.

Discrimination and inequality are part of the root causes of impoverishment, instability, conflict, and displacement

This paper concentrates on overcoming these inequalities and inequities. It explores the contribution that a focus on ensuring enjoyment by poor people of their fundamental human rights can play in achieving the aims of poverty elimination and an improved quality of life.

Considerable progress has been made over the last decade in complementing the focus on economic development and indicators such as GNP, with a concern for *human development* and indicators aimed at beginning the difficult task of measuring the quality of life. This paradigm shift is profound, but remains fraught with the complications of measuring quality rather than just quantity. Integrating indicators designed to measure the progressive realisation of such rights as the rights to food, housing, education, and health could play a key role in these efforts.

An important step was taken at the World Summit for Social Development when it was recognised that the enjoyment of human rights was a fundamental basis for social development. In the present paper the Author argues that a human rights approach to development provides a coherent framework both for the planning, implementation and evaluation of development programmes, and for ensuring cross-sectoral policy coherence in support of the rights and needs of poor people.

FROM LIBERTY RIGHTS TO HUMAN RIGHTS

As the Secretary of State acknowledged in her speech, for a human rights approach to be effectively used in development co-operation, an adjustment in the way we view human rights is required.

Western history has been greatly influenced by the rights theories of liberal philosophers giving rise to our belief in such rights as the rights to life, liberty and property, and freedom of assembly, expression, conscience and opinion.

We have brought this libertarian tradition into our perception of human rights. This has been both a strength and a weakness. We have tended to make the assumption that international human rights are the same as liberty rights, just subjected to the inevitable globalisation process that is the mark of our times. But this is both an over simplification, and an incorrect basis for a deeper understanding of international human rights. Internationally recognised human rights *include liberty rights,* but are *not limited* to these rights.

A fuller understanding of human rights does not require us to lose sight of those liberties and freedoms so dear to the British tradition, but neither should we allow our particular history and experience to mar our appreciation of the wider scope of human rights as a basis for human development.

Human rights are not just about liberty and freedoms but also about equality, equity and justice

SOME BASIC PRINCIPLES OF HUMAN RIGHTS AND HUMANITY

Human rights are premised on the *equal worth and dignity of all human beings*, and of our *common humanity.*

Equal worth:	**EQUALITY *and the principle of* NON-DISCRIMINATION**
	***Requires* EQUALITY OF OPPORTUNITY *and* EQUITABLE ACCESS TO PUBLIC RESOURCES**
	PARTICIPATION
Dignity:	**LIBERTY** **FREEDOM OF CHOICE** **AUTONOMY**
Common Humanity:	**MUTUAL RESPECT** **SOLIDARITY**

WHAT ARE HUMAN RIGHTS?

Human rights are a global vision backed by state obligations. The term "human rights" refers to those rights that have been recognised by the global community and protected by international legal instruments.

Human rights reflect the moral conscience of the world and
the highest common aspiration that
everyone should live in liberty and
free from want and fear

A common understanding of human rights and freedoms has been achieved and given legal force in international conventions. Human rights have thus been identified and defined, together with the obligations of states to ensure their realisation. However, the subject of human rights remains dynamic in the sense that the norms and standards are constantly being strengthened and expanded.

Internationally recognised human rights developed by the world community over the last 50 years, and protected by UN and other international conventions:

- represent a global agreement that recognition of the inherent dignity and of the equal and inalienable rights of all members of the human family is the foundation of freedom, justice and peace in the world

- establish defined obligations of states for ensuring the enjoyment of human rights which are the basis for human development

- provide a coherent theoretical and legal framework for practical action at the national and international levels

- establish objective criteria for good governance and the implementation of bi-lateral and multi-lateral development co-operation

- provide a sound basis for participation and partnerships in development

In 1948 the UN adopted the *Universal Declaration of Human Rights* as a "common standard of achievement for all peoples". Its provisions have been given legal force in two key covenants that were adopted in 1966 and came into force in 1976. Two further treaties provide additional protection of the rights of women and children. These four key texts are:

- *The International Covenant on Economic, Social and Cultural Rights*
- *The International Covenant on Civil and Political Rights*
- *The Convention on the Elimination of All Forms of Discrimination Against Women*
- *The Convention on the Rights of the Child*

Human rights include all those rights essential for human survival, physical security, liberty and development in dignity.

Human rights necessary for survival and dignified living include:

- the rights to life and liberty
- the right to a standard of living adequate for health and wellbeing of the individual and his/her family, including food and housing, and the right to the continuous improvements of living conditions
- the right to social protection in times of need
- the right to the highest attainable standard of physical and mental health
- the right to work and to just and favourable conditions of work
- the rights to privacy and to family life

Human rights also cover those rights and freedoms necessary for human dignity, creativity and intellectual and spiritual development e.g.

- the right to education and to access to information
- freedoms of religion, opinion, speech, and expression
- freedom of association
- the right to participate in the political process
- the right to participate in cultural life

They also include those rights necessary for liberty and physical security e.g.:

- freedom from slavery or servitude
- the right to security of person (physical integrity)
- the right to be free from arbitrary arrest or imprisonment
- freedom from torture and from cruel, inhuman or degrading treatment or punishment

Cross-cutting are the twin principles of ***equal rights*** of women and men, and the ***prohibition of discrimination*** of any kind on the grounds of race, colour, sex, language, religion, political or other opinion, national or social origin, property, birth or other status.

In recognition of the impact that the international system has on the enjoyment by individuals of their rights, Article 28 of the Universal Declaration of Human Rights states "everyone is entitled to a social and international order in which the rights and freedoms set forth in this Declaration can be fully realized".

All human rights are relevant
to securing a quality of life
commensurate with human dignity

During times of conflict the Geneva Conventions of August 1949, and their additional protocols, of June 1977, provide protection to combatants and civilians alike. They are founded on the ideal of respect for the individual and his/her dignity. Although not regarded as part of human rights law *per se*, these Conventions are relevant within the context of DFID's emergency assistance.

A further relevant text is the Convention Relating to the Status of Refugees, adopted by the UN on 28th July, 1951. It provides international protection for refugees who are outside their country of nationality and who are, owing to well-founded fear of being persecuted, unwilling to return to it.

THE UNIVERSALITY OF HUMAN RIGHTS

Human rights are inherent. ***Every man, woman and child is entitled to enjoy his or her human rights*** simply by virtue of being human. It is this ***universality of human rights*** which distinguishes them from other types of rights – such as citizenship rights or contractual rights.

The term universality of human rights is used to refer to the fact that every state throughout the world has a duty to respect and protect the human rights contained in international documents. These rights form a core minimum standard to be observed by all states, whatever their level of economic or political development.

HIERARCHIES AND THE INDIVISIBILITY OF HUMAN RIGHTS

There is a tendency to try to list human rights in order of their importance. However, any attempt at creating hierarchies of rights is doomed to failure. Each time one attempts to hold up a human right as being the most fundamental, it is possible to find another right that must be enjoyed as a pre-requisite of realisation of the right first identified. Human rights advocates therefore prefer not to get into the game of trying to construct hierarchies or to identify so-called "core human rights".

All human rights are core. Denial of one right invariably impedes enjoyment of others. For example, a malnourished girl will be unable to concentrate at school and to benefit from the education that would assist her to participate fully in civil society and the democratic process. This is why UN documents refer to the enjoyment of all human rights as being ***indivisible, interdependent and inter-related.***

STATE OBLIGATIONS

Once a state has adopted a particular international convention it is obliged to promote and protect the human rights covered by the convention. States are obliged to secure the human rights of ***all*** people within its jurisdiction, and not just its own citizens. However, under the International Covenant on Economic, Social and Cultural Rights, developing countries, with due regard to human rights and their national economy, may determine to what extent they would guarantee the economic rights recognised in the Covenant to non-nationals.

The constitutions of most modern states contain at least some provisions to protect human rights, and many states have introduced specific laws to prevent discrimination and protect individuals' human rights, either generally, or in specific circumstances.

The precise obligations of states vary from convention to convention. But in general terms, each state can be regarded as being obliged to **respect** the human rights of all people within its jurisdiction, to **protect** individuals from abuse by third parties, to **promote** respect for human rights in its laws, policies and actions, and to take the necessary measures to **ensure realisation** of human rights in practice. For instance, the International Covenant on Civil and Political Rights requires States Parties "to adopt such legislative or other measures as may be necessary to give effect to the rights recognized in the ...Covenant".

PROGRESSIVE ACHIEVEMENT OF ECONOMIC, SOCIAL AND CULTURAL RIGHTS

Recognising that states may not be able to ensure instant realisation of all economic, social and cultural rights, the International Covenant on these rights provides that all States Parties are obliged to **take steps, to the maximum of available resources, towards the progressive achievement** of the full realisation of these rights.

The provision concerning "the progressive achievement" of the full realisation of economic, social and cultural rights is very important. The South African Constitution of 1996 provides an excellent example of how these rights and obligations might be incorporated into national law. For example, article 26(1) of the Constitution states that everyone has the right to have access to adequate housing. Article 26(2) requires the state to take reasonable legal and other measures, within its available resources, to achieve the progressive realisation of the right. Article 26(3) provides that no one may be evicted from their home, or have their home demolished, without an order of court made after consideration of all of the relevant circumstances. In addition, no legislation may permit arbitrary evictions.

MARGIN OF DISCRETION

There is what is called a **margin of discretion,** which allows a state to choose the manner in which it fulfils its obligations under international human rights law. A state is able to decide which policies to adopt in order to ensure realisation of the rights within the context of the political, economic, religious, cultural, and other characteristics of the state. For example, if the obligation in question is that of guaranteeing access to health care for all, it is left to the state to decide **how** medical care is to be provided, i.e. whether through a public health service, private insurance schemes, or a mixture of the two.

Nevertheless, the state remains under a duty to act, and is accountable to the international community for its implementation of this obligation. The margin of discretion does not mean that a state is free to pick and choose which rights to implement, or that it might ignore the rights of a particular section of the community.

INTERNATIONAL OBLIGATIONS

As members of the UN, states have also undertaken to take joint and separate action to promote:

- Human rights globally, and
- Social development and better standards of living.

COST IMPLICATIONS OF
ECONOMIC, SOCIAL AND
CULTURAL RIGHTS

In the past, it has sometimes been argued that civil and political rights are of a different category to economic, social and cultural rights, and that the former merely imposes negative obligations on the state to abstain from a particular course of action. Economic, social and cultural rights, it is argued, impose positive obligations which have cost implications for states. ***Each of the two branches of rights impose both negative and positive obligations.*** There is no such thing as a free right. All human rights, civil and political as much as economic, social and cultural, involve expense.

For example, protecting civil and political rights involves state expenditure in terms of the provision and training of a police force, the establishment of a criminal process and prison service, and the operation of courts. Even the right to vote involves a state in costs, in terms of administration and the provision of accessible polling stations.

Conversely, the protection of many economic and social rights can be achieved simply by the introduction of appropriate legislation. For instance law can be introduced to prohibit discrimination in the enjoyment of these rights, to protect workers' rights and trade union rights, and the freedoms indispensable for scientific research and creative activity; as well as to prohibit such violations as arbitrary evictions from homes, or other actions which impede livelihood and survival.

HUMAN RIGHTS: A LEGITIMATE INTERNATIONAL CONCERN

Critics of integrating human rights into international policy tend to rely on three main arguments: that cultural relativity prohibits universal human rights; that a human rights approach to foreign policy, including development cooperation, results in the imposition of western values on other states; and that such a policy amounts to an interference in the domestic affairs of a foreign state.

This paper refutes these arguments. It argues that there is both a moral and legal duty on Britain and other states to be concerned with respect for human rights globally, and that the promotion of, and respect for, human rights is a legitimate subject of both foreign policy and development cooperation.

Furthermore, such a concern is called for by enlightened self-interest. Respect for human rights creates the climate in which political and economic freedoms can be exercised. This in turn supports international prosperity and trade. It also contributes to peace and security, and to the prevention of conflict and forced displacement.

CULTURAL RELATIVITY NO
BAR TO THE UNIVERSALITY
OF HUMAN RIGHTS

Recognition of the immense cultural diversity in the world leads some to question whether it is possible to talk about the "universal" system of values on which human rights norms are based. Some anthropologists and philosophers use the theory of cultural relativity to question the universal nature of human rights. Anthropologists have observed and documented the very real differences in the values acceptable within different groups of people and which have framed their cultures and traditions. It is a primary principle of anthropology not to import any value judgement from one culture to another.

However, individuals from faiths and cultures throughout the world do recognise universal human rights, and the 171 states participating at the World Conference on Human Rights in Vienna, 1993, agreed that "the universal nature of these rights and freedoms is beyond question".

To hold states accountable for their performance
with relation to global human rights standards
is not to impose the value system
of any one part of the world on another
but to refer to universal values
based on the distilled knowledge
and wisdom of all our cultures

CONVERGING AGENDA

The UN has recognised the link between human rights and development in various conferences as well as in the Declaration on the Right to Development and the Declaration on Social Progress and Development (see Annex 4). Particular sectoral conferences have used specific rights as their basis. These include the World Conference on Education for All: Meeting Learning Needs, Jomtien, 1990; the International Conference on Population and Development, Cairo, 1994; and the Fourth World Conference on Women, Beijing, 1995. The UN's recognition of this link culminated in the World Summit on Social Development, Copenhagen, 1995, which recognised enjoyment of human rights as a fundamental basis for development.

The human rights approach to development complements existing theories and models of development, for example Amartya Sen's entitlements and capabilities theory. There is a natural complementarity between the entitlement/capabilities approach which looks at the **problem** of poverty from the **point of view of the poor** and a human rights approach which combines a **vision of what ought to be** with an **emphasis on choices for people** and **solutions** in terms of the **steps to be taken** to achieve human rights and thereby development.

A similar cross-fertilisation of ideas between human rights and development can be seen in recent struggles for democracy and human rights within civil societies in a number of countries, and in the good governance policies introduced into development cooperation during the 1980's.

WHAT IS MEANT BY A HUMAN RIGHTS APPROACH TO DEVELOPMENT?

A human rights approach to development stresses **liberty, equality** and **empowerment.** This approach:

- Puts people first and promotes **human-centred development**

- Recognises the **inherent dignity** of every human being without distinction

- Recognises and promotes **equality between women and men**

- Promotes **equal opportunities and choices** for all so that everyone can develop their own unique potential and have a chance to contribute to development and social progress

- Promotes national and international systems based on **economic equity,** equity in the **access to public resources,** and **social justice**

- Promotes **mutual respect** between peoples as a basis for peace, justice, conflict resolution, and sustainable human development.

Past theories of the linkage between human rights and development have tended to focus on the linkages in terms of negative aid conditionalities, with the possibility of a withdrawal of aid in case of massive violations. This paper advocates a different approach to linking aid and human rights. It promotes a **positive** approach – one that will utilise human rights principles and legal norms as a **coherent framework for concrete action to eliminate poverty** and to achieve **sustainable improvement in the quality of life of the poor and socially isolated.** It is one that moves the focus:

- from **human wrongs** to **human rights**
- from **handouts** to **empowerment**
- from **charity** to **rights.**

It is an approach which requires a revitalisation of economic, social and cultural rights, and a recognition of their equal priority with civil and political rights. It is an agenda that moves from the **rhetoric** of human rights to **pragmatism** by promoting:

- Analysis of the enjoyment of human rights by poor people within a given state including, where possible, analysis in partnership with poor people of their actual experience with respect to enjoyment and denial of their fundamental human rights, using the yardstick of international human rights norms and standards

- Identification of the steps which states are obliged to take, in order to comply both with their legal obligations under international law, and also with the political commitments they have undertaken in this regard at international conferences

- Assistance to partner countries through development co-operation to help them to meet these obligations

- Identification of the best practices in achieving realisation of the rights affected and improving the quality of life of poor people

- The political will and allocation of sufficient resources to implement the strategies identified.

WHAT IS THE BENEFIT OF A HUMAN RIGHTS APPROACH?

Human rights and development are interdependent and mutually re-enforcing. Enjoyment of such rights as the right to education, to access to health care and services, to equitable property ownership, and to just and safe conditions of work, form the very basis upon which individuals can ensure for themselves and their families a standard of living adequate for health and wellbeing. People denied these rights will be unlikely to be able to provide for themselves, thus increasing poverty and expanding the need for welfare safety nets.

If these rights were to be fully realised without discrimination, the primary goals of human development would be met.

Respect for individual rights
not only sustains the development of individuals
but also encourages the initiative required
for economic and social progress

Securing human rights helps protect people from impoverishment and enables them to develop in accordance with their equal rights and dignity. A society which excludes any part of its whole membership from participation in its progress is an impoverished society.

Securing the realisation of women's human rights
on a basis of equality with men
is an essential pre-requisite
for sustainable development.

THE EXAMPLE OF HEALTH

Economic and social inequalities and inequities are observable through differential health status. Poor health frequently reflects poverty and social marginalisation. In turn, poor health exacerbates impoverishment and disadvantage. Health status indicators - which are measurable - are thus frequently an indication of the denial of the human rights that are so vital for survival and development in dignity.

The human rights approach to development
addresses the structural inequities
that cause impoverishment

The claim to the highest attainable standard of physical and mental health cannot be ensured simply through the provision of health care services – vital though these are. It requires drastic action to address the structural, legal, cultural and other inequities, and functional barriers, which deny the majority of the world's population full enjoyment of this right. It calls for the implementation of an effective common agenda, across sectors, for the promotion and protection of health and for the equitable betterment of the human condition.

Human Rights Approach to Development:

Is Coherent:

Human rights norms have been developed by the world community, and the associated obligations have been ***voluntarily undertaken by states.*** Human rights theory and law cover most aspects of human life, and provide a coherent framework for human development and international co-operation.

Contributes vision:

A human rights approach to development adds the vision of what development is striving to achieve. It sets the aim as the realisation by all people of all their human rights recognised under international law. It highlights the gap between what is and what ***ought to be.*** It is closing this gap by ***raising up*** the quality of people's lives to the standard required by human rights law, that should be the goal and raison d'etre of development efforts.

Provides an essential foundation for development:

A human rights approach focuses attention on the inequities, discrimination and systemic violations which are part of the causes of poverty and marginalisation. Its stress on ***participation*** and respect for individual ***autonomy*** and ***dignity*** strengthens development partnerships. Human rights norms provide ***benchmarks for measuring progress*** in the improvement of the quality of life.

The lens of human rights appraisal can provide insight into the ***causes of poverty.***

In so far as poverty results from a denial of human rights, international law helps identify the ***solutions,*** by setting out the steps to be taken by states to ensure enjoyment of human rights.

Is successful:

There are many examples of successful examples in which human rights have been integrated into development projects. These range from women's rights projects to those designed to empower street children to seek and enjoy their human rights. As the HIV/AIDS pandemic has shown, ***respect for human rights saves lives.***

Empowers, promotes self respect and is sustainable in human terms:

Individuals are **empowered** by learning of their human rights. By seeing the divide between the rights that they should enjoy and their current position, they are encouraged to seek their human rights.

People living in poverty or social isolation are encouraged to think of themselves as Victors rather than Victims (e.g. people living with HIV/AIDS).

Participation in the identification of priorities and in the planning, implementation and evaluation of projects helps poor people to have a sense of **ownership** in the process and outcome of development.

The Time is Right:

The agenda of development and human rights communities have been gradually converging. There is synergy in a joint approach to overcoming the inequities which subject millions of people to poverty.

There is increasing recognition of the need to ensure that the interests and rights of individuals are placed firmly at the centre of international and national policies.

A human rights approach to development partnerships is participatory, inclusive and pro-poor

PRACTICAL APPLICATION OF THE HUMAN RIGHTS APPROACH

The integration of human rights into development co-operation can be considered within seven inter-linked categories:

- Using development aid as a carrot and/or stick to promote respect for human rights and overcome abuse, i.e. linking development aid with positive and negative conditionalities

- Promoting human rights in times of conflict through an integration of a human rights component in peace-making and peace-keeping operations, and in the context of humanitarian assistance

- Assisting development partner governments to restructure their institutions, laws and policies in order to ensure good governance, the rule of law and respect for human rights at the national level - i.e. good governance projects

- Providing direct support for what might be called "traditional" human rights projects - e.g. projects aimed at promoting the independence of the judiciary, freedom of the press, police training in human rights and gender sensitivity, support for institutions of civil society concerned with the protection and promotion of human rights, and projects aimed at securing women's rights and the rights of the child

- Providing technical and financial assistance to partner governments in accordance with the obligation of international co-operation to achieve the progressive realisation of the rights recognised in the International Covenant on Economic, Social and Cultural Rights

- Addressing the structural, legal, socio-cultural and other systemic inequalities and the various manifestations of discrimination which are part of the root cause of impoverishment and social exclusion

- Mainstreaming human rights norms and principles into donors' policies, target setting, methodology and evaluation of development co-operation, and into the manner in which they perceive and conduct partnerships with Governments and civil society institutions in the developing world

The borders between these various categories are not distinct, and all may be regarded as making up the human rights approach to development proposed here.

Many donors are indeed already engaged to a greater or lesser extent with the first four categories. What is new in this Discussion Paper is the articulation of the remaining three categories.

This Discussion Paper advocates that, whilst negative conditionality may, as a last resort, continue to have its place in the range of options available to donors, this should not provide the focus of a human rights approach to development. Rather, development co-operation should be used for the positive promotion of human rights through projects falling within the remaining categories. Human rights should be mainstreamed throughout DFID's policies and programmes.

HUMAN RIGHTS: AN ESSENTIAL TOOL FOR HUMAN DEVELOPMENT

Human rights principles and legal standards provide an effective tool for achieving human development by providing objective global criteria for:

- identification of the causes of poverty and social isolation, and of appropriate solutions

- development of appropriate methodology for the design, implementation, and evaluation of development programmes and for the full participation of intended beneficiaries

- establishment of a focus on the poor and disadvantaged in order to implement equality

- ensuring priority attention is given to poverty elimination through implementation of the human rights of women and children, and a focus on the realisation of the right to an adequate standard of living, including food and housing, and the rights to education and health

- development and use of appropriate benchmarks and indicators for measuring progress in improving the quality of life of poor people in poor countries.

In this Author's view, not only is a human rights approach *effective,* but it is *essential* to the achievement of lasting progress.

WILL THE HUMAN RIGHTS APPROACH TO DEVELOPMENT BE WELCOMED BY DFID'S PARTNERS?

The human rights approach to development outlined in this Discussion Paper is likely to be welcomed by Southern partners, many of whom have long been advocating for greater attention to be paid to economic, social and cultural rights, and to other rights essential for development.

A positive approach to ensuring the realisation of the human rights of poor people will help overcome the perception held by some Southern countries that the West/North is only interested in criticising violations of human rights - particularly civil and political rights. The approach advocated in this Paper could, therefore, play an important role in overcoming the politicisation of human rights which has separated the world across East/West and North/South divisions.

OUTCOMES OF THE HUMAN RIGHTS APPROACH

A Human Rights Approach to Development will:

- Provide a firm foundation for sustainable human development

- Provide poor people with the opportunities and tools to help themselves, by focusing on securing enjoyment of their human rights

- Strengthen their self-esteem, and empower them to seek change and to participate in the wider development of their societies

- Focus development efforts on the needs identified by poor people themselves, and encourage their participation at every stage of planning, implementation, monitoring, and evaluation

- Prompt the legal reform essential to ensure the protection of human rights at the national level, and the practical implementation of these rights in state policy and action

- Prompt the social transformation necessary to overcome cultural causes of inequity – particularly the denial of women's equality with men

- Help assure a healthy and educated population able to contribute to the further economic and social development of their societies

- Promote human and institutional capacity building based on responsible citizenship, democracy and good governance

- Assist partner governments to develop the capacity to take the steps necessary to ensure to all the realisation of economic, social and cultural rights

- Raise global awareness of human rights and responsibilities and of the obligations of states in this regard, and prompt a better understanding of human rights and responsibilities among the public - in donor countries as well as in developing countries

- Focus on the implementation of the collective international obligations of securing universal respect for human rights, and of international co-operation to ensure the progressive realisation of economic, social and cultural rights

- Lead to further clarification of the effective steps which can be taken to ensure realisation by all people of all their human rights, thus providing guidance for the development of both national and international strategies

- Help bridge the divide between the aspiration of human rights instruments and the reality of people's lives

- Ensure that the concerns and contributions of people living in poverty and social isolation are adequately taken into account in the setting of human rights standards and in other normative development, and

- Help build the climate of respect for human rights, which is the foundation of development, democracy and peace.

A human rights approach is about putting people first

For this Author, a human rights approach to international policy is about putting people first. It is about putting the interests of people above economic and other interests.

It is not about applying some abstract philosophical concept; nor just about taking the moral high ground.

It is about ensuring that the impact of the policies are fully considered, and that they are designed to put the interests of people firmly at the top of the agenda. A human rights approach is about conducting international relations in a way that recognises that improving the quality of life enjoyed by individuals is central to an ethical foreign policy and development agenda.

The human rights approach advocated in this Paper reflects a vision of a just and equitable world in which all people can live in dignity and achieve their full potential.

1 INTRODUCTION

"...the peoples of the United Nations have in the Charter reaffirmed their faith in fundamental human rights, in the dignity and worth of the human person and in the equal rights of men and women and have determined to promote social progress and better standards of life in larger freedom."

Preamble, Universal Declaration of Human Rights

FIFTIETH ANNIVERSARY OF THE UNIVERSAL DECLARATION OF HUMAN RIGHTS

This year, 1998, marks the fiftieth anniversary of the Universal Declaration of Human Rights, the ground breaking document proclaimed by the United Nations on 10 December 1948, as a "common standard of achievement for all peoples and all nations." The Declaration was adopted in recognition that a world in which all human beings enjoy liberty and freedom from want and fear is the highest aspiration of all human kind.

Yet throughout the world, millions of people suffer daily from the ravages of deprivation and social exclusion, denied enjoyment of their human rights and dignity, and excluded from the benefits of the rapid progress which is a hallmark of our time.

The UN Development Programme (UNDP) estimates that a quarter of our human family lives in poverty, denied the vital rights to adequate food, drinking water, shelter and access to health care. Racism, intolerance, social prejudice and discrimination in all its forms cause untold misery. Oppression and injustice, like hunger, know no political boundaries, and no one region of the world has a monopoly on human rights - either in terms of respect or abuse.

A decade ago the former Secretary General of the Commonwealth, Sir Shridath Ramphal emphasised the stark and growing gap between those who "have" and those who "have not". In a paper presented at a Rights and Humanity lecture to mark the fortieth anniversary of the Universal Declaration he stated:

> "The unmet challenge of mass poverty and starvation in our one world, among one people, should surely be a matter for universal reproach. It cannot be a time for complacency; still less for smug satisfaction - unless misperception is distorting judgement. To further human development we must first understand our human condition better - more honestly, more dispassionately ... and we have to begin to understand our human reality and the need for change responsive to it. We must come to accept, in our hearts no less than our minds, our condition as a human family; our oneness; our inseparable humanity. We must begin to acknowledge what our unspoken judgement tell us, namely, that the national sovereignty which we prize so much may now be producing diminishing returns; that the adversarial system of relations between states which we superimposed on it, or which it imposed on us, is becoming not just outdated but far, far too dangerous.

We must acknowledge that, whatever our other achievements, our overall human development is at best dangerously uneven, at worst downright primitive."[1]

As we mark the fiftieth anniversary of the Universal Declaration one might be forgiven for asking what progress we have made. We are all aware that there remain immense problems.

More than one billion people live in abject poverty, most of whom go hungry every day. A large proportion, the majority of whom are women, have very limited access to income, resources, education, health care or nutrition, particularly in Africa and the least developed countries.[2]

In the last decade, the economic and social conditions of the most disadvantaged members of our human family have deteriorated alarmingly, whilst at the same time one quarter of the world's population have benefited from dramatic improvement in the quality of life.

- More than one-quarter of the world's population lives in poverty as measured by UNPD's human poverty index. This comprises three forms of deprivation – in the realms of life longevity, knowledge, and living standard. About one-third, 1.3 billion people, live on incomes of less than $1 a day.

- Eastern Europe and the countries of the Commonwealth of Independent States (CIS) have seen the greatest deterioration in the past decade. Income poverty has spread from a small part of their population to about a third, around 120 million people survive below a poverty line of $4 a day.

- In industrial countries, more than 100 million people live below the income poverty line, set at half the individual median income. Thirty-seven million are jobless.[3]

CURRENT GLOBAL SITUATION

In 1995, 117 Heads of State and Government met together with UN agencies, NGOs and other key actors of the world community to develop and adopt a strategy to overcome poverty and promote social development worldwide. The World Summit for Social Development, in calling for renewed emphasis to be paid to eradicating poverty, recognised that the world's current social situation was characterised by:

- Globalisation: a consequence of increased human mobility which has brought incredible prosperity and cultural exchange for some, but has also been accompanied by intensified poverty, unemployment and social disintegration for the majority. Threats to human well-being such as environmental degradation have also expanded beyond national boundaries and pose a greater risk than ever.

---

[1] Sir Shridath Ramphal, *Furthering Human Development*, paper presented at a series of lectures to mark the fortieth anniversary of the Universal Declaration of Human Rights organised by Rights and Humanity in co-operation with the United Nations Centre, London, at the Houses of Parliament, Westminster. Extracts from the speech are reproduced in *Rights and Humanity, Celebrating the Universal Declaration of Human Rights and the Achievements of the United Nations,* 1986.
[2] Copenhagen Declaration and Programme of Action adopted by the World Summit for Social Development, 1995. Paragraph 16 (b).
[3] Human Development Report, 1997.

- The growing polarisation between rich and poor: poverty, unemployment and social disintegration result in isolation, marginalisation and violence. Many people (including vulnerable groups like uneducated women and children) face growing insecurity about the future. Despite the fact that some developing nations may be catching up in the race for technological and economic advancement, the gap between the industrialised and the developing nations has widened over the last 10 years.

- Over 120 million people worldwide are officially unemployed and many more are underemployed. Many young people, including some with formal educational qualifications, have no hope of finding productive work.

- People with disabilities are one of the world's largest minorities at one in ten; they are often forced into poverty by lack of suitable employment, and face severe social isolation.

- Millions of people across the world, with a concentration in sub-Saharan Africa and the Middle East, are internally displaced or refugees from their home countries; the social consequences have a critical effect on the social stability and development of their home countries, their host countries, and their entire region.

- Widespread problems like the illicit drugs and arms trade, corruption, foreign occupation, terrorism, xenophobia and endemic communicable and chronic disease are major threats to social order and destroy the stability of families and society. Co-ordination and co-operation at the national level, and especially at the regional and international level are still underdeveloped and must be addressed urgently.[4]

PROGRESS IS ACHIEVABLE

At the same time, social indicators prove that progress is achievable. The United Nations Development Programme's 1997 Human Development Report points to the progress that has been made in the last half century. In almost all countries, poverty has been reduced in some respects. It highlights the accelerated progress in reducing poverty in the 20th century that began in Europe and North America in the 19th century as a result of the industrial revolution, with rising incomes, improvements in public health and education and eventually programmes of social security – what it refers to as the first Great Ascent from poverty and human deprivation. UNDP regards the second Great Ascent as beginning in the 1950s in the developing countries. The end of colonialism was followed by improvements in education and health and accelerated economic development that led to dramatic declines in poverty. By the end of the 20th century some 3 - 4 billion of the world's people will have experienced substantial improvements in their standard of living, and about 4 - 5 billion will have access to basic education and health care.

[4] Copenhagen Declaration and Programme of Action, adopted by the World Summit for Social Development, 1995.

The Human Development Report cites some of the key indicators of human development in the last few decades as follows:

- Since 1960, in little more than a generation, child death rates in developing countries have been more than halved.

- Malnutrition rates have declined by almost a third.

- The proportion of children out of primary school has fallen from more than half to less than a quarter.

- The share of rural families without access to safe water has fallen from nine-tenths to about a quarter.

Progress is to be found in all regions of the world:

- China, and another 14 countries or states with populations that add up to more than 1.6 billion, have halved the proportion of their people living below the national income poverty line in less than 20 years.

- Ten more countries, with almost another billion people, have reduced the proportion of their people in income poverty by a quarter or more.

- Beyond mere advances in income, there has been great progress in all these countries in life expectancy and access to basic social services.[5]

GROWING DISPARITIES BETWEEN RICH AND POOR

Set against these considerable achievements are the growing disparities between rich and poor.

Whilst the percentage of people living in poverty might have fallen in some countries, during the last three decades the gap between rich and poor has doubled, with the poorest fifth of the world's population receiving 1.4% of the global income, whilst the richest fifth receives 85%. The impact of these disparities, both within and between countries, is dramatic and is a cause of immense human suffering. It is also a cause of instability and potential conflict. Eliminating poverty therefore requires a commitment to overcoming the inequalities and inequities which are its foundation. The knock-on affect of these inequalities and related problems was recognised by the World Summit:

> "There is general agreement that persistent widespread poverty, as well as serious social and gender inequities, have significant influences on and are in turn influenced by demographic parameters, such as population growth, structure and distri-bution. There is also agreement that unsustainable consumption and production patterns are contributing to the unsustainable use of natural resources and environmental degradation, as well as to the reinforcement of social inequities and poverty, with the above-mentioned consequences for demographic parameters." [6]

5 Human Development Report, 1997, UNDP, page 2.

6 Copenhagen Declaration and Programme of Action adopted by the World Summit for Social Development, 1995, paragraph 20.

Inequality and inequities are human rights violations. We know that they are also potential causes of conflict and violence. Some regard poverty and exclusion itself as a form of violence, one which breeds further violence. As Padre Bruno Sechi, a pioneer of the education and empowerment movement for children living and working on the street in Brazil, has written:

> "The first and greatest violence is the systematic exclusion of people - a great number of people - by society. From this violence other violence directly and indirectly flows. Where you exclude, you must establish instruments to control those who are excluded so that they don't invade the peace of those who have access to opportunities and wealth." [7]

WHY DO THESE INEQUITIES PREVAIL?

If, as the UNDP statistics indicate, we have the knowledge and technical ability to reduce, even eliminate, poverty, why is it that poverty is so prevalent? Why is so little being done for the poor and isolated when the links between economic and social exclusion and conflict are so blatant? Why is the international community not up in arms about these violations of human rights?

The answers to these and similar questions may lie in the assumptions, perceptions and priorities which have dominated international thinking for the last couple of decades. There has been a tendency to oversimplify poverty - to see it simply in terms of income poverty rather than the myriad of deprivations and denials which make people feel impoverished and disempowered.

To some extent the political ideologies of the cold war have been replaced by economic ideologies which place reliance on the 'free' market to deliver human wellbeing. This has tended to put economic interests before human welfare and further marginalised the poor. In turn, this weakening of social cohesion undermines future prosperity.

It has become increasingly recognised that a concern for economic growth needs to be matched by attention to ensuring equitable distribution and access to public resources. We clearly need additional safeguards to protect the interests of the poor and vulnerable.

This is a fundamental function of human rights protection. Human rights are for everyone, as much for people living in poverty and social isolation as for the visible and articulate. The human rights framework therefore provides an important basis for poverty elimination.

THE SECRETARY-GENERAL'S UN REFORM PROPOSAL

The need to reappraise international policy has prompted the recent reforms within the UN.

[7] Quoted in *Children for Social Change: Education for citizenship of street and working children in Brazil,* by Anthony Swift·

As the Secretary-General, Kofi Annan, has recognised, developments in the present decade have underscored the fact that human rights are inherent to the promotion of peace, security, economic prosperity and social equity. In his report to the General Assembly, "Renewing the United Nations: A Program for Reform", the Secretary-General states "a major task for the future will be to enhance the human rights programme and integrate it into the broad range of the Organization's activities, including in the development and humanitarian affairs areas."

As a result, the issue of human rights has been designated as cutting across the four substantive fields of the Secretariat's work programme (peace and security; economic and social affairs; development co-operation and humanitarian affairs) and will need to be integrated into all aspects of development co-operation. This will provide a solid institutional basis from which the new High Commissioner for Human Rights, Mary Robinson, might carry out her mandate to promote and protect the realisation of the right to development, and to enhance support from relevant bodies in the United Nations system for this purpose.

The High Commissioner for Human Rights has the main UN mandate in terms of human rights. But to some extent, all UN agencies are involved in the promotion and realisation of human rights.

The equal worth and dignity of every human being forms one of the basic tenets of the world organisation, and each UN body is involved in some way in promoting enjoyment of human rights. However, the nature of their involvement differs. Some offices and bodies are charged directly with the task of enumerating human rights and ensuring their protection by international law. Other UN bodies are mandated to assist governments, particularly those of less-economically developed countries, in ensuring the realisation of such rights as the right to food (FAO), shelter (Habitat), health (WHO), special protection for children (UNICEF), labour rights (ILO), the rights of refugess (UNHCR) and education and cultural rights (UNESCO).

SECURING HUMAN RIGHTS - A MORAL AND LEGAL IMPERATIVE

The term "rights" is being used with increasing frequency in a wide variety of settings. The term may be used to describe a legal right or a moral claim, or merely an aspiration on behalf of an individual or group. Development practitioners come across the term "rights" in various settings. For instance, those working in agricultural development are familiar with the term "animal rights" as a claim for humane treatment of animals, and the term "intellectual property rights" in the context of seed development, animal breeding and so forth. These various aspects of rights discourse can be distinguished from *human* rights which have their own history and legal protection, dealt with more fully in chapters 2 and 3 of this paper. It is for this reason that the Author refers to a "human rights" approach to development rather than a "rights-based" approach.

The term "human rights" is correctly used to refer to all those rights recognised by the international community as being the birthright of every human being. Human rights include all those rights and freedoms necessary for liberty and autonomy, physical integrity, survival, and the development of the full human potential. Many such human rights have now been protected by international legal texts.

The global consensus on human rights has its roots in the world's diverse philosophies, religions and cultures. It therefore represents a truly global agreement on the steps necessary to achieve a more equitable world in which everyone might live in accordance with their rights and dignity.

The belief in the equal worth and dignity of every human being has fuelled the fight for many social and political reforms. These include:

- the abolition of slavery

- the civil rights movement in the USA

- the political and economic emancipation of women

- freedom from colonialism and political oppression

- the struggles for the rights of the poor through social justice movements, such as those based on liberation theology

- recognition of the rights and dignity of indigenous peoples, and of minority and other groups frequently denied equal rights

- the overthrow of communist dictatorships through, for example, Poland's "velvet revolution"

- the ending of the South African *apartheid* regime

For the millions of individuals, non-governmental organisations and governmental agencies throughout the world campaigning for justice and equality, human rights standards represent the moral conscience of the world.

Since the end of the Second World War there has been a considerable development of global consensus on the scope and nature of human rights and freedoms, and the methods by which they might be protected and enforced. Human rights have now been brought together in a large number of international instruments adopted by states – both at the UN level and regionally.

By these instruments states hve accepted the obligations to protect, respect, promote and ensure realisation of human rights. As members of the UN, states have also undertaken a collective obligation to secure human rights globally and to promote social development and better standards or living. These obligations form a firm basis for international human rights protection and development co-operation.

THE APPROACH TAKEN IN THIS PAPER

This paper advocates the use of human rights principles and legal norms as a coherent framework for poverty elimination and for the achievement of sustainable improvement in the quality of life of poor and socially isolated people.

Development assistance and human rights have been linked for some time by donor agencies imposing negative and/or positive human rights condition-alities. The human rights approach advocated in the present Paper builds on the promotion of positive conditionalities, but goes further. It promotes the use of development co-operation to assist partners to secure the realisation of all human rights - economic, social and cultural as well as civil and political rights - and articulates a human rights approach to the manner in which aid is delivered. It therefore complements existing good governance policies. At the same time, it is recognised that in extreme circumstances, the cessation of development aid may remain necessary in times of conflict and large-scale human rights violations.

The human rights approach articulated here combines a vision of *what ought to be* with an *emphasis on choices for people* and *solutions* in terms of the *steps to be taken* to achieve human rights and thereby development.

In the present paper the Author concentrates more on the *positive* relationship between human rights and development. It explores the contribution that a focus on ensuring enjoyment by poor people of their human rights can play in achieving the aims of poverty elimination and an improved quality of life.

This paper argues that a human rights approach to development both provides a coherent framework for the planning, implementation and evaluation of development programmes, and for ensuring cross-sectoral policy coherence in support of the rights and needs of poor people.

Broad and wide-ranging as the list of internationally recognised human rights may be, these are underpinned by certain key principles, such as:

- Respect for **equality, human dignity and autonomy**.

- **Gender equity** - this means that women and men must enjoy equal rights and opportunities.

- **Participation** by which all people should have active, free and meaningful participation in public life, in the decisions that affect their lives, and in development and its outcomes.

- The principle of **non-discrimination**, which requires that no-one should be discriminated against in enjoyment of his or her rights including access to public resources.

There are great potential benefits to basing development efforts on interna-tionally recognised human rights norms, and these fundamental principles which underlie them, because they have been articulated and adopted by states through the world, and recognised by actors at all levels of civil society.

Three main themes permeate this paper:

- The enjoyment of all human rights – civil, cultural, economic, political and social – is necessary for human development

- Everyone is entitled to enjoyment of human rights – women as well as men, children as well as adults, minorities as well as the majority

- The human rights approach to development needs to be reflected in a coherent policy across all government departments, and, for credibility, needs to be matched by a commitment to securing enjoyment of these rights at home

The inequalities and discrimination suffered by people living in poverty and social isolation are clearly visible in health status indicators. Therefore, throughout this Paper, health is used as an example to illustrate the relationship between human rights and development.

THE WAY FORWARD

At the launch of the 1997 Human Development Report, the Secretary of State stated:

> "Many poor countries need to re-order their public expenditure in a way that generates more benefits for the poor and generates more beneficial economic growth. The old pro and anti state arguments are over. We need an enabling state to reduce poverty and it is the duty of all governments to ensure that this is provided. The report is realistic about the need for faster economic growth. Poverty will not be eliminated without growth, but growth needs to be pro-poor.

> "The technical challenges for economic management are large but we have learned much from the excesses of the bloated state followed by a period of market idolatry. We are now ready for a better era of sensible regulation and economic structures that benefit the poor. But the most fundamental constraint is probably political. The report is right to devote a whole chapter to the politics of poverty eradication. Perhaps the most important statement in the whole report is the observation that what is lacking is not the resources or the economic solutions but the political momentum to apply them to the central task. We now understand the need for partnerships to pursue collective action. As the report says, there is a need to mobilise broad and diverse support. When enough people rally to the cause we would as a generation see the beginning of the end of abject poverty as part of the human condition.

> We have made a start. The Human Development Report is itself evidence of that. Ideas are changing. We need now to build up the momentum. Setting targets and monitoring progress will help provide the fuel for effective advocacy and persuasion."[8]

Poverty elimination is not about handouts but about addressing the inequalities and discrimination which cause impoverishment

---

[8] Speech by the Rt. Hon. Clare Short MP, Secretary of State for International Development

There are grounds for optimism. Hope is to be found both in the successes listed by UNDP and also in the myriad of self help projects in poor communities throughout the world, and in our own deprived inner cities. We must not accept that poverty is inevitable. Everyone has a role to play in overcoming this denial of human rights and dignity: trade unions, landless rural workers' movements, squatters' associations, women's organisations, and all those working from the grass roots up, as well as those working at the international and national policy level. We need what UNICEF once called a "grand alliance." We need a global commitment to securing justice and equality for all.

PART I - THE HUMAN RIGHTS FRAMEWORK

CHAPTERS 2, 3 & 4

2 RE-FOCUSING OUR PERCEPTIONS

"At great cost we have learned the importance of caring for the Earth. We must also learn to care for those who live upon it... those millions who are tortured by starvation, or imprisoned behind the bars of prejudice and discrimination."

HRH Crown Prince Hassan of Jordan,
a Patron of Rights and Humanity

FROM LIBERTY RIGHTS TO HUMAN RIGHTS

The Secretary of State for International Development has called for a human rights approach to human development. In her speech on 30 June 1997, the Rt. Hon. Clare Short stated:

> "We need a human rights based approach which ensures that our development effort will serve the needs and the rights of poor people. Human rights are central to development and to our objective of poverty elimination. However, our idea of human rights may need some adjustment."

In the UK our perceptions of human rights tend to be limited to those liberties and freedoms so hard won in our own political history. We were brought up with knowledge of the Magna Carta, the struggles between monarchs and parliaments over freedom of speech, and the suffragette movement.

But what did we learn about the Universal Declaration of Human Rights? How well are we versed in the fundamental human rights necessary for survival and development in dignity? What knowledge do our children have of the struggles to secure the human rights of landless peasants, or of the girls in Afghanistan denied their rights to go to school?

In Britain, this has led to what Professor Kevin Boyle has recently called a "culture of liberty" rather than a culture of human rights.[1]

Our history has been greatly influenced by the rights theories of liberal philosophers giving rise to our belief in such rights as the rights to life, liberty and property, and freedom of assembly, expression, conscience and opinion. We have brought this libertarian tradition into our perception of human rights. This has been both a strength and a weakness.

We have tended to make the assumption that international human rights are the same as liberty rights, just subjected to the inevitable globalisation process that is the mark of our times.

But this is both an over simplification, and an incorrect basis for a deeper understanding of international human rights. Internationally recognised human rights *include* liberty rights, but are *not limited* to these rights.

A fuller understanding of human rights does not require us to lose sight of those liberties and freedoms so dear to the British tradition, but neither should we allow our particular history and experience to mar our appreciation of the wider scope of human rights as a basis for human development.

[1] Opening Statement at Workshop on Rights-based Approaches to Poverty Elimination, organised by DFID and the British Council, 18 July, 1997, London.

Another influential European contribution to the notion of international human rights is that of "natural law" or the "law of God" espoused by Sophocles and many generations of Christians. The idea of natural law as a universal moral law which transcends the laws of states is one by which European political thinking has been permeated for more than two thousand years.[2] Natural law was freely invoked during the Nuremburg trials as the legal basis of at least some of the elements of the indictments of Nazi leaders, and formed a background to much of the post-war thinking about human rights.

These European contributions to the notion of human rights were clearly influential in the drafting of the international texts. But they were not the only philosophies that shaped the global consensus. From Eastern thought came recognition that a full understanding of human rights requires us also to consider the duties which each of us owes to others. From the South came the notion of "peoples" rights, the claim for self-determination, and recognition of the importance of community.

Box 1
A Glance at the History of Human Rights in Western Thought

- Influence of early Natural Law Theories:
  see e.g. Sophocles' Antigone - 441 BC
- Medieval Christendom - *Natural Rights:*
  Law of God perceived to have priority over the law of man giving rise to natural rights
- Age of Enlightenment -17th and 18th century philosophies and political revolutions:
  Rights of Man:
  Locke, Rousseau, Kant,
  Bill of Rights 1689, England
  Declaration of Independence, 1776,
  and Constitution, 1789, America
  Declaration of the Rights of Man and the Citizen, 1791, France
- Challenge of 19th century Legal Positivism:
  e.g. Jeremy Bentham viewed natural rights as nonsense, and the concept of natural rights being "inalienable" as "nonsense upon stilts"
- 20th century Enthronement of *Human Rights* - establishment of the United Nations, 1945 and adoption in 1948 of the *Universal Declaration of Human Rights*

HUMAN RIGHTS: A CHALLENGE TO THE ABUSE OF STATE POWER AND TO ECONOMIC INJUSTICE

In Britain we first claimed rights in the face of abuse of state power, which was at the time vested in the monarch, claiming rights such as freedom of speech and freedom from arbitrary arrest and imprisonment. The French Revolution broadened the debate under the slogan "Liberty, Equality, and Fraternity"; whilst the American Revolution added the ephemeral "pursuit of happiness".

---

[2] For an historical, but outdated, view of human rights, see "What are Human Rights?" by Maurice Cranston, published by The Bodley Head, 1973.

But by the time the drafters of the Universal Declaration of Human Rights set to work, other claims were being made, widening the discourse from civil and political concerns to the economic, social and cultural realms. The global community recognised that it is equally essential to ensure that economic or social power does not dispossess the less powerful of their ability to feed and clothe themselves. Nor should individuals be obstructed in their efforts to obtain education or employment, and to achieve health and to develop their full potential.

It is this wider subject of human needs and aspirations that is called *human rights.* In human rights theory the human being is viewed holistically, and human rights touch on every aspect of life.

Human rights are not just about liberty and freedoms but also about equity and justice

INTERNATIONAL PROTECTION OF HUMAN RIGHTS

Today, the term "human rights" is used in connection with those rights which have been recognised by the global community and protected by international legal instruments. It is in this sense that the term is used in this paper. Human rights reflect the moral conscience of the world and the highest common aspiration that everyone should live free from want and fear and have the opportunity to develop in dignity.

Human rights include all those rights essential for human survival, physical security, and development in dignity.

All human rights are necessary to secure a quality of life commensurate with human dignity

International human rights also recognise that: "All peoples have the right of self-determination. By virtue of that right they freely determine their political status and freely pursue their economic, social and cultural development."[3]

In recognition of the impact that the international system has on the enjoyment by individuals of their rights, Article 28 of the Universal Declaration of Human Rights states:

> "Everyone is entitled to a social and international order in which the rights and freedoms set forth in this Declaration can be fully realized."

---

[3] Article 1, common to both the International Covenant on Economic, Social and Cultural Rights and the International Covenant on Civil and Political Rights.

Box 2
Summary of Human Rights

Human rights necessary for survival and dignified living include:

- the rights to life and liberty
- the right to a standard of living adequate for health and wellbeing of the individual and his/her family
- the right to social protection in times of need
- the right to the highest attainable standard of physical and mental health
- the right to work and to just and favourable conditions of work
- the rights to food, and housing
- the rights to privacy and to family life

Human rights also cover those rights and freedoms necessary for human dignity, creativity and intellectual and spiritual development e.g.

- the right to education and to access to information
- freedoms of religion, opinion, speech, and expression
- freedom of association
- the right to participate in the political process
- the right to participate in cultural life

They also include those rights necessary for liberty and physical security e.g.:

- freedom from slavery or servitude
- the right to security of person (physical integrity);
- the right to be free from arbitrary arrest or imprisonment
- freedom from torture and from cruel, inhuman or degrading treatment or punishment.

Cross-cutting are the twin principles of the *equal rights* of *women and men*, and the *prohibition of discrimination* of any kind as to race, colour, sex, language, religion, political or other opinion, national or social origin, property, birth or other status.

ECONOMIC UNDER-DEVELOPMENT NO EXCUSE FOR ABUSE OF HUMAN RIGHTS

States which are accused of violations are frequently, but by no means always, those that are facing the most acute poverty. In the past, some states have tried to argue that they were not obliged to respect human rights as their economic development had not yet reached the necessary level. This is a spurious claim that clearly needs to be countered.

As the opening words of the Vienna Declaration and Programme of Action, adopted by the World Conference on Human Rights[4] in 1993 state:

> "The World Conference on Human Rights reaffirms the solemn commitment of all States to fulfil their obligations to promote universal respect for, and observance and protection of all human rights and fundamental freedoms for all in accordance with the Charter of the United Nations, other instruments relating to human rights, and international law. The universal nature of these rights and freedoms is beyond question." (Paragraph 1)

Indeed, the Declaration was even more precise on this point. In Paragraph 10 it confirmed that:

> "While development facilitates the enjoyment of all human rights, the lack of development may not be invoked to justify the abridgement of internationally recognised human rights."[5]

CREDIBILITY, OBJECTIVITY AND BRINGING RIGHTS HOME

The need for objectivity in any human rights work is clear. So too is the need for transparency in the principles on which development co-operation is based. In addition, in order to have credibility on the world stage, concerns for human rights overseas needs to be matched by firm action to make them a reality at home. The Labour Government's commitment to "Bring Rights Home" is therefore particularly important.

For too long there has been a marked tendency in Northern government circles to consider human rights as an issue solely of foreign policy, rather than a framework of obligations for domestic law and policy. This was reflected by the membership of government delegations at the World Conference on Human Rights in Vienna. Northern delegations were led by foreign office personnel, and the Conference was chaired by the Austrian Minister of Foreign Affairs. In contrast, Southern delegations comprised Ministers of Justice and representatives of other ministries of home affairs.

The television pictures of atrocities around the world have created in our minds the impression that human rights concerns are things occurring "over there somewhere". We rarely perceive the shortcomings of our own society – homelessness, racial discrimination, discrimination faced by people with disabilities, the increasing economic and social marginalisation of the most vulnerable members of our society - as being human rights concerns.

IMPORTANCE OF OBJECTIVITY IN AID CONDITIONALITIES

Controversies have emerged over the growing tendency of aid donors to link development assistance to the promotion of democracy, strengthening of civil society, and respect for the rule of law and human rights. The World Bank, OECD and EU have all supported some aspects of negative conditionalities. These policies have been introduced by donors in an attempt to promote good governance and respect for human rights, by linking aid to a recipient's performance in these areas.

---

[4] Attended by 171 States.

[5] The Vienna Declaration and Programme of Action, adopted by the World Conference on Human Rights, 1993, paragraph 10.

At the risk of over-simplifying what is a complex issue, it would appear that the policy has not always been consistently applied by all donors. This has led to considerable feelings of injustice. Some countries regard themselves as unfairly penalised by a donor's insistence of conditionality, whilst they observe other states, with similar or worse human rights records, being supported by the same international donors. The continued large scale assistance to Israel during its occupation of the West Bank and Gaza Strip, despite widespread violations of the rights of Palestinians in the Occupied Territories – which were well documented by the UN – was a particular thorn in the side of states against which conditionalities were enforced.

In the lead up to the World Conference on Human Rights in 1993, a number of Asian countries were vocal in criticising this aid conditionality, and were joined by several African and Latin American states. Their criticism was that there were insufficient criteria for the application of this policy, and that it was not applied consistently and objectively.

The problem was exacerbated by the focus of the international community on civil and political rights to the virtual exclusion of economic, social and cultural rights. Countries in the South felt that their priorities and concerns were being ignored, and that the human rights agenda was being dominated by the more powerful Northern states. The South only experienced human rights discourse from the sharp end of condemnation.

As a result, these countries felt disengaged from the global vision of human rights. This threatened to impede consensus on the fundamental principle of the universality of human rights during the preparations for the World Conference. Consensus was ultimately reached by balancing the firm statement on universality of human rights[6] with an additional paragraph (paragraph 5) stating that:

> "All human rights are universal, indivisible and inter-dependent and inter-related. The international community must treat human rights globally in a fair and equal manner on the same footing, and with the same emphasis." [7]

It is ironic that a policy designed to promote respect for human rights had the ultimate effect of jeopardising the global consensus that is the very basis of the international protection of human rights. This experience points to the necessity of scrupulous objectivity in the application of negative conditionalities relating to human rights and development. The implications of this lesson for the current negotiations over a renewed Lomé Convention should be considered.

The new policy of the UK's Department for International Development (DFID), with its focus on assisting developing country partners to ensure realisation of fundamental economic, social and cultural rights, is likely to play a critical role in healing this rift. In so doing, it will strengthen not only our efforts to ensure human development, but also the global commitment to human rights.

---

[6] "The universal nature of these rights and freedoms is beyond question". Paragraph 1, Vienna Declaration and Programme of Action

[7] This solution was hammered out at a multi-faith, multi-cultural International Round Table which was organised by Rights and Humanity as an emergency measure just prior to the World Conference. It brought together diplomatic and NGO representatives from all regional groupings. The Round Table, entitled "Strengthening Commitment to the Universality of Human Rights" was supported by the UK Foreign and Commonwealth Office and other donors. It was held in Jordan under the Chairmanship of HRH Crown Prince Hassan.

It is as well, therefore, that DFID's human rights approach to development is matched by the Government's commitment to addressing the economic and social problems faced by many people in Britain today. In so doing, the agenda should incorporate a concern for all human rights for all people.

A starting point would be to strengthen human rights education, and to ensure that the commitment to entrench the European Convention on Human Rights in domestic law is expanded to include those economic, social and cultural rights that are the foundations on which our liberties are built. A failure to do so will be to perpetuate the inequalities and privileges that are a denial of human rights and dignity. It is to ignore the very people most in need of protection - to fail to hear the cries of the destitute and rejected.

A NEW APPROACH

The history of concern for human rights in foreign policy is long. As we have seen, in more recent times concern for human rights has also been integrated into development assistance. To a lesser or greater extent donors have promoted respect for human rights, democracy and good governance through both negative and positive conditionalities, and through direct support for what might be termed "traditional" human rights projects, such as ensuring freedom of the press and the independence of the judiciary. This paper goes further.

This paper advocates the
use of human rights principles and legal norms
as a coherent framework for poverty elimination
and for the achievement of sustainable improvement
in the quality of life of poor and socially isolated people

With its emphasis on human development and poverty elimination, this approach is one that is likely to appeal greatly to DFID's partners as it facilitates a constructive dialogue concerning human rights realisation, rather than an adversarial approach. Furthermore, it reflects the concerns and priorities of the South.

FROM HUMAN WRONGS TO HUMAN RIGHTS

For human rights to be an effective basis for development, we need to implement ***pro-active*** strategies to ensure their enjoyment by people living in poverty and social isolation.

All too often when people hear the term ***human rights*** they think of a whole set of human ***wrongs*** – massacres, torture, arbitrary detentions, political oppression, aggressive dictatorship, extra-judicial killings, denial of a free press.

Government officials involved in human rights are seldom engaged until there is an urgent need for international action to do something about serious violations. Their attention tends to be focused on the most visible sectors of society - for example political dissidents, or journalists denied freedom of the press.

The daily abuse of the human rights of the poor and socially marginalised is all but ignored.

At the NGO level, there are some human rights groups focussing on minority and vulnerable people, but their work tends to focus on ex-post facto condemnation of abuse, or on seeking legal redress for human rights abuse. Similarly, the preoccupation of the international community tends to be on political action to embarrass, condemn, or isolate an offending state in the hope that it will stop the abuses, and that other states will be hesitant to violate the human rights of their peoples.

There is an urgent need to complement this work with strategies aimed more specifically at both ***preventing*** violations, and ensuring the ***practical realisation*** of human rights by people living in poverty and social isolation[8].

We need to adopt an ***holistic approach*** which can embrace the interdependence of all human beings and the indivisibility of all human rights, and which can address economic and social inequalities, together with environmental concerns, in the idiom of human rights.

We need more public awareness programmes, backed up at the international level by the ratification of treaties and the commitment of resources.

But is this sufficient?

It seems that we need something more profound – a shift in our thinking so that ***humanity,*** rather than economic considerations, can be central to our goals both as governments and as individuals. The Government's stress on human rights will play a critical role in this regard.

As the UN High Commissioner for Human Rights, Mary Robinson, stated in 1993:

> "There are natural limits to the effectiveness of national and international laws. We must strive to make them more effective to be sure. But at the end of the road it is our capacity as individuals to be concerned and moved by injustice that is the real driving force behind the human rights movement. We must ensure that the seeds of such individual responsiveness are firmly planted and nourished in our national cultures. This must be the goal of national education programmes. We must elevate the rights of others to a higher platform in our collective conscience." [9]

FROM CHARITY TO RIGHTS

A human rights approach to development is one that moves the debate from ***handouts*** to ***empowerment;*** from ***charity,*** to securing the ***rights*** of people to the requirements, freedoms and choices necessary for life and development in dignity.

---

[8] This is the principle mandate of the International Movement of Rights and Humanity.
[9] Presentation of the Concluding Remarks by the General Rapporteur, Mary Robinson, then President of Ireland, at the inter-regional meeting organised by the Council of Europe in preparation of the World Conference on Human Rights, 1993.

This shift in emphasis is particularly important for the ***self-esteem*** of poor people. The experience of using such an approach has shown that people feel ***empowered.*** By contrasting their current situation with what they are entitled to pursuant to human rights law, they are encouraged to work for change and seek their rights.

How poor people are educated about their rights is therefore very important. It is important not to create unrealistic expectations. It is equally vital to avoid stirring up the type of resentment over their condition that breeds violent confrontation.

It is particularly pertinent that the approach taken by DFID is one of assistance to partner governments in meeting the human rights requirements of poor people. If adequate steps are being taken to ensure realisation of their rights by poor people, ***and if they are a part of this process for progress,*** conflict is unlikely to occur.

The violations of the rights of the poor in Latin America have taught us that it is the indifference to social and economic injustice, and a government's consistent failure to take steps towards the enjoyment of fundamental human rights by poor people that leads to conflict. Too often poor people claiming their human rights have been subjected to brutal repression by police and security forces.

If the opinions of poor people were sought on priorities, if schools were being built and health services provided, if measures were being introduced to protect vulnerable people from police or domestic violence, then there would be no need for the poor to march on capitals in protest.

It is the insecurity of the threatened elite which causes conflict not the claim of the poor to their human rights

Thus rather than being an obstacle to a human rights approach to development, the lessons of the struggle of land-less peasants, forest-dwellers and the urban poor in Latin America have taught us the urgency to match claims for civil and political rights with human development projects targeted at achieving their economic, social and cultural rights.

If the repression experienced by poverty-stricken people in Latin America is not to be repeated in other parts of the world, ways must be found to ensure all human rights are secured for all people.

Just as peace is a pre-requisite for development, development is necessary for peace. Development and peace can only be realised fully if they are realised simultaneously. Both are essential for the full realisation of human rights. Conversely, a focus on the realisation of human rights provides a firm foundation for peace and development.

Article 22 of the Universal Declaration of Human Rights confirms:

> "Everyone, as a member of society, has the right to social security and is entitled to realization, through national effort and international co-operation and in accordance with the organization and resources of each State, of the economic, social and cultural rights indispensable for his dignity and the free development of his personality."

In the past, governments of the North, while signing up to the rhetoric that economic, social and cultural rights are of equal importance, have done little to promote them in practice. To some extent this is the inheritance of the impact of Western liberal rights theories mentioned above. An important focus of the Government's human rights policy should, therefore, be to ensure that equal priority is given to all human rights in both political statements and action, at home and abroad.

As Professor Philip Alston, the Chair of the UN Committee on Economic, Social and Cultural Rights, has written recently:

> "If we are told that girl children have very limited access to primary education in a particular country – Nepal, Pakistan, Afghanistan, or wherever – or that, despite formally equal access, only very few girls actually attend school, do we immediately say, 'This is a clear violation of their human right to education'? Or do we say, 'This is a great pity and we really hope that social programmes over the next fifty years will address the problem so that their great-grandchildren will benefit'? By contrast, if the same girls were being forced or sold into prostitution, we would immediately be outraged and say, 'Why isn't something being done? This is a violation of their human rights'."[10]

A view has sometimes been expressed that civil and political rights fall within the ambit of foreign policy, whilst development co-operation is concerned with the implementation of economic, social and cultural rights. This is too simplistic a view, and misses the inter-relationship and indivisibility of all human rights. Development co-operation can and should play an important role in promoting **all** human rights. Similarly, the defence of economic, social and cultural rights should not be left to development agencies alone. It should form a central part of a human rights-based foreign policy, and that of the UK Government's policy of "Bringing Rights Home".

Part of the historical hesitance of the West to give economic, social and cultural rights the priority they deserve has been due to a misunderstanding of their nature and of the associated state obligations. Leaving aside the ideological difficulties which permeated the Cold War period, the arguments against economic, social and cultural rights fall into two main concerns: the nature of the state duty imposed and the related cost implications; and the degree to which economic, social and cultural rights can be enforced through law (the justicibility argument).

---

[10] *Making Economic and Social Rights Count: A Strategy for the Future*, by Philip Alston in The Political Quarterly Vol 68, No.2 April – June 1997.

Each of these arguments has now been firmly discredited within UN human rights bodies and at recent UN conferences, but the misperceptions are still sometimes referred to in discussions about a human rights approach to development.

For instance, it has sometimes been argued that civil and political rights are of a different category to economic, social rights, and that the former merely impose negative obligations on a state to abstain from a particular course of action. In contrast, it is argued, economic, social and cultural rights impose positive obligations. This is a false distinction.

All human rights – civil, cultural, economic, political and social - impose both negative and positive obligations on states

Protecting the rights to life, physical integrity, and fair criminal process, for example, requires a state, not only to refrain from such atrocities as extra-judicial killings, but to take all those steps necessary to protect individuals' rights in these regards. States must, for instance, take the positive steps of training and supporting a police force, and judiciary, and establishing courts and the other essentials of a competent system of criminal justice.

Another related argument is that economic, social and cultural rights are too costly, in contrast to civil and political rights. It is incorrectly assumed that respect for the latter will involve the state in no cost. But there is no such thing as a free right. As we have seen, protecting civil and political rights involves state expenditure, for example with respect to the criminal process and prison service. Even the right to vote has cost implications for a state, in terms of administration and the provision of accessible polling stations.

Conversely, the protection of many economic and social rights can be achieved simply by the introduction of appropriate legislation. For instance, laws can be introduced to prohibit discrimination in the enjoyment of these rights; to protect workers' rights and trade union rights; protect the freedoms which are indispensable for scientific research and creative activity; as well as to prohibit violations such as arbitrary evictions from homes, or the deliberate denial of the means of livelihood and survival.

It is generally considered that states are obliged to provide the legal, economic, and social environment in which individuals might have an opportunity to meet their own needs, and that of their families.

The International Covenant on Economic, Social and Cultural Rights sets out the obligations of States Parties as being to ***take measures towards the progressive achievement of the rights recognised in the Covenant, to the maximum of available resources, including those available through international assistance.***

The Covenant does not goes as far as saying that states are obliged to provide everyone with free food, clothing and housing. In fact, there is only one provision in the entire Covenant that expressly calls for state provision. This is Article 13 concerning the right to education, which requires that "primary education shall be compulsory and available free to all". With respect to secondary and higher education, there is a commitment to the progressive introduction of free education.

Western lawyers based in capital cities, rather than those working at the grass roots, often lead the arguments about justicibility. It is thought that the lack of detail in the expression of economic, social and cultural rights inhibits the identification of the legal obligations of states, and therefore prevents the rights being enforceable through law. However, many economic and social rights are already protected by national laws, which provide redress for those whose rights are infringed. Most states protect some labour rights, and many national laws protect tenants from exploitation by landlords, to quote but two examples.

The lack of detailed articulation of the legal content of economic, social and cultural rights and of the associated state obligations is due as much to an inadequate emphasis on this branch of rights by Northern states, as to any inherent distinction between the two sets of rights. However, specialised agencies and the recent series of UN Conferences have made considerable headway in determining the state actions necessary for securing enjoyment of economic, social and cultural rights. Read together with the Covenant, these agreements go a long way to articulating the precise nature of state obligations.

A more recent argument which has been put forward to counter efforts to incorporate economic, social and cultural rights into national law, is that the level of enjoyment of these rights should be decided by parliament as a matter of policy, rather than by courts as a matter of law. This argument is used in the UK debate on a Bill of Rights, but, in this Author's view, is based on a misunderstanding of the nature of economic, social and cultural rights. Securing economic social and cultural rights is not just about handouts from the state, however vital these are in times of hardship. It is about ensuring equal opportunities and protection from discrimination, so that all people might adequately meet their own needs and those of their families. It is about lifting the barriers which keep people in poverty, and about overcoming the prejudice and social isolation which impedes a dignified life. Thus whilst the level of welfare entitlements correctly remains an issue for parliament, the legal protection of the rights to education, to work, to access to housing, for example, should be incorporated into national law and are an appropriate subject for courts.

All human rights are universal indivisible and inter-related

In 1995, 184 Heads of State and Government participated in the World Conference for Social Development in Copenhagen. They recognised that respect for *all* human rights was essential for human dignity, social development and justice. It is for this reason that the UN refers to all human rights as being *inter-related and indivisible.*

This clearly reflects the reality of peoples' lives. It is the nature of human rights that abuse of one right invariably impinges on the enjoyment of other rights. An uneducated women will be impeded from playing a full role in civil and political life; whilst freedom to join a trade union may mean little to a man unable to find any work. The enjoyment of **all** human rights must be seen as a whole. Each is equally worthy of protection and implementation.

In the debates over economic and social rights, cultural rights are frequently left out. It is as if people interpret these to be "soft" rights, related to having fun at a pageant or going to the opera. There is a perception that they are not of the same degree of importance as other human rights.

Of course the right to participate in cultural life includes the right to go to the theatre, but it is far too simplistic an analysis of cultural rights to see them as solely related to what might be described as culture with a capital "C".

For many millions of people, particularly indigenous peoples, access to their cultural heritage is a matter of survival. Those uprooted from their traditional homelands have the utmost difficulty adapting to life elsewhere. People whose livelihood is dependent on the forest suffer immense harm as a result of land clearance by loggers. This trampling of their fundamental human rights has dire consequences for their lives, and is responsible for their cultural, as well as economic, impoverishment.

FROM LEGALISM TO HUMAN DEVELOPMENT

Human rights, although protected by international law, are not just about conventions and law. The subject of human rights is a human subject: one that touches upon every aspect of human endeavour and aspiration.

We should not perpetuate the myth that human rights should be left to lawyers and diplomats

It is a subject that should shape the policy and action of every government department and sector of society.

The reiteration of human rights must be backed by concrete measures to promote their realisation in practice. This requires a pro-active approach focused on effective strategies for the promotion of the realisation by poor people of their human rights.

For an informed approach to the implementation of economic, social and cultural rights it is clearly necessary for other disciplines to play their role.

There is a potential synergy in bringing together the experiences of the human rights and development communities in a joint approach to poverty elimination and the achievement of social and economic justice.

A joint human rights and development approach
is needed to eradicate poverty and
achieve economic and social justice

FROM RHETORIC TO
PRAGMATISM

A human rights approach to development is a pragmatic approach to the elimination of poverty and the promotion of an improved quality of life by promoting:

- analysis of the enjoyment of human rights by poor people within a given state including, where possible, analysis in partnership with poor people[11] of their actual experience with respect to enjoyment and denial of their fundamental human rights, using the yardstick of interna tional human rights norms and standards

- identification of the steps which their states are obliged to take in order to comply both with their legal obligations under international law, and also with the political commit ments undertaken in this regard at international conferences

- assistance to partner countries through development co-operation to help them to meet these obligations
- identification of the best practices in achieving realisation of the rights affected and improving the quality of life of poor people

- the political will and allocation of sufficient resources to implement the strategies identified.

[11] A number of methodologies are currently employed to promote grass roots involvement in analysis and needs assessment, including proxy surveys.

Box 3
Strategies for Achievement of Enjoyment by Poor People of their Human Rights Include:

- the promotion of a human rights framework for policy and action, education in human rights and responsibilities, and the empowerment of individuals and peoples so that they are able to seek and enjoy their rights

- investment in the social sector so that there are sufficient schools and health care services accessible to poor people, and conditions in which they can meet their needs for housing, water and food and other fundamental requirements for a healthy life

- strengthening of the physical security of poor people, through, for example, police training in human rights, gender awareness, and community policing techniques

- legal reform to ensure that human rights are adequately protected by national law, and that speedy, accessible and affordable redress procedures are in place and accessible to poor people

- public education campaigns to combat prejudice and discrimination and to promote the development of a social and cultural environment in which all people – men and women, adults and children, the majority and minorities – might enjoy their equal human rights and dignity free from discrimination or abuse

- the strengthening of mechanisms to ensure poor people are empowered to participate in the decisions that affect their lives, in the local and national political process, and in cultural life.

3 A DEEPER UNDERSTANDING OF HUMAN RIGHTS

"All human beings are born free and equal in dignity and rights. They are endowed with reason and conscience, and should act towards one another in a spirit of brotherhood."

Article 1, Universal Declaration of Human Rights

HUMAN RIGHTS: A GLOBAL VISION BACKED BY STATE OBLIGATIONS

On a dull day when the rain is beating on your windows, re-reading the Universal Declaration of Human Rights can be inspiring. Its vision is of a world of equity and justice premised on the equality, worth and dignity of human beings. Its words reflect the optimism of the post-war period.

But the UN did not stop with vision. Over the last 50 years Member States have developed the international legal protection of human rights and enunciated clear obligations, which have been developed and voluntarily accepted by states from all regions of the world.

The global consensus on human rights has its roots in the philosophies, religions and cultures throughout the world. It therefore represents a truly global agreement on the steps necessary to achieve a more equitable world in which everyone might live in accordance with their rights and dignity.

Box 4
Some Basic Principles of Human Rights and Humanity

Recognition of
Equal Worth and Dignity of All Human Beings
and of our *Common Humanity*

Equal Worth:	*Equality* and the principle of *Non-Discrimination* Requires *Equality of Opportunity* and *Equitable Access to Public Resources* *Participation*
Dignity:	*Liberty* *Freedom of Choice* *Autonomy*
Common Humanity:	*Mutual Respect* *Solidarity*

INTERNATIONAL
ENTHRONEMENT OF HUMAN
RIGHTS

A concern for human dignity and justice has existed throughout civilisation, and states have taken action through their constitutions, national law, and policies to protect the rights of their citizens. But it was not until the atrocities of the Nazi era and the Second World War that the world community recognised the need to protect human rights at the international level. Until then international law had regarded the manner in which a state treated its own citizens as falling within the sovereignty of that state alone.

All that was to change with the creation of the United Nations. One of the first tasks assigned to the new organisation was what Winston Churchill called "the enthronement of human rights".

Article 1 of the United Nations Charter sets out the purposes of the UN, which, in addition to peace and security, include the aim:

> "(3) To achieve international co-operation in solving international problems of an economic, social, cultural, or humanitarian character, and in promoting and encouraging respect for human rights and for fundamental freedoms for all without distinction as to race, sex, language, or religion."

By Articles 55 and 56 of the Charter, all Member States pledge themselves inter alia to take *joint* and *separate action* to promote:

- universal respect for, and observance of, human rights and fundamental freedoms for all without distinction,

- higher standards of living, full employment, and conditions of economic and social progress and development, and

- solutions of international economic, social, health and related problems; and international cultural and educational co-operation.

This is the justification of international concern for human rights and forms part of the legal basis of the obligation of international development co-operation.[1]

The International Bill of Rights

Over the last 50 years, the UN has given the force of international legal protection to its vision of a world in which everyone might enjoy freedom from want and fear, and enjoyment of those other fundamental human rights necessary for human dignity and development.

In 1948 the UN General Assembly adopted the Universal Declaration of Human Rights as *"a common standard of achievement for all peoples and all nations"*. The provisions of the Universal Declaration were given legal force in two treaties adopted in 1966, and which came into force in 1976:

- **The International Covenant on Economic, Social and Cultural Rights (ICESCR)**
- **The International Covenant on Civil and Political Rights (ICCPR)**

[1] The Author is aware that not all states would recognise this article as imposing a legal obligation on them to co-operate on development. But the words clearly oblige states to promote social progress and development. However, the Charter does not go as far as saying that richer countries have an obligation to provide financial support for less developed countries. This may be implied, but is not explicit.

Together, the Universal Declaration and the two Covenants are referred to as the International Bill of Rights. As of February 1998 the ICESCR had 137 States Parties, and the ICCPR had 140 States Parties.

As we have seen, the scope of human rights protected by international law is much wider than is sometimes appreciated. Human rights are not limited to civil and political freedoms and liberties, but include those economic, social and cultural rights necessary for survival, human development, and dignity. These latter include the rights to adequate food, housing, health and education, and the rights and freedoms associated with participating in cultural and religious life. The human rights listed in Chapter 2, have now all been recognised and given the force of international law by the two covenants and subsequent instruments.

Other Major UN Texts

The UN has adopted a large number of other international instruments designed to protect human rights in specific circumstances, or to protect the rights of people particularly vulnerable to abuse of their rights. They include:

- **The Convention on the Elimination of Racial Discrimination (CERD) 1965**

- **The Convention on the Elimination of All Forms of Discrimination Against Women (CEDAW) 1979**

- **The Convention Against Torture and Other Cruel, Inhuman or Degrading Treatment or Punishment (CAT) 1984**

- **The Convention on the Rights of the Child (CRC) 1989.**

Regional Texts

The Council of Europe, the Organisation of American States, and the Organisation of African Unity have all adopted regional instruments to translate the international texts into additional obligations binding on States Parties within the region. For instance,

The Council of Europe has adopted:

- **The European Convention for the Protection of Human Rights and Fundamental Freedoms, 1950, and a series of Protocols thereto** (which primarily protect civil and political rights).

- **The European Social Charter (1961, Revised in 1996)** (with a focus on labour rights and some other economic and social rights).

The Organisation of American States has adopted:

- **The American Convention on Human Rights, 1969.**

- **Additional Protocol to the American Convention on Human Rights in the Area of Economic, Social and Cultural Rights, 1988 (Protocol of San Salvador).**

The organisation of African Unity has adopted:

- **African Charter on Human and Peoples' Rights, 1981.**

These Conventions have their own methods of review, and are helping to establish commitment to human rights in regions around the world.

Although there have been some attempts to develop a regional human rights convention for Asia, these have not to date been successful. This is partly as a result of the lack of homogeneity in the region with its many differing faiths, cultures, and levels of modernity. Such differences have made it difficult to reach consensus on a more detailed exposition of human rights and state obligations than that already accepted within the UN texts.

Additional Instruments

There are many other international instruments adopted by the UN and regional bodies. These include the International Convention on the Protection of the Rights of All Migrant Workers and their Families; the Declaration of the Rights of Persons Belonging to National or Ethnic, Religious and Linguistic Minorities; and the Declaration on the Rights of Disabled Persons.

The UN has also elaborated international human rights instruments governing, for example, the treatment of prisoners, minimum standards for the administration of juvenile justice, and the independence of the judiciary.

Several UN declarations are particularly relevant to the promotion of human development for instance the Declaration on the Right to Development, and the Declaration on Social Progress and Development. These latter two documents are reproduced in Annex 4.

The High Commissioner for Human Rights

In 1993 the UN General Assembly established the post of a UN High Commissioner for Human Rights, currently held by Mrs. Mary Robinson (former President of Ireland). The High Commissioner has the principle responsibilities within the UN for human rights under the direction of the Secretary General. The High Commissioner's mandate includes the responsibility "to promote and protect the realization of the right to development and to enhance support from relevant bodies of the United Nations system for this purpose". The resolution establishing the Office[2] requires the High Commissioner to:

> "Recognise the importance of promoting a balanced and sustainable development for all people and of ensuring realization of the right to development, as established in the Declaration on the Right to Development."

THE UNIVERSALITY OF HUMAN RIGHTS AND OTHER FUNDAMENTAL PRINCIPLES

Human rights are for everyone
as much for people living in poverty and social isolation
as for the visible and articulate

[2] UN General Assembly Resolution: A/RES/48/141 of 20 December 1993

Although legal instruments have ***recognised*** and ***confirmed*** human rights, the law is ***not the source*** of these rights. At a philosophical level, human rights are not granted by any human authority or government, but are derived from the essential dignity and nature of humankind.

There have been differing views about the original source of human rights. Some philosophers believe that they derive from human conscience and reason, reflected in the constant striving of the human race for justice and freedom. Moral and religious thinkers of differing faiths have stressed the inherent dignity and equality of humans – whether they regard this as stemming from the dignity of all creation, or from the creation of humans in the image of God.

These various ideas are captured in the founding document of modern day human rights – the Universal Declaration of Human Rights. It states in its first preambular paragraph that "recognition of the inherent dignity and of the equal and inalienable rights of all members of the human family is the foundation of freedom, justice and peace in the world". By Article 1, the Universal Declaration proclaims:

> "All human beings are born free and equal in dignity and rights. They are endowed with reason and conscience and should act towards one another in a spirit of brotherhood."

Human rights are inherent

Thus today, an answer to the question "who grants human rights?" is that they arise from the recognition of their existence by the world community, expressed through numerous UN and other international documents, and adopted by states from every region of the world representing the rich diversity of the world's faiths and cultures.

Just as law is not the source of human rights, neither can law justifiably deprive individuals of their fundamental human rights and freedoms. These are deemed inalienable, and cannot be abrogated by human law. The earlier South African laws on *apartheid* violated human rights despite the fact that they had been duly passed by the South African parliament of the time. Similarly, the promulgation of German laws could not prevent the Nazi atrocities from amounting to blatant violations of human rights.

Every man, woman and child is entitled to enjoy his or her human rights simply by virtue of being human

It is this ***universality of human rights*** which distinguishes them from other types of rights – such as citizenship rights or contractual rights.

The term universality of human rights is used to refer to the fact that every state throughout the world must recognise, respect and protect the legal standards contained in international human rights documents. These rights form a core minimum standard to be observed by all states, whatever their level of economic or political development.

Human rights are premised on the recognition of the equal worth and dignity of every human being, regardless of any distinguishing characteristic. This gives rise to the twin principles of *equality* and *non-discrimination*.

WOMEN'S RIGHTS ARE HUMAN RIGHTS

Despite these fundamental principles of equality and non-discrimination, women throughout the world suffer gross inequities, and are denied full enjoyment of their human rights on a basis of equality with men. In order to prompt the necessary action to achieve women's equal rights the UN adopted the Convention on the Elimination of Discrimination Against Women (CEDAW) in 1979. It came into force in 1981. By February 1998 it had 161 States Parties.

States Parties undertake to pursue a policy of eliminating discrimination against women in all fields. In order to overcome existing inequality, the Convention recognises the possibility of taking measures of affirmative action or "positive discrimination". States Parties also undertake to take measures to suppress all forms of traffic in women.

Part II of CEDAW contains provisions relating to political rights, including the right to vote and to be eligible for election to all publicly elected bodies, the right to participate in the formulation of government policy and to hold public office at all levels, and the right to participate in non-governmental organisations concerned with public and political life.

Part III addresses social and economic rights in the fields of education, employment, health care and economic and social life, and requires States Parties to take into account the particular problems faced by rural women.

Part IV covers civil and family rights. It provides for equality before the law, and elimination of discrimination in all matters relating to marriage and family relations.

At the UN, women's issues have been primarily the concern of the Commission on the Status of Women. The Commission on Human Rights, on the other hand, deals with human rights concerns. For many years, the latter refused to take up issues relating to women's human rights on the basis that these fell within the remit of the Commission on the Status of Women. As a result, women's human rights became marginalised in the UN. At the Vienna World Conference on Human Rights a major shift was prompted by a global advocacy lobby united under the slogan "Women's Rights are Human Rights". As a result, women's rights have now been "mainstreamed" in the UN, and are now covered by the UN human rights bodies.

Another significant success at Vienna was recognition that violence against women is a human rights concern. For too long it had been argued that what took place behind closed doors, or within the family, was a private matter, and of no concern to the state, thus falling outside human rights.

THE RIGHTS OF THE CHILD

The recognition of the particular vulnerability of children to abuse of their rights led to the adoption of the Convention on the Rights of the Child (CRC) in 1989. By February 1998, this Convention had 191 States Parties, more than any other human rights instrument.

The Convention defines a child as "every human being below the age of eighteen years unless, under the law applicable to the child, majority is attained earlier". States Parties undertake to pursue a policy of protecting the child from all forms of discrimination and to provide appropriate care. Provision is also made for the right of a child to acquire nationality, to leave any country and enter his or her own country, and to enter or leave the territory of another State Party for the purposes of family reunification. States Parties commit themselves to taking measures to combat the illicit movement of children abroad.

The CRC also covers civil and family rights and social and economic rights. It provides for the rights to freedom of expression, thought, conscience and religion. It also contains provisions relating to social and economic rights in the fields of adoption, welfare, education, health, and economic and social development. Particular attention is drawn to children seeking refugee status, and the rights of a child with mental or physical disability.

An important provision of the Convention is contained in Article 12 by which States Parties commit themselves to assuring to children who are capable of forming their own views the right to express those views freely in all matters which affect them. Further, the views of the child shall be given due weight in accordance with the age and maturity of the child.

Under the CRC, the child should be protected from narcotic drugs, sexual abuse, sale or traffic in children, ill-treatment and cruelty. States Parties undertake not to impose capital punishment for offences committed by persons below eighteen years of age.

PROTECTION FROM VIOLENT ABUSE

Massive violations of human rights may amount to crimes against humanity which are prohibited by customary international law.

Additional international instruments have been adopted to protect individuals from violent abuse. The Convention on the Prevention and Punishment of the Crime of Genocide was adopted by the UN on 9 December 1948, the day before the Universal Declaration of Human Rights was proclaimed. States Parties undertake to bring the perpetrators to justice before a competent tribunal, such as the International Criminal Tribunals for Rwanda and the former Yugoslavia.

The prohibition of torture is also strengthened in the Convention against Torture and Other Cruel Inhuman or Degrading Treatment or Punishment adopted by the General Assembly on 10 December 1984. As of February 1998 it had been ratified by 104 states.

During times of conflict the Geneva Conventions of August 1949, and their Additional Protocols of 8 June 1977, provide protection to combatants and civilians alike. They are founded on the idea of respect for the individual and his/her dignity. Persons not directly taking part in hostilities and those put out of action through sickness, injury, captivity or any other cause must be respected and protected against the effects of war; those who suffer must be aided and cared for without discrimination.

The Additional Protocols extend this protection to any person affected by an armed conflict. They furthermore stipulate that the parties to the conflict and the combatants shall not attack the civilian population and civilian objects and shall conduct their military operations in conformity with the recognised rules and standards of humanity.

Although not regarded as part of human rights law per se, these Conventions are relevant within the context of DFID's emergency assistance. A further relevant text is the Convention Relating to the Status of Refugees adopted by the UN on 28 July 1951. It provides international protection for refugees who are outside their country of nationality and who are, owing to well-founded fear of being persecuted, unwilling to return to it. The United Nations High Commissioner for Refugees (UNHCR) has the international mandate to protect and assist refugees.

The position of individuals uprooted from their homes and livelihoods but who remain within their countries is not covered by the 1951 Convention. However, the UNHCR's mandate has been extended by various UN resolutions to cover internally displaced persons. Whilst the formal legal protection of internally displaced persons remains weak, the provisions of international human rights treaties apply both in times of conflict and in times of peace, and so can be relied upon in conjunction with the Geneva Conventions and, where appropriate, the Refugee Convention.

HIERARCHIES AND THE INDIVISIBILITY OF HUMAN RIGHTS

There is a tendency to try to list human rights in order of their importance. However, attempts at creating hierarchies of rights are doomed to failure. It is attractive to consider the right to life as the most precious, but without enjoyment of the right to food, the right to life is meaningless. Similarly, as Amartya Sen and others have illustrated, denial of a free press is significantly associated with famine as it hampers the alerting mechanisms.[3]

Each time one attempts to hold up a human right as being the most fundamental, it is possible to find another right that must be enjoyed as a pre-requisite to realisation of the right first identified. Human rights advocates therefore prefer not to get into the game of trying to construct hierarchies or of identifying "core" rights. In any case, it would be very difficult to get any real consensus on such a listing.

UN documents refer to the enjoyment of all human rights as being interdependent and inter-related. Denial of one right invariably impedes enjoyment of others. For example, a malnourished girl will be unable to concentrate at school and to benefit from the education that would assist her to participate fully in civil society and the democratic process.

[3] *Poverty and Famine: An Essay on Entitlement and Deprivation,* Amartya Sen, Clarendon Press, Oxford, 1981

Once a state has adopted a particular international convention it is obliged to ensure that the human rights protected by the convention are enjoyed by persons within the jurisdiction of the state. States are obliged to secure the human rights of *all* people within their jurisdiction, not just their own citizens. However, under the International Covenant on Economic, Social and Cultural Rights, developing countries, with due regard to human rights and their national economy, may determine to what extent they would guarantee the economic rights recognised in the Covenant to non-nationals.

The constitutions of most modern states contain at least some provisions to protect human rights, and many states have introduced specific laws to prevent discrimination and protect individuals' human rights, either generally, or in specific circumstances.

The precise obligations of states vary from convention to convention. But in general terms, state obligations can be regarded as falling into four components:

Obligation to **RESPECT**

States are obliged to ensure that human rights are fully respected in the context of state policies, laws and actions, and those of its public officials. This obligation requires states to ensure that none of its Ministries or public servants violate human rights by their policies or actions.

Obligation to **PROTECT**

States are obliged to ensure that enjoyment, by everyone without discrimination, of all their human rights is protected from abuse by third parties – i.e. from the actions of individuals and groups at all levels of society, including corporations, institutions, and public and private bodies. This protection should be through the introduction of laws to protect human rights, and the provision of affordable and accessible redress procedures in the event of abuse of the rights.

Obligation to **PROMOTE**

The Universal Declaration of Human Rights and subsequent texts have called on states to promote respect for human rights through teaching and education. Furthermore, in the provision on the right to education, States Parties to the ICESCR agree that education "shall be directed to the full development of the human personality and the sense of its dignity, and shall strengthen the respect for human rights and fundamental freedoms" (Article 13).

Obligation to **ENSURE REALISATION**

States are obliged to take the necessary steps to ensure the realisation of human rights. For instance, the ICCPR requires

States Parties "to adopt such legislative or other measures as may be necessary to give effect to the rights recognized in the ... Covenant".

Recognising that States may not be able to ensure instant realisation of all economic, social and cultural rights, the ICESCR provides that all States Parties should *take steps, to the maximum of available resources, towards the progressive achievement* of the full realisation of these rights.

(i) Law, policy and action

Compliance by a state of its obligations under international human rights law can be regarded as requiring:

- *a review of national law, policies and actions* to ensure that they adequately protect and respect the equal rights of everyone and protect against discrimination in enjoyment of rights
- *analysis of the realisation of the rights* within all sectors of the community (best achieved in partnership with represenatives of civil society including people living in poverty and social disadvantage) in order to identify any groups not adequately enjoying their rights
- *development of strategies for ensuring realisation* of the rights of people not fully enjoying their human rights
- *promotion of the observance of human rights* through education and training in human rights and responsibilities.

(ii) Progressive Achievement of Economic, Social and Cultural Rights

As we have seen the International Covenant on Economic, Social and Cultural Rights obliges states to take steps towards achieving progressively the full realisation of economic, social and cultural rights. The obligation, contained in Article 2(1) can be broken up into the following components. States are obliged to:

- *take steps*
- *individually and through international assistance and co-operation (especially economic and technial)*
- *by all appropriate means*
- *including particularly the adoption of legislative measures*
- *to the maximum of their available resources*

Thus the state is obliged to *take some steps* towards the realisation of the right. It is not permitted to ignore the problem. Each state should develop a plan for realising the rights, and if it is unable to afford all the measures necessary, it should seek international development assistance – either in the form of economic aid or technical assistance. They should set *goals* and *targets* and *timeframes* for their national plans in this regard, which could form a basis of multi-lateral and bilateral development agreements.

This approach is in line with that of the UN Committee on Economic, Social and Cultural Rights which is responsible for reviewing States Parties' reports on the steps they have taken to implement their Covenant obligations. Such goals and targets, if considered by the Committee to be adequate, could form the basis of **benchmarks** for the progressive realisation of economic, social and cultural rights.

These could assist in developing **quality of life indicators** for inclusion in the human development indices currently used by UNDP.

(iii) Protection Against Discrimination

Although the term "progressive achievement" is used, the obligation to guarantee some rights in the Covenant is **immediate**.[4] For instance, the obligation concerning enjoyment of all human rights without discrimination is an immediate obligation.

States are obliged to take immediate steps to ensure that:

- no one suffers discrimination in enjoyment of their rights
- the equal rights of women are guaranteed.

(iv) Modifying Social and Cultural Patterns

The Convention on the Elimination of All Forms of Discrimination Against Women requires States Parties to take all appropriate measures:

> "to modify the social and cultural patterns of conduct of men and women, with a view to achieving the elimination of prejudices and customary and all other practices which are based on the idea of inferiority or superiority of either of the sexes or on stereotyped roles for men and women" (Article 5)

This is a critical provision, as enjoyment by women of their human rights is frequently impeded by custom and social or cultural traditions.

(v) Specific Measures

States need to take special steps in order to ensure the enjoyment of particular rights. Sometimes, these measures are spelt out in the relevant international instrument. For instance, the ICESCR lists some of those steps to be taken by states to achieve the full realisation of the right to the highest attainable standard of physical and mental health. In a list that is clearly outdated, these steps include those necessary for:

- the reduction of the stillbirth-rate and of infant mortality
- the improvement of environmental and industrial hygiene
- the prevention, treatment and control of epidemic, endemic, occupational and other diseases, and the creation of conditions which would assure to all medical service and medical attention in the event of sickness.

---

[4] Limburg Principles on the Implementation of the International Covenant on Economic, Social and Cultural Rights, 1986. Expert meeting convened at the University of Limburg, the Netherlands. Part I. A. paragraph 8.

(vi) International Obligations

In addition to their duties to respect, protect, promote and ensure realisation at the national level, states are under international obligations with respect to human rights. As we have seen at the beginning of this chapter, by Articles 55 and 56 the member states of the UN pledge themselves to take joint and separate action to promote:

- universal respect for, and observance of, human rights and fundamental freedoms for all without distinction,
- higher standards of living, full employment and conditions of economic and social progress and development,
- solutions of international economic, social, health and related problems as well as international cultural and education co-operation.

These complementary duties form the basis of the duty of international co-operation and of development assistance.

In addition, as we have seen, the ICESCR also refers to international obligations. The full text of Article 2(1) provides:

> "Each State Party to the present Covenant undertakes to take steps, individually and through international assistance and co-operation, especially economic and technical, to the maximum of its available resources, with a view to achieving progressively the full realisation of the rights recognised in the present Covenant by all appropriate means, including particularly the adoption of legislative measures."

In this author's view[5], since donor states are also party to the ICESCR, they are under an obligation, to the maximum of their available resources, to assist less developed countries in ensuring the realisation of economic, social and cultural rights. There has been general agreement within the development community that donor states should aim to meet the target of 0.7% of their GNP as a contribution to development co-operation. This then should be the current target for complying with this obligation of development assistance.

Further support for the view that, together with the UN Charter quoted above, the ICESCR imposes a **duty** of international assistance and co-operation is found in an earlier article. Article 1 of the Covenant recognises that all peoples may freely dispose of the natural wealth and resources *"without prejudice to any obligations arising out of international economic co-operation"*. If there were no such obligations, there would have been no need for states to have included this phrase.

This view is also supported by state practice. Although the amount of aid may not be as high as proposed by the UN, the richer states **are** providing economic and technical assistance.

Whatever its legal nature, the obligation of development assistance and co-operation is at the least a moral imperative. It is called for by our common humanity, recognition of the equal rights of everyone, and the imperative of solidarity with the poor.

---

[5] See footnote 1 at the beginning of this chapter.

MARGIN OF DISCRETION

There is what is called a ***margin of discretion,*** which allows a state to choose the manner in which it fulfils its obligations under international human rights law. A state is then able to decide which policies to adopt in order to ensure realisation of the rights within the context of the political, economic, religious, cultural, and other characteristics of the state. For example, if the obligation in question is that of guaranteeing access to health care for all, it is left to the state to decide ***how*** medical care is to be provided, i.e. whether through a public health service, private insurance schemes, or a mixture of the two.

Nevertheless, the state remains under a duty to act, and is accountable to the international community for its implementation of this obligation. ***The margin of discretion does not mean that a state is free to pick and choose which rights to implement, or that it might ignore the rights of a particular section of the community.***

MONITORING AND ENFORCEMENT OF HUMAN RIGHTS OBLIGATIONS

States are accountable to the international community for their human rights record. There are a number of UN bodies and mechanisms which monitor and seek to enforce international human rights standards. The UN High Commissioner for Human Rights has the role of coordinating the human rights work of the UN. The mandate of the High Commissioner includes promoting the enjoyment of all human rights, enhancing international cooperation on human rights and engaging in discussions with governments. She also has particular responsibility for promoting and protecting the realisation of the right to development.

The enforcement of human rights however, is notoriously weak, particularly at the international level. There is no world court on human rights, although some regional bodies have human rights courts. Ideally, states should provide human right mechanisms at the national level, so that anyone suffering abuse of their rights can have access to redress. However, this is unlikely to be effective when the law or policy of the government is itself the vehicle of violation.

National laws that violate human rights cannot be justified on the basis that they were duly passed by the legislature, as we have seen from the example of South Africa's former *apartheid* policy and the extermination laws of the Nazi regime. Similarly, current laws that deny women equal rights or in other ways encourage women's subordination, or that of other groups, offend human rights.

In this way, internationally recognised human rights – i.e. those enunciated in international texts adopted by the world community – form a higher standard by which national laws might be judged. States are accountable to the international community for dereliction in protecting these rights. International human rights mechanisms provide opportunities by which national law, policy, or practice can be judged against objective international standards.

A series of bodies have been established by the UN to monitor and enforce international human rights standards. These activities can be viewed in three groups:

- investigations of allegations of violations of human rights by the Commission on Human Rights and its Sub-Commission;
- review by various treaty-monitoring bodies of States Parties' reports on measures taken to implement their obligations under various conventions;
- individual complaints mechanisms.

Monitoring Human Rights Violations

In addition to their promotional work, the Commission on Human Rights and its Sub-Commission on the Prevention of Discrimination and Protection of Minorities also undertake monitoring activities.

The Commission annually establishes a working group to consider situations of alleged gross violations of human rights referred to it by its Sub-Commission, and it has various other working groups which examine the situation in a particular country, or which work on a particular issue. The Commission also establishes other **ad hoc** arrangements to deal with situations in particular countries, which may, with the co-operation of the government concerned, include on site visits and investigations of special rapporteurs, representatives or envoys. Such mechanisms can have an impact on the behaviour of states, albeit less speedily and effectively than desired. In situations of continued gross violations, the issue can be referred to the Security Council which may impose sanctions.

The Sub-Commission on the Prevention of Discrimination and the Protection of Minorities also has a monitoring role. For many years the Sub-Commission had working groups investigating the situation in Southern Africa, the Israeli-occupied territories of the West Bank and Gaza, and practices under the **apartheid** regime. The work of these groups substantially contributed to the awareness and political commitment that paved change.

Reporting Procedure before Treaty-Monitoring Bodies

In addition, there are a number of procedures which depend on the voluntary co-operation of states. The two International Covenants and a number of other conventions, have each set up a mechanism through which the implementation of the obligations of States Parties can be monitored. The Committee on Human Rights, for example, oversees the implementation of the ICCPR, and the Committee on Economic, Social and Cultural Rights reviews implementation of the ICESCR.

States parties are required to report at regular intervals on the legal and other steps that they have taken to implement their obligations under the particular convention. The reports are reviewed by the relevant committee, which comprises independent experts. The Committees may make recommendations to the state, which is required to change its law or practice if found to be in breach of human rights standards.

There are currently six UN Treaty-Monitoring Bodies which monitor states parties' compliance with the obligations undertaken by the various conventions:

- The Human Rights Committee
- The Committee on Economic, Social and Cultural Rights
- The Committee on the Elimination of Racial Discrimination
- The Committee on the Elimination of Discrimination Against Women
- The Committee on the Rights of the Child
- The Committee Against Torture

Several Committees have adopted an approach of "constructive dialogue" by which they seek to influence states parties by encouraging a sharing of experience of how particular difficulties are addressed in other countries. Although the failure of states to produce their reports is a continuing problem, a surprising number do participate in the work of the various committees. These latter are able to point to a number of significant successes in promoting cessation of violations or other necessary reform at the national level.

Individual Complaints

The UN mechanisms permit individual complaints in order both to consider situations of widespread massive violations, and to offer redress to individuals whose rights have been violated. The procedure established by UN ECOSOC Resolution 1503 is designed for consideration of systematic, massive violations of human rights. The procedure involves the entire hierarchy of the UN from the Sub-Commission to the General Assembly. It is intended to identify and, if possible, correct "situations which appear to reveal a consistent pattern of gross violations of human rights". Any individual or group may submit communications provided certain requirements are met.

A number of conventions have protocols permitting individual complaints. The ICCPR, for instance, has an Optional Protocol which permits individuals alleging a violation of their rights to bring a complaint before the Human Rights Committee. Many human rights advocates are supporting the introduction of a similar optional protocol to allow individual complaints under the ICESCR and CEDAW.

The Committees also play an important role in interpreting the legal meaning of provisions in the international instruments, and their application in particular circumstances. This has led to a body of jurisprudence ranging from legal opinion (sometimes in the form of "General Comments" adopted by a Committee), to decisions in specific cases.

INTERNATIONAL HUMAN RIGHTS JURISPRUDENCE

Some of the most effective enforcement mechanisms are at the regional level. The OAS and Council of Europe have both established human rights courts to enforce their respective regional conventions. The Inter-American Court of Human Rights (based in San José, Costa Rica) and the European Court of Human Rights (based in Strasbourg, France) both allow individuals to bring complaints alleging a violation of their rights. These provide effective mechanisms for the protection of individual rights in these regions. UN and other international human rights bodies have contributed, through their decisions and legal opinions, to the understanding of the nature and contents of human rights and state obligations. These collectively make up the jurisprudence of international human rights law that provides a guide to the measures which states must introduce to ensure realisation of the rights. For instance, in a helpful opinion on the right to life, the UN Human Rights

Committee[6] has stated:

> "The right to life has been too often narrowly interpreted. The expression 'inherent right to life' cannot properly be understood in a restrictive manner and the protection of this right requires that states adopt positive measures. In this context, the Committee considers that it would be desirable for states parties to take all possible measures to reduce infant mortality and to increase life expectancy, especially in adopting measures to eliminate malnutrition and epidemics."

INDIVIDUAL
RESPONSIBILITIES

International human rights law is a part of public international law which binds states rather than individuals. International conventions are a form of international contract between states. Each is bound to account to the others for compliance with the obligations undertaken. It is this contractual inter-state responsibility which provides the legal base for the review by states of the performance of other States Parties to international human rights texts.

Individuals, although bearers of the human rights protected by the legal instruments, are not generally regarded as subjects of international law, and as a rule, cannot be accountable at the international level for a denial of human rights.

However, the position of individuals in international law is changing. First, under a number of human rights conventions, individuals have the right of complaint for alleged violations of human rights. Second, international criminal law is presently being developed under which individuals, such as war criminals, might be prosecuted.

However, this is not to say that individuals are not under a duty to respect the rights of others. Far from it. It is just that this duty is normally enforced under a wide range of national laws – race and sex discrimination provisions, criminal, tort, family, employment, trade union law and so forth.

HUMAN RIGHTS ARE NOT
DEPENDENT ON THE
PERFORMANCE OF DUTIES

What needs to be emphasised is that an individual does not lose his or her human rights as a result of a failure to respect the rights of others. A person guilty of harming another, is still entitled to the protection of human rights law concerning the fair conduct of criminal proceedings. The right to freedom from torture, and from cruel, inhuman, and degrading treatment or punishment is inalienable. According to international human rights standards, there are no circumstances in which torture can be justified.

However this is not to say that all human rights and freedoms are absolute. International human rights law recognises both the individual liberties and freedoms that are the basis of human potential and creativity, and the need to protect the common good.

---

6 The Human Rights Committee is a body of independent experts established by the UN. It reviews the reports of State Parties on the measures they have taken to guarantee the human rights protected by the International Covenant on Civil and Political Rights.

BALANCING INDIVIDUAL
RIGHTS AND THE COMMON
GOOD

The Universal Declaration of Human Rights states in Article 29:

> "Everyone has duties to the community in which alone the free and full development of his personality is possible."

Like any law, international human rights law seeks a balance between conflicting interests – between enjoyment of the rights of one, and the rights of another; between individual rights and the common good.

This latter point is important to stress, as critics sometimes fear that a human rights approach means asserting individual liberty at the cost of common welfare. But in fact international human rights law provides for those circumstances in which liberties and freedoms might be curtailed.

Article 29 goes on to state:

> "In the exercise of his rights and freedoms, everyone shall be subject only to such limitations as are determined by law solely for the purpose of securing due recognition and respect for the rights and freedoms of others and of meeting the just requirements of morality, public order and the general welfare in a democratic society"

The right to liberty does not imply that a duly convicted criminal may not be imprisoned. Rather it decrees that no one should be ***arbitrarily*** deprived of his or her liberty. Human rights law, therefore sets out minimum standards for the protection of fair treatment in criminal hearings.

Article 30 provides:

> "Nothing in this Declaration may be interpreted as implying for any State, group or person any right to engage in any activity or to perform any act aimed at the destruction of any of the rights and freedoms set forth herein."[7]

Similarly, the Preambles to the ICESCR and ICCPR include the following paragraph:

> "Realising that the individual, having duties to other individuals and to the community to which he belongs, is under a responsibility to strive for the promotion and observance of the rights recognized in the present Covenant".

INDIVIDUAL RIGHTS AND THE
PROTECTION OF THE PUBLIC
HEALTH: THE EXAMPLE OF
AIDS

Applying this balance between the rights of individuals and the welfare of the community is not always straight forward as the experience of responding to the HIV/AIDS pandemic has illustrated.

---

[7] A somewhat similar provision is contained in Article 5(1) of the ICCPR.

The obligation to protect the public health, confirmed in Article 12 of the ICESCR, is a fundamental responsibility of states.

Prior to major medical advances, particularly the development of antibiotics, it was sometimes necessary to isolate persons with contagious diseases in order to curtail the spread of infection. Most states have public health laws which grant wide powers to public health authorities. These sometimes include isolation.

The strategies of isolation and quarantine lie deep in the traditions of public health. However, as strategies to prevent the spread of HIV they have been severely criticised. Similarly, coercive measures such as mandatory testing for HIV antibodies, whether directed against a whole population, targeted groups, or individuals considered to be at risk of infection, have also been criticised as unnecessarily restricting individual rights and freedoms.

The "public good" exception to individual rights covered by Article 29 of the Universal Declaration is expanded by Article 4 of the International Covenant on Econonmic, Social and Cultural Rights and Article 12 of the International Covenant on Civil and Political Rights. The latter permits a restriction on an individual's freedom of movement if it is necessary for a number of grounds, including public health. Article 19 has a similar provision with respect to freedom of expression, and by Articles 21 and 22 this is expanded to restrictions on the right of peaceful assembly and of freedom of association with others. These provisions require such restrictions to be:

- in conformity with law
- necessary in a democratic society
- for such purposes as the protection of public health or to protect the rights and freedoms of others

Subsequent human rights jurisprudence has added the requirement that:

- the restrictions proposed are **proportionate** to the expected benefit of the policy
- the measure proposed is the **least intrusive** and restrictive option
- there is **no arbitrary discrimination** against any individual or group.

It is sometimes argued that it is necessary to restrict the liberty of people with HIV in order to protect the rights of others, but public health experts and human rights lawyers alike agree that in the vast majority of cases this is not necessary, as HIV is not contagious in normal social settings.[8] Indeed, it is considered counterproductive, as individuals fearing a restriction of their liberty will be unlikely to present themselves voluntarily for HIV testing, or for sexual and reproductive health services. This risks the knock-on effect of a possible increase in the rates of STD (and therefore HIV) transmission.

---

[8] As long ago as 1988 WHO recommended: "Persons suspected or known to be HIV-infected should remain integrated within society to the maximum possible extent and be helped to assume responsibility for preventing HIV transmission to others. Exclusion of persons suspected or known to be HIV-infected would be unjustified in public health terms and would seriously jeopardise educational and other efforts to prevent the spread of HIV." Social Aspects of AIDS Prevention and Control Programmes, WHO, Geneva, 1 December, 1988. WHO/SPA/GLO/87.2

Protection of individual rights
is integral to effective public health measures

It is therefore argued that since there is no public health justification for restricting the rights of individuals with HIV, such a restriction would, in the absence of some other compelling reason, amount to a violation of their human rights.

RESPONSIBILITIES OF CORPORATIONS AND INTERNATIONAL FINANCIAL INSTITUTIONS

Attempts are currently being made within the human rights community to find ways of extending individual responsibility to corporations, particularly multinational companies. The activities of Shell in Ogoniland in Nigeria have shown how devastating the actions of large corporations can be on the lives of people. A way **must** be found to make these bodies accountable for the abuses of rights they inflict.

Similarly, human rights advocates are striving to hold the international financial institutions (IFIs) accountable for the human rights impact of their policies and programmes. This was prompted by the adverse consequences of the imposition of economic structural adjustment programmes on the poor and vulnerable sectors of society.

It has been argued that since the IFIs are not formally a part of the UN they are not bound by the duty to respect human rights contained in the UN Charter. In contrast, this Author argues that individual states that serve on the Board of the IFIs carry with them into the boardroom their responsibility to ensure respect for human rights. They are therefore jointly liable to ensure that the policies and programmes of the IFIs do not impede enjoyment of human rights. Human rights impact assessments should be drawn up to complement those on environmental impact.

Some progress has been made in calling on IFIs to consider the social development impact of their policies. At the World Summit for Social Development held in Copenhagen in March 1995, the participating states adopted the following text:[9]

> (a) "The World Bank, the International Monetary Fund, the regional and subregional development banks and funds, and all other international finance organizations should further integrate social development goals in their policies, programmes and operations, including by giving higher priority to social-sector lending, where applicable in their lending programmes;

> (b) The Bretton Woods institutions and other organisations of the United Nations system should work together with concerned countries to improve policy dialogues and develop new initiatives to ensure that structural adjustment programmes promote sustained economic and social development, with particular attention to their impact on people living in poverty and vulnerable groups."

[9] The Copenhagen Declaration and Programme of Action, paragraph 92.

THE DYNAMIC NATURE OF
HUMAN RIGHTS LAW

As the last section illustrates, human rights law is at the same time ***concrete*** in that it has promulgated identifiable norms and standards developed and agreed to by the international community, and ***dynamic*** in that it is being developed to strengthen the international protection of human rights and to meet new needs as they are recognised.

International lawyers use the terms "hard" law and "soft" law. Hard law refers to those rights and responsibilities already covered in legally enforceable international instruments, whilst soft law is the term given to emerging rights and obligations contained in declarations of the UN General Assembly. These declarations reflect a political commitment, and are frequently the first step in developing an international legal instrument. For instance, the Declaration on the Rights of the Child of 1959 is the precursor of the Convention on the Rights of the Child adopted by the UN in 1989.

This is not always the case. In 1969, the Declaration on Social Progress and Development was adopted by the UN, and in 1986, the General Assembly adopted the Declaration on the Right to Development[10]. However, these texts have not been translated into legal texts. Their provisions, therefore, whilst persuasive are not technically legally binding on states. However, in the absence of a UN human rights court to enforce legal obligations, human rights are enforced through political pressure rather than legal action. The distinction between hard law and soft law is therefore less important than it might otherwise be.

In addition to these instruments, the documents adopted by UN conferences are also persuasive. It is at conferences such as the Fourth World Conference on Women in Beijing that the international community agrees to take specific measures for the realisation of human rights.

In addition, such conferences provide the opportunity to develop concepts and thus lay the foundation for the further enunciation of internationally recognised human rights. For instance, there was an attempt at Beijing to develop human rights in the context of sexual and reproductive health. However, after considerable debate on this controversial issue, the language finally adopted did not go much further than that already agreed at the International Conference on Population and Development in Cairo, in 1994.

PRINCIPLE OF
NON-REGRESSION

There is a principle of international law which human rights advocates hold dear. It is the principle of ***non-regression***. This principle of state practice requires that norms already adopted should not be undone at a later date.

During the recent series of UN conferences, acceptance of this principle was much in evidence. All states appeared to accept that it was in their interests not to open up a discussion about language already agreed elsewhere. If one state did this, then other states would do so as well. This could simply lead to a re-arguing of the negotiations undertaken at a previous conference.

It is through the negotiations at these conferences, and the enunciation in UN declarations and conventions that international human rights law is able to develop.

[10] These Declarations are discussed in Chapter 5 below.

4 HUMAN RIGHTS IN INTERNATIONAL POLICY - A REVIEW OF SOME CURRENT APPROACHES[1]

"Democracy, development, the pursuit of peace and protection of human rights are universal values. We at the United Nations believe this as a matter of fact and a matter of faith.

We seek to promote these universal values not because we believe all humans are the same, or that all cultures are identical, but because we know that all humans need food, need freedom, need a sustainable future."

UN Secretary General Kofi Annan.

LEGITIMACY OF INTERNATIONAL CONCERN FOR HUMAN RIGHTS

As a recent survey published by the Economist magazine has noted, the relationship between human rights and diplomacy has a long tradition. Ever since the French Revolution there have been attempts to spread respect for the rights of individuals through relationships with other states. From the early nineteenth century this has prompted the development of two schools of thought about the relationship between human rights and foreign policy: one concerned with the universal rights of man in the formulation of foreign policy; the other with order, which was seen to be best maintained through a balance of power in which states do not challenge each other's legitimacy. The two sides persist today and might be called 'liberals' and 'realists'.[2]

Critics of integrating human rights into international policy tend to rely on three main arguments: that cultural relativity prohibits universal human rights; that a human rights approach to foreign policy results in the imposition of western values on other states; and that such a policy amounts to an interference in the domestic affairs of a foreign state.

This paper refutes these arguments. It argues that there is both a moral and legal duty on the United Kingdom and other states to be concerned with respect for human rights globally, and that the promotion of, and respect for, human rights is a legitimate subject of both foreign policy and development cooperation.

Furthermore, such a concern is called for by enlightened self-interest. Respect for human rights creates the climate in which political and economic freedoms can be exercised. This in turn supports international prosperity and trade. It also contributes to peace and security, and to the prevention of conflict and forced displacement.

[1] This chapter is based on *Securing All Human Rights for All People: A Government Obligation Under International Law*, a background paper prepared by the Author for the One World Action Seminar with the Foreign Secretary, Robin Cook, *Foreign Policy in the 21st Century*, London, 29 October, 1997.
[2] See *Human Rights and Diplomacy*, Economist Magazine, 12 April 1997

CULTURAL RELATIVITY NO
BAR TO THE UNIVERSALITY
OF HUMAN RIGHTS

Recognition of the immense cultural diversity in the world leads some to question whether it is possible to talk about the "universal" system of values on which human rights norms are based. Some anthropologists and philosophers use the theory of cultural relativity to question the universal nature of human rights. Anthropologists have observed and documented the very real differences in the values acceptable within different groups of people and which have framed their cultures and traditions. It is a primary principle of anthropology not to import any value judgement from one culture to another.

However, individuals from faiths and cultures throughout the world do recognise universal human rights, and the states participating at the World Conference on Human Rights agreed that "the universal nature of these rights and freedoms is beyond question".

To hold states accountable for their performance
with relation to global human rights standards
is not to impose the value system of any one part of the world
on another, but to refer to universal values, based on the
distilled knowledge and wisdom of all our cultures

An issue that is frequently raised in this context is that of traditional practices such as female genital mutilation. It has long been recognised that such practices are harmful to the health of women and girls. As a result, the UN and other international agencies have developed strategies to combat these practices. Further, such practices have been recognised as a form of violence against women and condemned in international human rights fora. But, it is sometimes argued that these international initiatives are interfering with the cultures of other societies.

It is not possible here to consider all the implications raised by these issues. However, what can be stated is that when an individual donor, such as DFID, assists states to develop appropriate strategies or supports projects designed to overcome such practices, it is not imposing its own domestic values. It is acting in accordance with the global consensus that such practices are harmful to health, and violate the rights of women and girls.

Clearly, particular sensitivity is required in promoting respect for universal human rights in situations that raise issues of culture.

HUMAN RIGHTS: A GLOBAL
AGENDA

One of the arguments states sometimes put forward for refusing to respect the human rights of everyone within their jurisdiction is that the very notion of human rights is a Western concept, which is neither relevant nor binding on states in other parts of the world.

This criticism is linked with the concern in several regions that the various forms of Western cultural imperialism are trampling traditional local values. Some would say that these include a particularly Western interpretation of human rights with a stress on individuality, which is not fully shared by other societies that place more emphasis on duties and communities. Such critics have been particularly vocal in parts of Asia, and the Islamic world.

Although there are real concerns behind such viewpoints, these arguments do not so much deny the universality of fundamental human rights, as point to the need for sensitivity in the development and implementation of human rights standards. In order for human rights to be viewed as genuinely universal in nature, it is essential that in the drafting of human rights texts, the voices of all faiths and cultures are heeded, and that the standards that have already been developed are objectively enforced.

But is it true to say that the concept of human rights is solely a Western notion? Certainly not at this date in history. Although historically the political reforms in Europe and North America during the eighteenth and nineteenth century played an important role in shaping modern concepts of human rights and democracy, these have by no means been the only influences. The modern theory of human rights goes far beyond the confines of liberal rights theory associated with the West, and owes much to the influence of philosophies and values from elsewhere in the world, and to notions of equity and social justice.

Whilst in Eastern societies greater emphasis may be placed on human duties than on rights, and in many African societies, stress is laid on social responsibilities – to the family and the community – these notions are in no way incompatible with current human rights thinking. The influence of these varying approaches can be seen in the Universal Declaration of Human Rights. For instance, as we have seen, Article 29 (1) provides:

> "Everyone has duties to the community in which alone the free and full development of his personality is possible."

More recently, the human rights community has benefited from the contribution of indigenous people throughout the world, who also lay emphasis on the nature of human responsibilities, particularly regarding the world's populace as custodial guardians of the environment for the benefit of future generations.

The global nature of human rights is also evidenced in political action by states. All Member States of the UN have pledged themselves to respect human rights. States from all regions of the world now take active part in international debates concerning the development of international human rights texts, and participate in the UN human rights bodies responsible for overseeing the development, protection and enforcement of human rights globally.

Similarly, the fact that 171 states took part in the World Conference on Human Rights in Vienna in 1993, and unanimously adopted the Vienna Declaration and Programme of Action, is proof that the human rights regime is now genuinely accepted world-wide. In adopting the Vienna Declaration and Programme of Action the participating states endorsed a global human rights agenda for implementation into the next century.

As the Vienna Declaration stresses:

> "...while the significance of national and regional particularities and various historical, cultural and religious backgrounds must be borne in mind, it is the duty of States, regardless of their political, economic and social systems, to promote and protect all human rights and fundamental freedoms."[3]

The Vienna Declaration also confirms:

> "Human rights and fundamental freedoms are the birthright of all human beings; their protection and promotion is the first responsibility of all Governments."[4]

Furthermore, individuals throughout the world claim the importance of human rights to their lives.

Not surprisingly, criticisms of the universality of human rights are most frequently heard from states that do not wish to comply with their obligations to respect human rights, or who are trying to avoid international condemnation of their record in this regard.

A human rights agenda, if objectively implemented, should not be regarded as imposing purely western values on other countries. Rather, it holds states accountable for obligations that they have freely undertaken at the international level

In order not to be seen as imposing a western agenda, it is vital that equal priority is given to all human rights - civil, cultural, economic, political and social. A focus in international policy on a few selected civil and political freedoms merely exacerbates the criticisms of the imposition of a western agenda.

Sceptics sometimes question whether it is appropriate to impose current international human rights standards on countries at different levels of development.

It is well to remember that the full realisation of human rights is a long term agenda. As our own historical experience illustrates, human rights protection often evolves over time as societies recognise additional injustice and inequalities. It is well to recall that child labour remained a reality in Britain until the reforms of the nineteenth century. Universal suffrage was not achieved until 1918, and protection from racial and sex discrimination came even later. Today, the rights of people with disabilities, minorities, asylum seekers and the homeless remain inadequate.

The difficulties of implementing fully the protection of all human rights in the circumstances of abject poverty are illustrated by the current discussions on child labour.

[3] Paragraph 5(1), Vienna Declaration and Platform for Action, adopted at the World Conference on Human Rights, June 1993.
[4] Paragraph 1(1), Vienna Declaration and Platform for Action.

The immediate introduction of law to prohibit child labour could have severe consequences for the livelihoods of the children affected and their families, and is not, therefore, considered to be the best answer in many cases. There have been circumstances in which well-intentioned projects designed to rescue children from factory work have left them without an income, and have resulted in forcing them into prostitution.

At the same time, as we have seen, lack of economic development is not an excuse for governments to fail to act. It is incumbent on states in which child labour remains a problem to take appropriate steps towards its abolition, whilst giving urgent attention to the needs of the children.

The international community needs to act sensitively in such a situation by *supporting* states seeking to introduce reforms, rather than by condemning such states as violators of children's rights.

LEGAL JUSTIFICATION FOR INTERNATIONAL CONCERN AND ACTION

Observers from the 'realist' school of international relations frequently criticise a concern for human rights overseas, as being interference in the 'internal affairs' of a country.

Similarly, in earlier years, some states sought to avoid international attention being paid to their human rights record by arguing that the way in which it treated its citizens was a matter falling solely within the state's sovereignty. Such states would seek to rely on Article 2 (7) of the UN Charter that provides:

> "Nothing contained in the present Charter shall authorise the United Nations to intervene in matters which are essentially within the domestic jurisdiction of any state ...". [5]

However, respect for internationally recognised human rights cannot be regarded as "essentially within the domestic jurisdiction of any state". Respect for human rights is an international issue and concern. The Charter obligations concerning human rights have made that clear. Since the adoption of the UN Charter, the universal character of human rights, and the legitimacy of international concern for their respect, has been developed in numerous global and regional human rights instruments, commencing with the Universal Declaration of Human Rights.

The legitimacy of international concern for human rights was emphasised by the World Conference on Human Rights, Vienna, in 1993. Paragraph 4 of the Vienna Declaration and Programme of Action provides:

> "The promotion and protection of all human rights and fundamental freedoms must be considered as a priority objective of the United Nations in accordance with its purposes and principles, in particular the purpose of international co-operation. In the framework of these purposes and principles, *the promotion and protection of all human rights is a legitimate concern of the international community*. ..." [6]

---

5 This provision expressly exempts enforcement actions taken by the UN following determination by the Security Council of the existence of any threat to the peace, breach of the peace, or act of aggression.
6 Emphasis added.

The relationship between this legitimate international concern for the protection of human rights and the principle of state sovereignty can be stated thus:

State sovereignty ensures that each State may determine how best to protect the rights of its own citizens; but protect them it must. A failure by a State to protect human rights justifies international concern and action.

More recently, the legitimacy of the role played by individuals and non-governmental organisations (NGOs) in drawing attention to abuse of rights has been vindicated. By the Helsinki Final Act, participating states expressly recognised the right of individuals to monitor the human rights record of states. Similarly, the World Conference on Human Rights recognised:

> "... the important role of non-governmental organisations in the promotion of all human rights and in humanitarian activities at national, regional and international levels. ... Non-governmental organisations and their members genuinely involved in the field of human rights should enjoy the rights and freedoms recognised in the Universal Declaration of Human Rights, and the protection of the national law. These rights and freedoms may not be exercised contrary to the purposes and principles of the United Nations. Non-governmental organisations should be free to carry out their human rights activities, without interference, within the framework of national law and the Universal Declaration of Human Rights." [7]

Constant vigilance is required to ensure that spurious reliance is not placed on the principle of state sovereignty and non-interference with domestic affairs in an attempt to prevent legitimate concern and humanitarian action on the part of the international community.

There is, however, a distinction between international 'concern' on the one hand, and 'action' on the other. This distinction is perhaps the most crucial and difficult aspect in the international protection of human rights and humanitarian relief assistance. For although the UN Charter emphasises the right – indeed the duty – of member states to 'take joint and separate action' for the achievement of the goals of the Organisation, the form that such action might take is not fully spelt out.

Action at the international level, be it in the form of diplomatic representations to a violating government, a complaint before an international human rights forum, or condemnation by an international body of a government committing gross violations, would certainly appear to be permissible action. Authority for such international activities may be found in the various instruments protecting human rights and those establishing international enforcement procedures.

---

[7] Vienna Declaration and Programme of Action, Paragraph 38.

But as we have seen in the former Yugoslavia, Somalia and Rwanda, it is less clear what action individual states, or the UN collectively, can take to operate effectively within a country in which genocide or mass violations of human rights are occurring.

A thorough review[8] of both the legal basis and the logistics of such international operations is required in order that the lessons of these interventions can be learnt, and procedures be established to enable the international community to respond speedily and effectively to the humanitarian needs of the future.

THE REQUIREMENT OF GIVING EQUAL PRIORITY TO ALL HUMAN RIGHTS FOR ALL PEOPLE

ALL HUMAN RIGHTS

To some extent, the inheritance of western liberal traditions has led Western governments to sign up to the rhetoric that economic, social and cultural rights are of equal importance, but to do little to promote them in practice.

An important focus of the Government's human rights policy should be to ensure that **equal priority is given to all human rights** in both political statements and action, at home and abroad. This is essential for the credibility of the human rights agenda, for a policy which only promotes those liberal values of particular significance to the west, will risk being seen as imposing a western agenda.

But this is not the only reason why civil, cultural, economic, political, and social rights should be given equal priority. We have witnessed the truth that liberty is not simply the absence of coercion, but includes the freedom and ability to take up opportunities.

The human rights community now recognises the need to balance individual liberties with provisions to promote equity and social justice

This cannot be achieved through the promotion of civil and political rights alone. These rights are vital, but they are not sufficient to secure freedom from hunger, the indignity of unemployment, and the agony of watching a child die for lack of essential immunisation or health care.

In 1993, the current High Commissioner for Human Rights, Mrs. Mary Robinson, spoke of a visit to Somalia she had recently made:

> "My inner sense of justice and equality was outraged by what I had seen …Are we not diminishing our own sense of humanity by failing to address the starvation and destitution of so many of our fellow human beings? How can we assert the universality of human rights by ignoring the life chances of millions of people?"[9]

---

[8] Similar to that undertaken in the Joint Evaluation of Emergency Assistance to Rwanda, Synthesis Report by John Eriksson *et al.*

[9] Presentation of the Concluding Remarks by the General Rapporteur, Mary Robinson, then President of Ireland, at the inter-regional meeting organised by the Council of Europe in preparation of the World Conference on Human Rights, 1993.

ALL PEOPLE On a similar point, a concern for human rights in international policy must encompass a concern for ***all people***.

A coherent policy is one that gives as much emphasis to using the tools of foreign and domestic policy to protect women's human rights, as it does to protect those of men. It is one which gives as much emphasis to overcoming atrocities against the poor and vulnerable, as protecting the rights of the more visible political dissidents, journalists, and human rights defenders.

As the Rt. Hon. Clare Short has reminded us:

> "Human rights are not satisfied until they are realised equally by every individual".[10]

This point is particularly important in the manner in which the rights of women are treated in foreign policy. It is essential that the achievement of women's rights is not seen to be solely a development issue. Whilst it is true that respect for women's rights is beneficial for economic and social development, this should not be the sole basis of concern for their protection.

To paraphrase the famous quote that the civilisation of a country can be measured by the manner in which it treats its minorities, the effectiveness of human rights policies can be judged by the degree of protection they afford to the voiceless and powerless – the poorest and most vulnerable people in our societies.

THE NEED FOR INTER-DEPARTMENTAL COHERENCE

The UK Government has stressed the importance of coherence in policy between various departments of the Government. This is particularly important, as the protection of human rights is a cross-cutting concern. The Foreign Office, DFID, Ministry of Defence, Department of Trade and Industry, to name but some departments, all have their roles to play in the international promotion and protection of human rights.

The inter-linkages are particularly obvious in times of mass violations of human rights and the type of complex emergencies that emerged during the conflicts in the former Yugoslavia and in Rwanda. Compartmentalisation is simply not possible. There are considerable links between the political steps necessary to prevent and end conflict and those intended to build and keep the peace, on the one hand, and emergency humanitarian efforts and co-operation for reconstruction and development, on the other. Coordination between these various initiatives is vital.

---

[10] *Democracy, Human Rights and Governance*, Speech by Rt. Hon. Clare Short, Secretary of State for International Development, at the Public Sector Management For The Next Century Conference, University of Manchester, 30 June 1997.

It is particularly important that there is close co-operation and coordination between DFID and the Foreign Office in implementing the human rights approach to international policy. For this reason, before turning to the implementation of the new human rights approach to development, it is useful to review some aspects of the more traditional activities undertaken by governments, and to consider their impact on the development agenda.

CONTRIBUTING TO THE INTERNATIONAL PROTECTION OF HUMAN RIGHTS

As we have seen, the UN Charter imposes obligations on member states with respect to the international protection of human rights. Implementing these obligations has traditionally been regarded as part of the role of the Foreign and Commonwealth Office, and for a number of years has been the particular responsibility of the Human Rights Policy Department of the FCO.

In implementing this duty of international protection, states traditionally undertake activities such as:

- Contributing to international standard setting through the drafting of new instruments
- Reporting to treaty monitoring bodies on the steps taken to implement obligations under specific treaties
- Participating in the work of international human rights fora, such as the UN Commission on Human Rights, and supporting the UN Centre for Human Rights
- Raising human rights violations with appropriate UN bodies, including where necessary, the Security Council
- Supporting international criminal tribunals
- Introducing measures to prohibit the export of instruments of torture, and ban the sale of any equipment to countries known to use such equipment for internal repression or other violation of human rights.
- Promoting international arms control measures
- Supporting positive measures to promote and protect human rights such as: training in human rights and responsibilities for police; measures to strengthen the independence of the judiciary; support for human rights NGOs and grass-roots organisations representing minorities or other disadvantaged people; and programmes to promote women's rights, and encourage freedom of expression.

International Standard Setting

Despite major progress in normative development over the last 50 years, there remain some significant gaps and weaknesses in the international protection of human rights. These weaknesses are particularly recognisable by the disadvantaged status of particular sectors of society. For example, additional attention needs to be given to the protection of minorities, asylum-seekers, and people living with disabilities. Further, the protection of human rights during internal armed conflict and complex emergencies needs to be strengthened.

The whole area of economic, social and cultural rights needs to be further developed. This could be assisted by the proposed optional protocol to grant individual petition under the ICESCR. Similarly, the initiative for an optional protocol to the Convention on the Elimination of All Forms of Discrimination Against Women (CEDAW) should be supported.

Strengthening legal protection in these regards should therefore form part of the wider human rights approach to development. Although standard-setting is primarily a role undertaken by the FCO rather than DFID, the experience of DFID in understanding the disadvantages suffered by, and aspirations of, people living in poverty and social isolation, could clearly strengthen any resulting international texts. Similarly, DFID might consider supporting grass-roots representatives to enable them to participate in the drafting of new texts.[11]

In engaging in standard setting, governments would be well advised to heed the advice of the High Commissioner for Human Rights, Mary Robinson. In the lead up to the World Conference on Human Rights in 1993, she called for a "listening approach to human rights", that is, one in which we listen to other points of view, and are mindful that in our various traditions, the approaches we adopt in the process of consensus building might themselves differ.

Dealing with Human Rights Violations

A number of options are available to Governments for dealing with human rights violations. These range from quiet diplomacy at one end of the spectrum, to UN interventions sanctioned by the Security Council, at the other. Sometimes the choice of option is comparatively easy. On other occasions it is fraught with difficulties, both political and ethical - some of which are considered more fully below.

Experience has indicated that bilateral human rights policies are rarely effective on their own. Working through multi-lateral organisations is therefore important. Both the EU and the Commonwealth have integrated a concern for human rights into their activities.[12] However, for multi-lateral action to be credible, it must be consistently applied.

DEVELOPMENT ASSISTANCE IN TIMES OF HUMAN RIGHTS VIOLATIONS

In situations of conflict, violence, and other mass violations of human rights, the opportunities for development are remote. Even the provision of emergency humanitarian relief may be impeded.

Three differing situations arise when:

- a donor withdraws development assistance in order to send a message to a regime violating human rights to indicate that the situation is unacceptable - negative conditionality

[11] For instance, a number of international donors supported representatives of indigenous peoples' organisations to participate in the UN Working Group on Indigenous Peoples during the 1980s.
[12] For instance, see the Lomé Convention of the EU, and the Harare Communiqué of the Commonwealth.

- the conditions within a country have deteriorated to such an extent that it is no longer logistically possible to ensure that assistance reaches the intended beneficiaries, which raises difficulties for humanitarian assistance

- embargoes or sanctions have been imposed on a state by the UN Security Council.

Difficulties arise in determining when such conditionalities and sanctions should be imposed, and who should decide.

DEVELOPMENT ASSISTANCE AND NEGATIVE CONDITIONALITY

In recent years the promotion of human rights and democracy has become a critical objective of the development assistance of a number of donors. These policies have, to a greater or lesser extent, made the provision of assistance dependent on the human rights record and democratisation process in the recipient country. In times of violations of human rights, donors have sometimes wished to send a political message that the situation is unacceptable by reducing, withdrawing, postponing, or threatening to reduce or withdraw, development assistance.

The consideration of such conditionalities raises a number of issues about the criteria to be used, and the impact of the conditionalities, particularly on the poor and vulnerable.

Criteria for judging violations

What criteria should be introduced to assess the human rights performance of an aid recipient country? And what type of violations should prompt the withdrawal of assistance? For instance, how can the comparative seriousness of unexplained deaths of political opponents in police custody be weighed against the forcible eviction of slum dwellers from their homes? And what is to be done in a situation in which a country has made progress in one area of human rights at the same time as limiting enjoyment of other rights? How do we judge the human rights situation in a country in which there has been a marked improvement in securing equitable access to public services, but at the same time, press freedom has been curtailed? Is the latter to be considered more significant than the former? If so, do we not fall, once again, into the trap of giving precedence to one set of rights over another?

A simple answer might be to wait until an international human rights body has condemned the particular transgression, but this would impose a considerable delay, and in any case, there is no guarantee that these bodies would be any more objective than donor governments.

These and other questions will have to be answered, perhaps on a case-by-case basis. What can be stressed, however, is that donors must ensure that the application of human rights conditionalities is both politically neutral and seen to be objective. To a certain extent, the intervention of multilateral bodies will assist in this regard, but clear and transparent guidelines are required on how these conditionality policies are to be implemented, and these should be accessible to aid-recipient countries.

An evaluation of Norwegian aid commissioned by the Norwegian Ministry of Foreign Affairs, and undertaken by Hilde Selbervik, reviews three Norwegian programme countries. The review shows that the lack of operational guidelines and country-specific strategies in the field of human rights and democratisation leads to incoherence and *ad hoc* intervention. The study recommends the development of a detailed set of general guidelines, which should be more operational than the rudiments already existing.[13]

This need for more operational guidelines has been recognised by a number of donor countries, and steps are underway to fill this gap. There is also a need to strengthen institutional capacity and competence in the field of human rights and democracy within development assistance administrations.

In order to avoid flavouring aid conditionalities with a solely northern perspective on human rights violations, it is essential that development partner countries be involved in the process of drawing up these guidelines. Only in this way will donors be able to avoid a charge that human rights conditionalities in development assistance policies are but one more way of imposing Northern values and interpretations on countries on the South.

Impact on the Poor and Vulnerable

Insofar as development assistance is targeted at assisting the poorest sectors of society, is there not a risk that the withdrawal or reduction of development aid through the imposition of conditionality could have the unjust result of causing the poor to suffer on account of the sins committed by their government?

The impact of the withdrawal of assistance on the poor and vulnerable should, therefore, be given particular consideration. Ethical policies require a consideration of the *impact* of the policy, as much as the moral basis of the policy.

The detrimental impacts of negative aid conditionalities on the most vulnerable members of society have been known to the international community for some time.

Negative aid conditionalities impact adversely on the poor but have almost no impact on the behavior of states

What is more recently coming to light is the fact that negative conditionality has had almost no impact on altering the behaviour of governments and leaders that consistently abuse the human rights of their people.

David Gillies has examined the human rights policies and programmes of the Netherlands, Canada, and Norway. In a study reviewing the period 1973-1994, he focused on cases where bilateral development aid had been used deliberately as a tool in the furtherance of democracy and human rights. Gillies identified 25 cases where negative aid conditionalities had been imposed. In 23 of these cases aid was reduced, suspended, threatened with suspension, or terminated altogether.

[13] *Aid as a Tool in the Promotion of Human Rights and Democracy: What can Norway Do?* Evaluation Report 7.97, Chancellor Michelson Institute, published by The Royal Ministry of Foreign Affairs, Norway, October, 1997

The other 2 cases were examples of non-action despite threats to take action. The subsequent human rights record and the rate of democratisation process in the respective recipient countries was then compared to the position prior to the donor's action. Although Gillies's analysis does not comprise all cases linking human rights and development in this period, his findings for those cases studied were unequivocal in every case - ***the human rights situation and condition of governance continued to be poor, or even worsened.***[14] This point was endorsed by the conclusions of Selbervik's Norwegian study.

As Gillies argues in a different study, such conditionality should be "a lever of last resort in extreme cases of unequivocal state culpability in the perpetration of deliberate, systematic or persistent human rights violation."[15]

Based on an analysis of Norwegian policies and practices, Selbervik's study made the following recommendations in order to improve Norwegian support for human rights and democratisation:

- A detailed set of general guidelines for support within the human rights sector should be worked out and made more operational than the rudiments already existing;
- A thorough overall assessment should be made of the human rights situation and the democratisation challenges of each programme country with a view to defining the problems and need for support;
- Detailed country-specific strategies for the human rights and democratisation sector (as is done for other sectors) should be worked out. This is necessary due to the wide variations between programme countries in terms of a number of factors: need and prospects for making an impact; entry points and channels; the donor's position in the country in absolute and relative terms etc.;
- Based on the overall assessment and the country-specific strategies appropriate entry points should be identified and projects designed to address the problems encountered. Project areas and design should be discussed in a dialogue with the authorities concerned and civil society organisations;
- For each programme country a decision should be made as to prioritisation of the human rights and democratisation sector. If accorded high priority, the competence and capacity commensurate with the task at hand should be made available so as to be able to make an impact;
- Interventions and measures should as far as possible be co-ordinated with other donors in order to avoid overlap and duplication of effort. It would be worth while to consider what other donors are doing within this sector and to draw upon their experiences.[16]

---

[14] *Between Principle and Practice*, 1996, as cited by Selbervik, *ibid*
[15] David Gillies, *Human Rights, Democracy and "Good Governance": Stretching the World Bank's Policy Frontiers,* International Centre for Human Rights and Democratic Development, Canada, 1993.
[16] Selbervik, 1997, *ibid*, at page 75

Even when development assistance is not provided, donors may be involved in providing emergency humanitarian assistance. Particularly difficult issues are raised by attempts to provide humanitarian assistance in times of widespread violation of human rights and complex emergencies.

Many would argue that, in some circumstances, to continue relief aid props up an oppressive regime. The withdrawal of aid, on the other hand, can provide a clear signal to the violating government that such abuse can not be tolerated.

There may be situations in which there are calls from the country concerned for international sanctions. South Africa during the *apartheid* regime is a case in point. Similarly, during the current conflict in Siérra Leone, some people within the country are calling on donors to take decisive action. They are prepared to make short term sacrifices in order to achieve the longer term goal of democracy and respect for human rights.

This is a difficult area, as the only relief available to those suffering abuses of their human rights by an oppressive regime, may be assistance from the international community.   At the same time, the situation might be complicated by the logistical difficulties of aid delivery to the intended beneficiaries.

Donors are under an ethical duty to take appropriate measures to ensure that aid reaches the intended beneficiaries. It is generally agreed that development and relief assistance should not be continued where there is clear evidence of misuse, or there is reason to believe that the aid will be diverted from its intended beneficiaries. On the other hand, a purely theoretical possibility that the aid will be misused should not itself lead to a withdrawal of aid. It may be that local or international NGOs will be more successful in delivering the assistance direct to the poor and oppressed. Routing aid through NGOs should therefore be considered.

Where it is impossible even for NGOs to reach the intended beneficiaries, donors may be under pressure to withdraw humanitarian aid altogether. This issue is hotly debated, as it raises difficult ethical issues of turning one's back on people in need.

In order to ensure consistency and a coherent policy in this regard, there is need for agreement, both at the national and international levels, about the criteria to be adopted to determine when to withdraw, and when to recommence humanitarian assistance. The UK's commitment to the development of guidelines for the provision of humanitarian assistance in times of conflict and human rights violations is particularly important in this regard.

As the situation in a country deteriorates, a spectrum of options available to the international community continues with the engagement of the Security Council. Where the violations amount to a threat to the peace, breach of the peace, or act of aggression, the Security Council may, pursuant to Article 41 of the UN Charter, call upon the members of the UN to apply sanctions. These measures may include complete or partial interruption of economic relations, and of rail, sea, air, postal, telegraphic, radio, and other means of communication, and the severance of diplomatic relations.

Peace keeping action is another option. Should the Security Council consider that the measures outlined above would be inadequate, or where they have proved to be inadequate, it may take such action by air, sea, or land forces as may be necessary to maintain or restore international peace and security. Such action may include demonstrations, blockade, and other operations by air, sea, or land forces of Members of the United Nations.[17]

A state must cease providing development assistance once the UN has introduced sanctions. By Article 2 of the UN Charter, Member States commit themselves to give the UN "every assistance in any action it takes in accordance with the present Charter". States "shall refrain from giving assistance to any state against which the United Nations is taking preventive or enforcement action."

Humanitarian Impact of Trade Embargoes and Economic Sanctions

A human rights approach requires that, in considering the imposition of sanctions, the international community should consider the impact such actions will have, particularly on the poor and vulnerable.

Many studies have been conducted on the humanitarian impact of sanctions. They have shown that in most cases it is the poor and vulnerable that suffer the main hardship, rather than the governments at which the sanctions were aimed.

Some writers have gone as far as saying that sanctions "... place us squarely in the dilemma of having to choose methods of killing some people to save others".[18] In Iraq, estimates suggest that infant deaths may have doubled or tripled since sanctions were imposed; in the month of January 1996 alone, more than 6000 children under the age of five reputedly died as a direct result of sanctions.[19]

In addition, whilst 'humanitarian exemption clauses' (i.e. excluding humanitarian items from the sanctions regime) is attractive in theory, in practice such exemptions have not always led to a marked increase in the quality of the conditions of those most affected by the imposition of sanctions. Reasons for this are numerous, and have been explored in detail elsewhere.[20] A case in point is that of the exemptions allowed within the sanctions imposed on Iraq. The exemptions initially included supplies strictly for medical purposes and, in humanitarian circumstances, foodstuffs. Subsequently, these exemptions were expanded to include supplies for essential civilian needs subject to certain 'notification' and 'no objection' procedures. However, observers consider that very few of these items have yet reached those most in need, and one study suggests that it took almost seven years before the first food supplies reached Iraq.[21]

[17] UN Charter, Article 42
[18] T. Getman and L. Witte, 1995. *A Humanitarian Community Position Paper on Sanctions.* World Vision US.
[19] From the Ramsay Clark report on civilian impact of UN sanctions, March 1,1996, to the members of the Security Council. Cited in: *The Children are Dying; The Impact of Sanctions on Iraq,* 1996, World View Forum.
[20] See *Sanctions - Still Stacking Up The Bodies; The Failure of the Concept of Humanitarian Windows,* World Vision; *A Safer Future* by Edmund Cairns, 18 September 1997
[21] See *A Safer Future,* ibid.

While adults can conceivably survive for long periods of hardship and privation, children have far less endurance and resistance. In a report on the Impact of Armed Conflict on Children for the UN General Assembly, Graça Machel points to studies of Cuba, Haiti and Iraq following the imposition of sanctions: each nation showed a substantial rise in the proportion of children who were malnourished. For example, in Haiti after 1991, the figure rose from 5% to 23%.[22]

Machel recommends that any sanctions regime undertaken should be precisely targeted at the vulnerabilities of the political or military leaders whose behaviour the international community wishes to change. This could include arms embargoes or the freezing of overseas corporate and individual assets. These measures are less likely to harm children and other vulnerable civilians in the targeted country.[23]

She also recommends a system of child impact assessment before the imposition of sanction regimes, and continuous monitoring during the life span of the regime against the standards laid out in the Convention on the Rights of the Child. She recommends that, at the very least:

> "...such assessments should measure changes in access to essential medicines...especially items that may serve both civilian and military purposes, such as chlorine for water purification...water quality or quantity...and the infant mortality rate".[24]

A controversial but very significant point that Machel raises is the autonomy of humanitarian agencies. She considers that humanitarian assistance programmes of the United Nations specialized agencies and of NGOs should be exempt from approval by the Security Council Sanctions Committee.

In summary, a human rights approach should pay attention to the likely effect of the sanctions on the population of the country concerned. There must be consideration of the balance between the potential benefit of sanctions, and the impact on the rights and needs of people facing oppression and living in poverty and social isolation. In this context, further consideration should be given to directing sanctions to political leaders rather than to the civilian population. The international community must also consider how to ensure that the humanitarian needs resulting from an imposition of sanctions are fully met, and that the necessary resources are made available.

THE POSITIVE PROMOTION OF HUMAN RIGHTS THROUGH INTERNATIONAL POLICY

As the Foreign Secretary has stated:

> "We should not fall into the ...error of imagining that we have done our bit for human rights by refusing to have anything to do with those countries with an unsatisfactory performance on human rights. This may provide us with clean hands, but it is unlikely to provide their people with better rights".[25]

---

[22] Machel, Graça, *Promotion of the Rights of Children: Impact of Armed Conflict on Children*, Report to the General Assembly of the Expert appointed by the UN Secretary General, UN document A/51/306, 26 August, 1996.
[23] Machel, *Ibid*, para. 130
[24] Machel, *Ibid*, para. 132
[25] Speech by the Foreign Secretary, Rt. Hon. Robin Cook, Locarno Suite, Foreign and Commonwealth Office, London, 17 July 1997

A wide spectrum of other options is also open to the Foreign and Commonwealth Office and to DFID to *promote* respect for human rights.

As the Rt. Hon. Tony Lloyd, Minister of State, Foreign and Commonwealth Office, has reminded us, megaphone diplomacy can sometimes be counterproductive. This is certainly the case in dealing with sensitive issues, such as the promotion of women's rights in Islamic countries, and the prevention and redress of domestic violence and of female genital mutilation.

Both DFID and the Foreign and Commonwealth Human Rights Policy Department already support a wide range of activities to promote respect for human rights, ranging from educational projects, through projects to promote gender equity, and training in human rights for police officers, to steps to secure an independent judiciary and free press. They also support NGOs and other actors of civil society. Support for the establishment of National Human Rights Commissions and other national procedures can also assist in the prevention and redress of violations.

These activities form an essential part of an effective human rights policy. They play a key role in promoting a culture of human rights and democracy. They also contribute to conflict prevention and the avoidance of the forced displacement of people - which should be principle goals of international policy.

In the Author's view, DFID should give priority to developing these positive measures to promote respect for human rights and democracy, in conjunction with mainstreaming a human rights approach into all its policies and programmes. This is not to say that the more traditional negative conditionalities will never be appropriate. Rather, that they should be seen as the option of last resort.

PART II - A CONVERGING AGENDA

CHAPTER 5

5 HUMAN RIGHTS AND DEVELOPMENT: A CONVERGING AGENDA

"We Heads of State and Government are committed to a political, economic, ethical and spiritual vision for social development based on human dignity, human rights, equality ...".

Opening words of the Copenhagen Declaration and Programme of Action, adopted at the World Summit for Social Development, 1993

HUMAN RIGHTS AND DEVELOPMENT THEORY: DISTINCT BUT COMPLEMENTARY

Human rights and development theories have emerged from distinct disciplines, resulting in the application of different criteria for establishing the cogency of theoretical models and for measuring their success. This has sometimes impeded dialogue and comprehension between the two disciplines.[1]

Nevertheless, we have witnessed a convergence in the theory and practice of human rights and development, particularly as they relate to the lives of people living in poverty and social isolation. This has been particularly evident in the series of recent UN Conferences that have specifically referred to the nexus between human rights and development.

For instance, the World Declaration on Education for All and Framework for Action to Meet Basic Learning Needs, adopted at Jomtien in 1990, clarified the steps to be taken to implement the right to education. Similarly, the final report of the World Food Summit adopted in 1996, set out commitments by states concerning the implementation of the right to food.

The 1993 World Conference on Human Rights (WCHR) recognised that:

> "democracy, development and respect for human rights and fundamental freedoms are interdependent and mutually reinforcing."[2]

This confluence of human rights and development concerns was particularly marked at the World Summit for Social Development (WSSD). Heads of State and Government committed themselves "to a vision for social development" based on, among other things, "human dignity, human rights and equality".

---

[1] In an attempt to explore issues of joint concern *Rights and Humanity* has, since 1989, been organising a series of meetings for development theorists and practitioners and human rights advocates to consider human rights as a framework of economic and social justice and development. This led to the establishment of the Human Rights and Development Forum convened by *Rights and Humanity* in 1992. The Forum brings together development agencies such as OXFAM, Save the Children, and Christian Aid, and human rights groups, including Rights and Humanity, Amnesty International, Minority Rights Group, Change, Article 19, and the Commonwealth Human Rights Initiative in a common exploration of issues relating to human rights and development.
[2] Vienna Declaration and Programme of Action, paragraph 8.

Among the many references to human rights in the Declaration and Programme of Action of the WSSD is the important Commitment 1, by which participating states committed themselves to the creation of "an economic, political, social, cultural and legal environment that will enable people to achieve social development".

To this end, States undertook at the national level to:

> "Reaffirm, promote and strive to ensure the realization of the rights set out in relevant international instruments and declarations, such as the Universal Declaration of Human Rights, the International Covenant on Economic, Social and Cultural Rights, and the Declaration on the Right to Development, including those relating to education, food, shelter, employment, health and information, particularly in order to assist people in poverty."

The International Conference on Population and Development (ICPD),[3] held in Cairo, 1994, put stress on empowering women and providing them with more choices through expanded access to education and health services and promoting skills development and employment. It made the shift from seeking solely to achieve demographic targets to meeting the needs of individual women and men.

It utilised an holistic approach, recognising the numerous linkages between population and development and setting these in the wider context of women's human rights and human development. The programme of action includes goals in regard to education - especially for girls - and for the further reduction of infant, child and maternal mortality levels. It also addresses issues relating to population, the environment and consumption patterns; the family; internal and international migration; prevention and control of HIV/AIDS; information, education and communication; and technology, research and development.

This Conference marked a significant step forward by viewing population and development from a human rights perspective.

At the Fourth World Conference on Women, held in Beijing in September 1995, under the themes of equality, development and peace, States reaffirmed their commitment to eliminating discrimination against women and to removing all obstacles to equality. The need to ensure a gender perspective in all relevant state policies and programmes was also recognised. The Beijing Declaration and Platform for Action[4] identifies twelve "critical areas of concern" in overcoming obstacles to women's equality, defines strategic objectives, and sets out the steps to be taken by Governments, the international community, non governmental organisations and the private sector for the removal of existing obstacles.

---

3 5 – 13 September, 1994. 179 States participated, and adopted the Programme of Action.
4 Adopted by the 189 participating states.

At both Cairo and Beijing considerable emphasis was placed on defining human rights in the context of women's sexual and reproductive health. This was a controversial issue. The use of progressive language was resisted, to varying degrees, by Islamic countries, the Vatican and a number of Catholic countries. The fact that agreement was eventually reached on this issue, was an indication of the recognised importance of women's human rights within the wider agenda of population, development, and peace.

At the UN Conference on Human Settlements (Habitat II), in 1996, there were differences of opinion about the right to housing. This right was strongly opposed by the USA. But it had already been accepted in the International Bill of Rights, and other states felt equally strongly that recognition and protection of this right must form the basis of human settlement strategies. Article 61 of the Istanbul Declaration and Global Plan of Action reflects this latter view. It states:

> "Since the adoption of the Universal Declaration of Human Rights in 1948, the right to adequate housing has been recognized as an important component of the right to an adequate standard of living. All Governments without exception have a responsibility in the shelter sector, as exemplified by their creation of ministries of housing or agencies,by their allocation of funds for the housing sector and by their policies, programmes and projects. ... Within the overall context of an enabling approach, Governments should take appropriate action in order to promote, protect and ensure the full and progressive realisation of the right to adequate housing."

One of the actions to be taken by States is:

> "Providing legal security of tenure and equal access to land for all, including women and those living in poverty, as well as effective protection from forced evictions that are contrary to the law, taking human rights into consideration and bearing in mind that homeless people should not be penalised for their status."

The inclusion of commitments to ensuring respect for human rights within the context of these conferences, shows the general acceptance that respect for human rights is an essential basis for the strategies aimed at achieving human development.

Box 5.

Convergence of Human Rights and Development Agenda:

Some Milestones

- Jomtien Declaration on Education for All, 1990, recognised the right to education as a basis for international and national strategies

- In the Harare Communiqué, 1991, Commonwealth Heads of Government pledged themselves to extend benefits of development within a framework of respect for human rights

- World Conference on Human Rights, 1993, recognised that development and respect for human rights are interdependent and mutually re-inforcing and confirmed that women's rights are human rights

- World Health Organisation's Task Force in Health and Development adopted a human rights approach, 1993

- World Health Organisation's Global Commission on Women's Health adopted a human rights approach to protecting women's health, 1993

- International Conference on Population and Development, 1994, confirms the centrality of women's rights as a basis for development and population policies

- World Summit for Social Development, 1995, recognised human rights as a basis for development

- Beijing Women's Conference, 1995, confirmed women's human rights as essential basis for sustainable development

- The Development Assistance Committee (DAC) of the OECD prompted wider discussions of human rights and development, 1996

- HABITAT II, 1996, confirmed the right to housing as an important component of the right to an adequate standard of living

- World Food Summit, 1996, set out state commitments concerning implementation of the right to adequate nutrition

- A concern for human rights incorporated into the WHO 9th General Programme of Work, and the Renewed Health for All Strategy, 1997

The time is right to promote
a human rights based approach to development
in order that the experience of both human rights
and development theory and practice
can be brought to bear
on the urgent priority of poverty elimination

HUMAN RIGHTS APPROACH COMPLEMENTS EARLIER THEORIES

PARTICIPATION AND
EMPOWERMENT

Across a range of areas of social science there has, over the last decade, been a move towards an approach that seeks to be more empowering.

Particularly during the last decade of human rights advocacy, considerable stress has been placed on the principle of *participation.* The position of the right to participate as a human rights norm is strengthened by its increasing inclusion in human rights instruments. The International Bill of Rights confirms that "every citizen shall have the right and the opportunity … to take part in the conduct of public affairs, directly or through freely chosen representatives", and to take part in cultural life. The Declaration of the Right to Development proclaims that "every human person and all peoples are entitled to participate in, contribute to and enjoy development"; and also provides that "States should encourage popular participation in all spheres as an important factor in development and in the full realisation of all human rights."[5]

This principle of participation
is the practical manifestation of
an individual's equality and autonomy

At the same time, at the project end of social welfare, justice and development, there has been a marked move away from what might be described as the "soup kitchen" or "handout" approach to helping people, towards empowerment and other strategies to promote the fuller enjoyment of human rights.

For many years there has been a growing recognition among development practitioners that the best way of helping people is to involve members of the beneficiary target group in the development and implementation of assistance programmes, and in other ways to help themselves.

[5] Articles 1(1) and 8(2) respectively.

An earlier focus on *economic* development, and indicators such as GNP, is now being complemented by efforts to promote *human* development, and indicators aimed at the difficult task of measuring the quality of life. This paradigm shift is profound, but remains fraught with the complications of measuring quality rather than just quantity.

Within the health field, the global health community has moved from a narrow focus on curative care, to one which emphasizes protection and promotion of the health of all people. The Alma Ata Declaration on Primary Health Care of 1979,[6] was the milestone in this regard. This reflects the general disillusionment with the "top-down" approach. In contrast, the Primary Health Care strategy is aimed at tackling issues of inequities, reaching all people, satisfying their needs, and supporting capacity-building.

DEMOCRACY, HUMAN RIGHTS AND GOOD GOVERNANCE

A similar cross-fertilisation of ideas between human rights and development can be seen in the recent struggles by civil societies in a number of countries for democracy and human rights, and in the good governance policies introduced into development co-operation during the 1980s.

As we have seen, the promotion of respect for democracy, human rights and the rule of law has formed an increasingly important dimension of the policies of the World Bank, the OECD, the European Union and many bilateral donors.

The Good Government policy introduced by the former UK Government, for example, covered such issues as legitimacy, accountability, and competence of government, as well as respect for human rights, democratic principles and the rule of law. However, the term "Good Government" tended to be interpreted to refer to the *process* of governance, rather than the content of policy.

This Author has argued elsewhere[7] that in her view this interpretation was too restrictive. If human rights were to be adequately integrated into development, it was necessary to consider both the process of governance and the *content* of policy and action. It is through both aspects that states must implement their obligations to ensure enjoyment of all human rights - including economic, social and cultural rights.

The more restrictive view had the tendency of viewing human rights as limited to a sub-set of rights associated with the democratic process.The new human rights approach to development widens the inclusion of human rights within the policy and practice of development cooperation.

---

[6] *WHO, Alma Ata 1978: Primary Health Care.*
[7] *Good Governance and Human Rights: Two Sides of the Same Coin?* by Julia Häusermann, in *Good Governance*, report of a One World Action Seminar, London, March 1994.

A human rights approach to development
moves on from a focus on the civil and political rights
prioritised in earlier good government policies
to an holistic view of human rights
recognising the indivisibility of civil, cultural,
economic, political and social rights

ENTITLEMENTS, CAPABILITIES, AND HUMAN RIGHTS

The authoritative contribution of Amartya Sen's entitlements and capabilities theories has had a significant impact on development thinking, and on the indicators used by UNDP in recent Human Development Reports.

An important aspect of Sen's work has been to move the attention from measuring income to measuring a human being's experience of lack of income. He analyses poverty and famine from the human, rather than the strictly economic, dimension. Sen's term "entitlements" is used to refer to a person's legal rights of ownership within the national setting.[8] In a later work, Dreze and Sen added the concept of "extended entitlements":

"While the concept of entitlement focuses on a person's legal rights of ownership, there are some social relations that take the broader form of accepted legitimacy rather than legal rights enforceable in a court." [9]

They give the example of a male householder traditionally receiving more food than other members of the household:

"Despite their legally weaker form, such socially sanctioned rights[10] may be extremely important in determining the amount of food or health care or other commodities that different members of a family get ... 'Extended entitlements' is the concept of entitlements extended to include the results of more informal types of rights sanctioned by accepted notions of legitimacy."

The enjoyment of entitlements is further developed in the concepts of "functioning" and "capabilities." For Sen:

"The functioning of a person refers to the valuable things the person can do or be (such as being well nourished, living long and taking part in the life of a community). The capability of a person stands for the different combinations of functionings the person can achieve; it reflects the freedom to achieve functionings.

---

[8] Sen, Amartya. 1981. *Poverty and Famines: An Essay on Entitlement and Deprivation.*
[9] Dreze, Jean and Sen, Amartya . 1989. *Hunger and Public Action*, at page 10
[10] Contrast this use of the term "rights" with a **human rights** usage.

> In the capability concept the poverty of a life lies not merely in the impoverished state in which the person actually lives, but also the lack of real opportunity – due to social constraints as well as personal circumstances – to lead valuable and valued lives.
>
> Capability is a broad concept, and it incorporates the concerns that are associated with what is often called 'the standard of living', but goes beyond it. Living standards relate specifically to the richness of the person's own life, whereas a person may value his or her capability also to be socially useful and influential (going well beyond the pursuit of his or her own living standards)."[11]

In this way Dreze and Sen bring in a much needed "quality of life" component into the understanding of poverty, which is similar to a human rights view of deprivation.

However, there is an important distinction between the entitlements and capabilities theories, on the one hand, and the human rights approach to development proposed here. The former is concerned with the reality of people's lives, i.e. what *is*. The latter is concerned with international law, and what ***ought to be***.

For this reason, the author would propose avoiding use of the term "entitlements" within the explanation of a human rights approach. Whilst at a philosophical and legal level it is correct to say that individuals are "entitled" to enjoy their human rights, the use of the term "entitlements" might lead to confusion with Sen's usage of the term, which has now found broad favour in development circles.

Another way of looking at the distinction is that whilst Sen's theory looks at an individuals's command over commodities or capabilities, a human rights approach looks at what needs to be done to improve the situation. The focus on human rights, which implies choices for people, and on state obligations is therefore a pragmatic, rather than descriptive approach. A human rights approach does not supersede the entitlements and capabilities theories. It complements these earlier approaches.

There is a natural complementarity between:
the entitlement/capabilities approach
which looks at the problem of poverty
from the point of view of the poor
and a human rights approach
which combines a vision of what ought to be
with an emphasis on choices for people
and solutions in terms of the steps to be taken
to achieve human rights and thereby development

[11] *Hunger and Public Action,* at page 12.

HUMAN RIGHTS AND STATE OBLIGATIONS: A COHERENT BASIS FOR DEVELOPMENT

HUMAN RIGHTS AND SOCIAL
PROGRESS

In a number of ways human rights protection has, over the last thirty years, been somewhat ahead of development theory in terms of recognising the relationship between enjoyment of human rights and the achievement of development.

For instance, at a time when development theory and practice remained much influenced by a focus on economic growth and the trickle down theory (which so clearly failed to meet the needs of the poor), the Declaration on Social Progress and Development was adopted by the UN General Assembly in 1969. It proclaims:

Article 1   "All peoples and all human beings, without distinction shall have the right to live in dignity and freedom and to enjoy the fruits of social progress and should, on their part, contribute to it.

Article 2   Social progress and development shall be founded on respect for the dignity and value of the human person and shall ensure the promotion of human rights and social justice, which requires:

(a) The immediate and final elimination of all forms of inequality, exploitation of peoples and individuals....

(b) The recognition and effective implementation of civil and political rights as well as of economic, social and cultural rights without any discrimination."

THE RIGHT TO
DEVELOPMENT

The Declaration on the Right to Development was adopted by the UN General Assembly[12] on December 1986. It explicitly reconfirmed the existence of a human right to development, and elaborated the content of the right and state obligations.

At the time, the Declaration was controversial. Much of the controversy was around the question of the bearers of the right to development. Was it only individuals? – the view of the North – or were states also bearers of the right to development? The wording as adopted remains somewhat ambiguous on this point by referring to individuals and "peoples".

However, the Declaration contains some concepts that have taken root in human rights and development theory. For instance, Article 1 states:

"The right to development is an inalienable human right by virtue of which every human person and all peoples are *entitled to participate in, contribute to and enjoy* economic, social, cultural and political development, in which all human rights and fundamental freedoms can be fully realized." (Emphasis added.)

[12] The United States voted against the Declaration, and a number of northern donors - including the UK, Denmark, Finland, Germany, Iceland, Japan and Sweden - abstained.

Article 2 of the Declaration provides:

> "1. The human person is the central subject of development and should be the active participant and beneficiary of the right to development.
>
> 2. All human beings have a responsibility for development, individually and collectively, taking into account the need for full respect for their human rights and fundamental freedoms as well as their duties to the community, which alone can ensure the free and complete fulfilment of the human being, and they should therefore promote and protect an appropriate political, social and economic order for development.
>
> 3. States have the right and the duty to formulate appropriate national development policies that aim at the constant improvement of the well-being of the entire population and of all individuals, on the basis of their active, free and meaningful participation in development and in the fair distribution of the benefits resulting therefrom."

Despite the earlier controversies, the right to development was unequivocally confirmed by the 171 States (including the USA and UK) that participated in the World Conference on Human Rights in 1993. The World Conference confirmed:

> "...the right to development, as established in the Declaration on the Right to Development, as a universal and inalienable right and an integral part of fundamental human rights.
>
> As stated in the Declaration on the Right to Development, the human person is the central subject of development.
>
> While development facilitates the enjoyment of all human rights, the lack of development may not be invoked to justify the abridgement of internationally recognized human rights.
>
> States should cooperate with each other in ensuring development and eliminating obstacles to development. The international community should promote effective international cooperation for the realization of the right to development and the elimination of obstacles to development."[13]

The right to development was similarly reconfirmed by consensus at the International Conference on Population and Development (Cairo), the World Summit for Social Development (Copenhagen), and the Fourth World Conference on Women (Beijing). Thus today there can be no doubt that the right to development is firmly entrenched in international human rights protection.

---

[13] Article 10, paragraph 10, Vienna Declaration and Programme of Action.

The multi-faceted nature of the right was confirmed in October 1995, by the UN Working Group on the Right to Development, which stated that:

> "the right to development is multidimensional, integrated, dynamic and progressive. Its realization involves the full observance of economic, social, cultural, civil and political rights. It further embraces the different concepts of development of all development sectors, namely sustainable development, human development and the concept of indivisibility, interdependence and universality of all human rights. . . Realization of the right to development is the responsibility of all actors in development, within the international community, within States at both the national and international levels, within the agencies of the United Nations system."

HUMAN RIGHTS LEGAL TEXTS

Although these Declarations do not yet have the force of law, a number of human rights legal instruments have been adopted which specifically deal with the rights and development needs of the people living in poverty and vulnerability. Indeed the whole of the International Covenant on Economic, Social and Cultural Rights might be regarded as an agenda for development.

In addition, civil and political rights are essential for development. As Amartya Sen has reminded us, freedom of the press is vital in the prevention of famine:

> "the role of newspapers and public discussions...can be extremely crucial in identifying famine threats (an energetic press may be the best 'early warning system' for famine that a country can devise), [and] can also help to keep the government on its toes so that famine relief and preventative measures take place rapidly and effectively."[14]

The enjoyment of all human rights is essential for full human development

Without wishing to imply any hierarchy of rights, some human rights can be highlighted as having particular relevance to current development priorities with regard to protecting the freedoms, dignity and security of poor people, and the achievement of poverty elimination.

PHYSICAL SECURITY AND GOOD GOVERNANCE: SOME KEY HUMAN RIGHTS

A number of rights protected by the provisions of the International Covenant on Civil and Political Rights are of particular importance in securing the rights of people living in poverty and social isolation, and to securing good governance.

---

[14] Sen, Amartya. 1981. Poverty and Famine: An Essay on Entitlement and Deprivation.

The International Covenant on Civil and Political Rights provides, for example:

- Every human being has the inherent right to life (Article 6).

- No one shall be subjected to torture or to cruel, inhuman or degrading treatment or punishment (Article 7).

- No one shall be held in slavery; no one shall be required to perform forced or compulsory labour (except where imposed as a punishment for a crime) (Article 8).

- Everyone has the right to liberty and security of person (Article 9); all persons deprived of their liberty shall be treated with humanity and with respect for the inherent dignity of the human person (Article 10);

- Everyone lawfully with the territory of a State shall, within that territory, have the right to liberty of movement and freedom to choose his residence; everyone shall have the right to leave any country, including his own (Article 12).

- All persons shall be equal before the courts and tribunals. In the determination of any criminal charge against him or of his rights and obligations in a suit of law everyone shall be entitled to a fair and public hearing by a competent, independent and impartial tribunal established by law (Article 14).

- No one shall be subjected to arbitrary or unlawful interference with his privacy, family, home or correspondence, nor to unlawful attacks on his honour and reputation. Everyone has the right to the protection of the law against such interference or attacks (Article 17).

- Everyone shall have the right to freedom of thought, conscience and religion (Article 18).

- Everyone shall have the right to hold opinions without interference, and to freedom of expression; this right shall include freedom to seek, receive and impart information and ideas of all kinds, regardless of frontiers, either orally, in writing or in print, in the form of art, or through any other media of his choice (Article 19).

- The right of peaceful assembly shall be recognised (Article 21). Everyone shall have the right to freedom of association with others, including the right to form and join trade unions for the protection of his interests (Article 22).

- Every citizen shall have the right and the opportunity, without discrimination, to take part in the conduct of public affairs, directly or through freely chosen representatives; to vote and to be elected at genuine periodic elections (Article 25).

- All persons are equal before the law and are entitled without any discrimination to the equal protection of the law (Article 26).
- Persons belonging to ethnic, religious and linguistic minorities shall not be denied the right, in community with the other members of their group, to enjoy their own culture, to profess and practise their own religion, or to use their own language (Article 27).

POVERTY ELIMINATION: SOME KEY HUMAN RIGHTS AND STATE OBLIGATIONS

Labour rights are protected both by the ICCPR (Article 22 – the right to form and join trade unions) and the ICESCR (Article 6 – the right to work). These rights have been further elaborated in a wide range of ILO conventions which confirm five core labour standards.

Box 6.

Some Core Labour Standards Protected By ILO Conventions

There are a number of important concepts that are protected by the ILO Conventions. They are as follows:

1. The right to organise and to bargain collectively
   ILO Convention concerning freedom of association and protection of the right to organise, 1948, no. 87.
   ILO Convention concerning the application of the principles of the right to organise and to bargain collectively, 1949, no. 98.

2. Equal remuneration for men and women for work of equal value
   ILO Convention concerning equal remuneration for men and women workers for work of equal value, 1951, no. 100.

3. Non-discrimination in respect of employment and occupation
   ILO Convention concerning discrimination in respect of employment and occupation, 1958, no. 111.

4. Protection of children and adolescents
   ILO Convention concerning minimum age for admission to employment, 1973, no. 138.

5. Abolition of forced labour
   ILO Convention concerning forced or compulsory labour, 1930, no. 29.
   ILO Convention concerning the abolition of forced labour, 1957, no. 105.

Box 7.
Some Relevant State Obligations

• The Right to Education

Article 13 ICESCR

(2) The State Parties to the present Covenant recognize that, with a view to achieving the full realisation of this right:

(a) Primary education shall be compulsory and available free to all;

(b) Secondary education in its different forms, including technical and vocational secondary education, shall be made generally available and accessible to all by every appropriate means, and in particular by the progressive introduction of free education;

(c) Higher education shall be made equally accessible to all, on the basis of capacity, by every appropriate means, and in particular by the progressive introduction of free education;

(d) Fundamental education shall be encouraged or intensified as far as possible for those persons who have not received or completed the whole period of their primary education;

(e) The development of a system of schools at all levels shall be actively pursued, an adequate fellowship system shall be established, and the material conditions of teaching staff shall be continuously improved; ...

• The Right to the Highest Attainable Standard of Physical and Mental Health

Article 12, ICESCR

(2) The steps to be taken by States Parties to the present Covenant to achieve the full realization of this right shall include those necessary for:

(a) The provision for the reduction of the stillbirth-rate and of infant mortality and for the healthy development of the child;

(b) The improvement of all aspects of environmental and industrial hygiene;

(c) The prevention, treatment and control of epidemic, endemic, occupational and other diseases;

(d) The creation of conditions which would assure to all medical service and medical attention in the event of sickness.

• The Right to Work

UN Charter

Member States commit themselves to the promotion of full employment.

Article 23, UDHR

(1) Everyone has the right to work, to free choice of employment, to just and favourable conditions of work and to protection against unemployment.

Article 6 ICESCR

(1) States Parties...recognize the right to work, which includes the right of everyone to the opportunity to gain his living by work which he freely chooses or accepts, and will take appropriate steps to safeguard this right.

(2) The steps to be taken ... shall include technical and vocational guidance and training programmes, policies and techniques to achieve steady economic, social and cultural

development and full and productive employment, under conditions safeguarding fundamental political and economic freedoms to the individual.

Article 7 ICESCR

The States Parties recognize the right of everyone to the enjoyment of just and favourable conditions of work, including fair wages, safe and healthy working conditions, equal opportunities, reasonable limitation of working hours.

• Land Rights

Article 17, UDHR

(1) Everyone has the right to own property alone as well as in association with others

(2) No one shall be arbitrarily deprived of his property.

(Although not expressly stated, States need to protect individuals' land rights so as to prevent the poor and vulnerable from being evicted from their land. Land reform may also be necessary to ensure access to land for poor people).

• Adequate Standard of Living including food and housing

Article 11, ICESCR

(1) States Parties…recognize the right of everyone to an adequate standard of living for himself and his family, including adequate food, clothing and housing, and to the continuous improvement of living conditions. The States Parties will take appropriate steps to ensure the realization of this right, recognizing to this effect the essential importance of international co-operation based on free consent.

(Although there is no specific reference to a "right to water", access to adequate clean water is generally regarded as being a part of the requirements of an adequate standard of living.)

• The Right to Freedom from Hunger

Article 11(2), ICESCR

States Parties…shall take, individually and through international co-operation, the measures, including specific programmes, which are needed:

(a) To improve methods of production, conservation and distribution of food by making full use of technical and scientific knowledge, by disseminating knowledge of the principles of nutrition and by developing or reforming agrarian systems in such a way as to achieve the most efficient development and utilisation of natural resources;

(b) Taking into account the problems of both food-importing and food-exporting countries, to ensure an equitable distribution of world food supplies in relation to need.

• The Right to Social Security

Article 22, UDHR

Everyone, as a member of society, has the right to social security…

Article 25, UDHR

(1) Everyone has the right to…security in the event of unemployment, sickness, disability, widowhood, old age or other lack of livelihood in circumstances beyond his control.

Box 8.

Equal Rights of Women

Articles 2 and 3, ICESCR and ICCPR

States Parties to the present Covenant undertake to ensure the equal right of men and women to the enjoyment of all economic, social and cultural rights [civil and political rights] as set forth in the present Covenant.

Article 2, Convention on the Elimination of Discrimination Against Women (CEDAW)

States Parties...undertake:

(a) To embody the principle of the equality of men and women in their national constitutions or other appropriate legislation if not yet incorporated therein and to ensure, through law and other appropriate means, the practical realization of this principle;

(b) To adopt appropriate legislative and other measures, including sanctions where appropriate, prohibiting all discrimination against women;

(c) To establish legal protection of the rights of women on an equal basis with men and to ensure through competent national tribunals and other public institutions the effective protection of women against any act of discrimination;

(d) To refrain from engaging in any act or practice of discrimination against women and to ensure that public authorities and institutions shall act in conformity with this obligation;

(e) To take all appropriate measures to eliminate discrimination against women by any person, organization or enterprise;

(f) To take all appropriate measures, including legislation, to modify or abolish laws, regulations, customs and practices which constitute discrimination against women;

(g) To repeal all national penal provisions which constitute discrimination against women.

This Convention also sets out a number of specific measures to be taken by states to ensure equal enjoyment by women of each of these rights. For example,

Article 5(a) requires States parties to take all appropriate measures:

"To modify the social and cultural patterns of conduct of men and women, with a view to achieving the elimination of prejudices and customary and all other practices which are based on the idea of the inferiority or the superiority of either of the sexes or on stereotyped roles for men and women".

Article 4(1) states that:

"Adoption by States Parties of temporary special measures aimed at accelerating de facto equality between men and women shall not be considered discrimination as defined in the present Convention, but shall in no way entail as a consequence the maintenance of unequal or separate standards...".

In addition, the Convention requires States Parties to take all appropriate measures to secure equality in such areas as: suppressing all forms of traffic in women and exploitation of prostitution of women (Art.6); the elimination of discrimination against women in the political and public life of the country (Art.7); ensuring to women the opportunity to represent their Government at the international level and to participate in the work of international organisations (Art. 8); education (Art.10); employment (Art.11); health care (Art. 12); the right to family benefit, financial credit, and to participate in recreational activities, sports and all aspects of social life (Art. 13); equality with men before the law (Art.15); eliminating discrimination in all matters relating to marriage and family relations (Art.16).

The Rights of the Child

The Convention on the Rights of the Child, Article 4

States Parties shall undertake all appropriate legislative, administrative, and other measures for the implementation of the rights recognized in the present Convention. With regard to economic, social and cultural rights, States Parties shall undertake such measures to the maximum extent of their available resources and, where needed, within the framework of international co-operation.

THE RIGHT TO PARTICIPATE

As we have seen above, the ICESCR and the ICCPR contain provisions concerning the right of individuals to participate in cultural life and political life, respectively. A wider right of participation is also explicitly mentioned in the Convention on the Rights of the Child. Article 12 (1) provides:

> "States Parties shall assure to the child who is capable of forming his or her own views the right to express those views freely in all matters affecting the child, the views of the child being given due weight in accordance with the age and maturity of the child."

Similarly, CEDAW has a number of references to the obligations of States Parties to ensure the participation of women in the formulation of government policy and public functions, at all levels of government, and in non-governmental organizations and associations concerned with the public and political life of the country. States Parties also confirm the opportunity for women to represent their governments at the international level and in the work of international organizations.[15]

The need for participation of all sectors of society has also been recognised as indispensable to achieving the progressive realisation of economic, social and cultural rights. As the Limburg Principles on the realisation of economic, social and cultural rights have emphasised, popular participation is required at all stages, including the formation, application and review of national policies.[16] For a number of years, the UN Committee on Economic, Social and Cultural Rights[17] has been questioning governments about the participation of NGOs and other sectors of society in the preparation of state reports to the Committee on the measures they have taken to implement the provisions of the Covenant.

Participation is a key theme running throughout the UN Declaration on Social Progress and Development[18]. For example, it states that social progress and development requires:

- The active participation of all elements of society, individually or through associations, in defining and in achieving the common goals of development with full respect for the fundamental freedoms embodied in the Universal Declaration of Human Rights (Article 5(*c*)).

- The education of youth in, and promotion among them of, the ideals of justice and peace, mutual respect and understanding among peoples; the promotion of full participation of youth in the process of national development (Article11(d)).

- The adoption of measures, to ensure the effective participation, as appropriate, of all the elements of society in the preparation and execution of national plans and programmes of economic and social development (Article 15(a)).

---

[15] Articles 7 and 8 of CEDAW.
[16] Limburg Principles on the Implementation of the International Covenant on Economic, Social and Cultural Rights, 1986.
[17] This is the UN committee which monitors state compliance with the provisions of the ICESCR.
[18] See Annex 4 for the full text of the Declaration on the Right to Development.

- The adoption of measures for an increasing rate of popular participation in the economic, social, cultural and political life of countries through national governmental bodies, non-governmental organizations, co-operatives, rural associations, workers' and employers' organizations and women's and youth organizations, by such methods as national and regional plans for social and economic progress and community development, with a view to achieving a fully integrated national society, accelerating the process of social mobility and consolidating the democratic system (Article 15(b)).

The Declaration on the Right to Development also stresses the importance of participation. Article 8 (2) provides:

> "States should encourage popular participation in all spheres as an important factor in development and in the full realization of all human rights."

ICESCR AND INTERNATIONAL DEVELOPMENT CO-OPERATION

There are a number of references to international assistance and co-operation within the text of the International Covenant on Economic, Social and Cultural Rights, and it appears to have been expected that the implementation of the Covenant would form a formal part of development co-operation.

The references to international development co-operation and assistance are primarily in the context of the implementation of state obligations concerning specific rights. But by Article 23 of the ICESCR, the States Parties also agree that:

> "...international action for the achievement of the rights recognized in the present Covenant includes such methods as the conclusion of conventions, the adoption of recommendations, the furnishing of technical assistance and the holding of regional meetings and technical meetings for the purpose of consultation and study organized in conjunction with the Governments concerned."

The drafters of the Convention left the details of the steps to be taken by states to ensure realisation of the rights to be worked out later by states in co-operation with the relevant Specialised Agencies. For instance, ILO has consistently contributed to the enunciation and protection of labour rights, and UNESCO has promoted the adoption of conventions and recommendations with respect to the human rights falling within its mandate.

It was assumed that WHO would play a similar role with regard to human rights and health. That it has, to date, failed to do so is to be regretted. However, WHO has now taken on board the benefit of utilising a human rights approach to health, and may well play a more active role in this regard in the future.

Although it is not possible here to go into these other legal instruments, the state obligations contained in the ICESCR should be read in conjunction with those in ILO and UNESCO conventions and recommendations. In addition, documents adopted at UN Conferences set out specific goals and targets relevant to the realisation of these rights.

PART I I I - THE HUMAN RIGHTS APPROACH
TO DEVELOPMENT

CHAPTERS 6, 7, 8 & 9

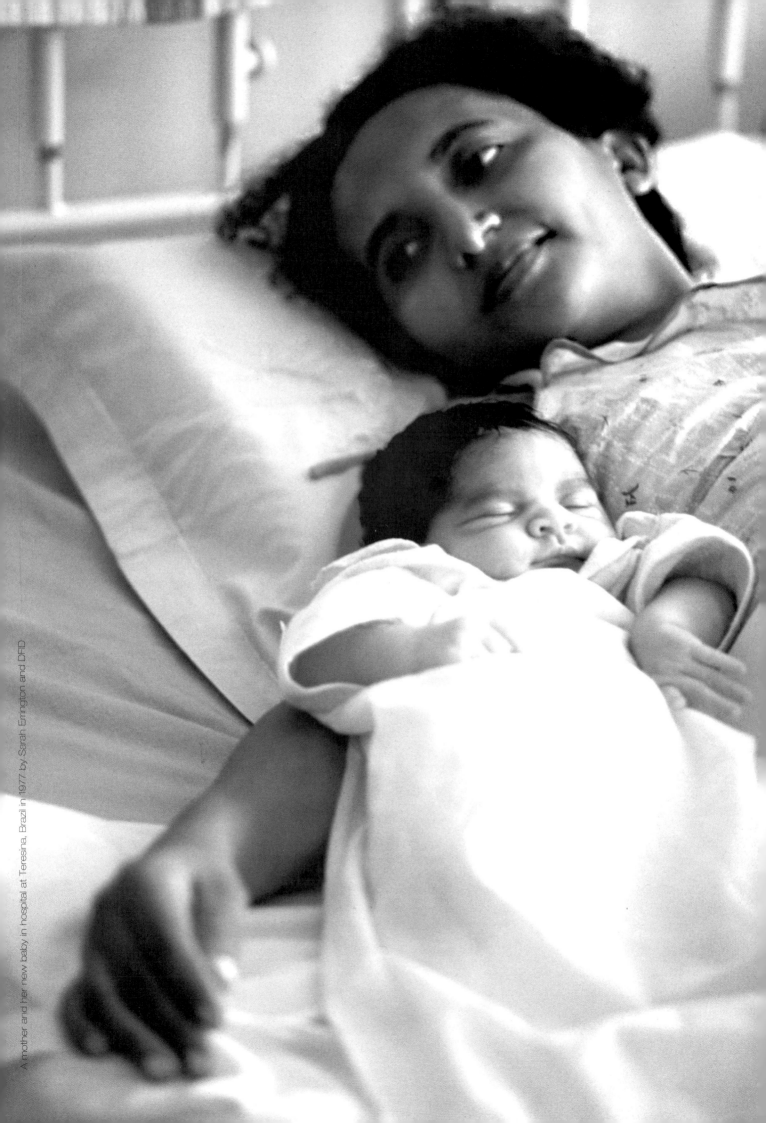

6 CENTRALITY OF HUMAN RIGHTS IN DEVELOPMENT

"Human rights begin with breakfast."

President Leopold Senghor, former
President of Senegal

RELATIONSHIP BETWEEN HUMAN RIGHTS AND DEVELOPMENT

The relationship between human rights and development is at once both simple and complex. The negative relationship between human rights and development is self-evident. The very definition of poverty used by UNDP - poverty means the denial of choices and opportunities for a tolerable life – is a statement of denial of the human rights and freedoms necessary to enjoy a quality of life commensurate with human dignity.

Enjoyment of such human rights as the right to education, access to health care and services, to property ownership, and to just and safe conditions of work, form the very basis upon which individuals can ensure for themselves and their families a standard of living adequate for health and wellbeing. People denied these rights will be unlikely to be able to provide for themselves, thus increasing poverty and expanding the need for welfare safety nets.

The enjoyment of human rights is essential for human survival and development in dignity

In addition, for an individual to develop his or her full potential, to have the opportunity to contribute to society and to secure a quality of life commensurate with human dignity, a wide range of other rights and freedoms need to be enjoyed. These include protection of physical security and the freedoms and liberties indispensable for dignity and for entrepreneurial and creative activity, as well as the right to participate in the political process.

Poverty is a violation of human rights

Poverty is itself a violation of human rights. In addition, it causes vulnerability to a denial of a wide range of other human rights. Conversely, discrimination, inequalities and other violations exacerbate poverty. The relationship between human rights, poverty and development is thus circular. Breaking this circle by securing the enjoyment of human rights by people living in poverty and social isolation is an effective tool in overcoming poverty and in promoting human development.

Box 9

The Relationship Between Human Rights, Development and Poverty Elimination

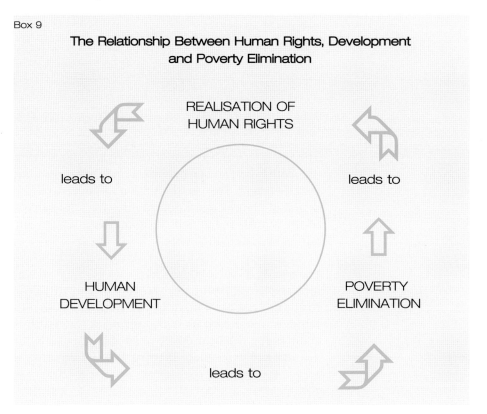

People living in poverty are in double jeopardy. They suffer a violation of their economic rights, but they are also at risk of discrimination and a denial of other civil and political rights. People living in abject poverty who daily suffer abuses of those fundamental rights necessary for survival - such as the right to adequate housing, food and clothing, and to social security in times of need - are in no position to contribute to their own development or that of their society.

POVERTY CREATES VULNERABILITY TO VIOLATIONS OF OTHER HUMAN RIGHTS

Discrimination and inequality
are part of the root causes of
impoverishment, instability, conflict, and displacement

The vulnerability of poor children to abuse of their human rights so dramatically illustrated by forced prostitution, child labour, and the plight of street children, highlights the urgency of measures to protect the enjoyment of their human rights, so that they might develop in safety and dignity.

Indeed, the whole issue of security is crucial. People living in poverty and social isolation are particularly vulnerable to violence and physical attacks. Street children in Latin America have been subjected to atrocious violence and even death by police. Such brutality can go unheeded when the victims are voiceless and powerless. Women who lack an independent income, or the legal rights to child custody on divorce, may be forced to remain in violent relationships, with serious consequences to their physical and mental health, and that of their children.

The rights of the less politically articulate members of our societies are all too often violated with impunity by more privileged classes. Poverty frequently goes hand-in-hand with illiteracy, which adds to the sense of powerlessness of poor people. The destitute are the first to suffer in times of famine or national disaster. They are vulnerable to exploitation, and – as the Bhopal tragedy taught us – are likely to be most at risk from the inappropriate siting of hazardous industries.

DISCRIMINATION AND INEQUALITY ARE ROOT CAUSES OF POVERTY

The correlation between discrimination, social marginalisation and poverty is well recognised. Throughout the world, people who are marginalised socially, and whose human rights are inadequately protected in national law, are the most vulnerable to poverty.

This is particularly visible with respect to women and minorities, but applies equally to people with disabilities, minorities, recent immigrants and asylum seekers, and others facing prejudice and inequality.

Securing human rights helps
protect people from impoverishment
and enables them to develop
in accordance with their equal rights and dignity

The disadvantaged legal, social and cultural status of women considerably inhibits their potential for enjoyment of their human rights on a basis of equality with men. This denial of rights has been recognised as being a major cause of the feminisation of poverty. A woman who is denied enjoyment of her right to education may be left with few employment choices. This is compounded by inequalities in the laws of property ownership and inheritance.

But economic factors are not the only cause of impoverishment. For instance, a woman who is denied the choice of contraception is denied the opportunity to make free choices about a whole range of other aspects of her life, including work. She is therefore denied full enjoyment of her human rights, and her development is impaired. And so the list goes on.

Securing realisation of women's human rights
on a basis of equality with men
is an essential pre-requisite for sustainable development

The income disparities and other inequities which exist within and between societies - which leave over one billion people living below the poverty line - are a shocking reminder of the injustice of our international and national societies.

IMPACT OF POVERTY AND
DISCRIMINATION ON
HEALTH[1]

There is a direct relationship between the enjoyment of human rights and health status. Violence, conflict, torture and other violations of physical integrity have inevitable adverse consequences for life and health - both physical and mental. Enjoyment of the right to the highest attainable standard of physical and mental health is dependent on many other human rights, including the rights to adequate food, clothing and housing, the rights to education, to work, and to just and favourable conditions of work. In effect:

Everyone should be able to live and work in environments
where known health risks are controlled
and health is promoted as an individual and social good

The relationship between health and the standard of living was recognised in the Universal Declaration of Human Rights adopted by the United Nations General Assembly in 1948, Article 25 (1) of which provides *inter alia:*

> "Everyone has the right to a standard of living adequate for the health and well-being of himself and his family, including food, clothing, housing and medical care and necessary social services."

Setting the standard of adequacy by reference to health and well-being illustrates recognition of the strong relationship between economic factors and health status.

The impact of poverty on physical and mental health is immense. In this regard it is vital that poverty is understood in more than just an economic sense. Poverty is multi-dimensional - a denial of the choices and opportunities necessary for health, well-being and development in dignity.

This multidimensional poverty is exacerbated by a lack of the education and information which would enhance opportunities, and by the inequalities and discrimination which deny access to resources, technology and essential services. At the same time, poverty exacerbates these inequities, by denying individuals opportunities and access to basic goods and services.

Furthermore, discrimination and social rejection also have negative health consequences. They contribute to increased rates of anxiety, depression, and chronic stress, as well as to alcohol and drug abuse, and suicide.

---

[1] The sections on health in this Chapter draw on a background paper prepared by the Author in consultation with WHO in preparation for an Informal Consultation on the Right to the Highest Attainable Standard of Physical and Mental Health held at WHO 4 - 5 Dec 1997, Geneva.

Economic and social inequalities and inequities are observable through differential health status. Poor health frequently reflects poverty and social marginalisation. In turn, poor health exacerbates impoverishment and disadvantage. Health status indicators - which are measurable - are thus frequently an indication of the denial of the human rights which are so vital for survival and development in dignity.[2]

Clearly, not all morbidity and mortality is caused by inequity and discrimination. However, what can be said is that preventable ill-health is associated with poverty and disadvantage. Studies from throughout the world illustrate the disadvantaged health status of impoverished women, minorities, indigenous people, and other groups who experience discrimination and inequalities. Health status data provides an important indicator of inequities and discrimination which are both the root causes of preventable ill-health and an impediment to human development. They therefore provide an entry point to breaking the vicious circle of discrimination and poverty.

Health promotion has long been a major objective of development policies and programmes. These will be considerably strengthened by a human rights approach.

The achievement of the highest attainable standard of health needs to be promoted as a social "good"[3] and a goal of development. It has an intrinsic value in and of itself[4]. This truth requires that the right to health, like other human rights, is recognised to be non-negotiable. Health is not a mere consumer good, but is a fundamental human right, which cannot be set aside for economic gain, nor in the interests of economy. It is therefore not necessary to rely on the grounds of efficiency or profit in order to advocate that health is given the priority it deserves in development policy.

Box 10

The Right to the Highest Attainable Standard of Health

- 1946, the Constitution of the World Health Organisation, states that "the enjoyment of the highest attainable standard of health is one of the fundamental rights of every human being".
- 1948 the Universal Declaration of Human Rights recognises that "Everyone has the right to a standard of living adequate for health and well-being ..."
- 1966 the International Covenant on Economic, Social and Cultural Rights gave legal force to this right by Article 12 which recognises the "right of everyone to the enjoyment of the highest attainable standard of physical and mental health".

This right is frequently referred to in short hand as the "right to health".

[2] It is for this reason that *Rights and Humanity* has focused on health in its efforts to show the nexus between human rights and development.

[3] See *Health in Development. Prospects for the 21st Century*. Report of the first meeting of the Task Force on Health in Development. 27-30 June 1994, Geneva, Switzerland. WHO/DGH/94.5.

[4] *Health the Courage to Care. A critical analysis of WHO's leadership role in international health by the Task Force on Health in Development*. WHO, Geneva, 1997. WHO/HPD/97.3. .

The fundamental basis of all human rights is recognition of the equal worth and dignity of everyone, and of the universality of human rights by which all men, women and children are equally entitled to enjoyment of their fundamental rights and freedoms without discrimination on any ground.

To talk of the universal enjoyment of the right to
the highest attainable standard of physical and mental health
is not to claim that everyone can enjoy an equal health status -
each of us is biologically and genetically different

Neither is it to claim a right always to be healthy

Rather, the right is a claim of each individual
to his or her own highest potential
physical and mental health

The right to health should not be equated simply
with the right to access to health care services

The claim to the highest attainable standard of physical and mental health cannot be ensured simply through the provision of health care services – vital though these are. It requires drastic action to address the structural, legal, cultural and other inequities, and functional barriers, which deny the majority of the world's population full enjoyment of this right. It calls for the implementation of an effective common agenda, across sectors, for the promotion and protection of health and for the equitable betterment of the human condition.

Just as the attainment by any individual
of his or her highest attainable standard of health
is a pre-requisite for the full enjoyment of other human rights

so is enjoyment of other human rights necessary for the
realisation of the highest attainable standard of
physical and mental health

The relationship between health status, human rights and the wider environment can be illustrated by a cone in which the pinnacle is the achievement of the highest attainable standard of physical and mental health. This is supported by a second tier which represents the enjoyment of all those human rights necessary to achieve this outcome, including, but by no means limited to, the right of access to medical service and medical attention in the event of sickness. This tier also includes such other rights as the right to adequate food and housing and the right to education, as well as those civil and political rights which protect physical integrity, individual freedoms, and access to information.

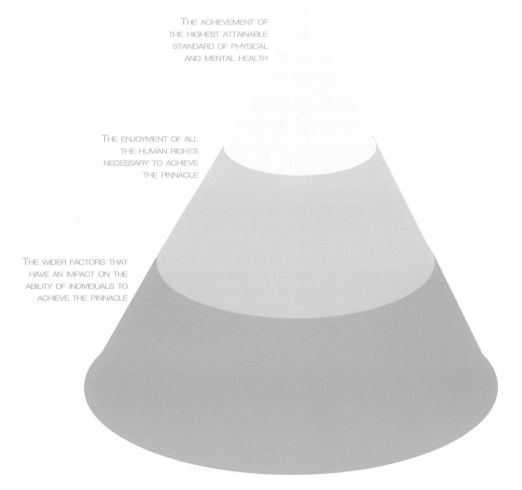

THE ACHIEVEMENT OF
THE HIGHEST ATTAINABLE
STANDARD OF PHYSICAL
AND MENTAL HEALTH

THE ENJOYMENT OF ALL
THE HUMAN RIGHTS
NECESSARY TO ACHIEVE
THE PINNACLE

THE WIDER FACTORS THAT
HAVE AN IMPACT ON THE
ABILITY OF INDIVIDUALS TO
ACHIEVE THE PINNACLE

The base tier represents all the wider international and national economic, political, legal, social, cultural and physical factors that have an impact on the ability of individuals to achieve their highest potential of physical and mental health. For instance, structural adjustment policies and other macro-economic policies, as well as environmental concerns often have an impact on the ultimate achievement of the highest attainable standard of physical and mental health.

These factors together provide the basis of a comprehensive understanding of the right to the highest attainable standard of physical and mental health. Health and other human rights can only be fully realised if they are realised simultaneously. All are essential for human development.

EXAMPLE OF WOMEN AND AIDS

The HIV/AIDS pandemic raises one of the most graphic examples we have to date of the way in which the denial of equality and legal rights has adverse health consequences. It is clear that HIV infection is following the fault-lines in our societies. Women are at particular risk of HIV infection as a result of the denial of their equal rights.

In a number of studies for the UN from 1988 onwards, Rights and Humanity identified that a woman's ability to protect herself from the risk of infection is directly linked to the protection of her rights by law, and her economic and social status[5] The lack of equality of access by women to literacy and health care restricts women's access to knowledge about HIV/AIDS, and the measures that may be taken to avoid infection.

However, this is not the only reason why women are at risk. A number of studies from Africa and Latin America and other regions of the world with high rates of heterosexual transmission of HIV indicate that the major risk factor for HIV infection in married women, and their children, is the pre-marital and extra-marital sexual activity of their husbands or partners. Why can these women not protect themselves?

Women's lack of education and training, combined with legal and social obstacles to employment, force many women to be economically dependent on men. Combined with this is the social conditioning that prevents women gaining assertiveness skills. Even when a woman knows or suspects that her partner may be placing her at risk, she may be unable to negotiate safe sex.

Furthermore, in those situations in which a woman is denied her equal right to the custody of her children on divorce, or to a share in matrimonial property, her choices are stark. She must either, stay with her husband and risk being infected, or risk losing her home and her economic support base, which in itself increases her vulnerability.

Securing protection of women's rights
in national law and ensuring women's social empowerment
so that they might assert their rights
is an essential tool for preventing the further spread of HIV

SOME WEAKNESSES OF EARLIER DEVELOPMENT MODELS

It can be argued that a failure to focus on overcoming these inequalities and inequities has weakened previous development efforts. The experience of the last decades has been, rather than the achievement of sustainable development, an ever-widening gap between rich and poor members of our societies.

[5]See, for example, *Effects of the Acquired Immunodeficiency Syndrome on the Advancement of Women*, by Julia Häusermann, Report on behalf of the UN Secretary-General to the Commission on the Status of Women, Thirty-third session, Vienna, 29 March – 7 April, 1989 UNDoc./E/CN.6/1989/6/Add.1. See also *Women and AIDS: A Human Rights Perspective*, by Julia Häusermann and Renée Danziger, paper presented at the VII International Conference on AIDS, Florence, 16-21 June 1991.

Non-discrimination is a fundamental principle of human rights law. Despite the importance given to this principle and to the affirmation of the equal rights of all individuals – women and men; minority and majority – the aspirations of international human rights law have been far from fully realised. Over one quarter of the world's population lives in abject poverty and suffers widespread denial of their rights. Countless people face discrimination and social rejection in their daily lives.

Development efforts that fail to take into account the root causes of impoverishment and marginalisation are doomed to failure. It is like trying to attach a sticking plaster to wet skin. If the underlying inequities are not resolved, such projects will provide, at best, temporary solutions.

SYSTEMIC VIOLATIONS

The suffering of people living in poverty is not caused solely by deliberate oppression by the state. Perhaps most often it stems from inequities in international and national economic and social systems. The manner in which the international economic system impacts on the most vulnerable sectors of society is a case in point.

This Author refers to these violations of human rights as "systemic violations". Such violations are well illustrated by the adverse consequences on the lives of poor people of the introduction, without adequate social safety nets, of economic structural adjustment programmes. The adverse human impact of these policies, promoted by part of the international community, had to be addressed by the introduction by other international agencies of social safety nets to meet the urgent needs of the most vulnerable sectors of society.[6]

This experience of structural adjustment programmes has illustrated the importance of main-streaming a concern for human rights throughout international and national policies and actions. It is critical that all sectors, departments and agencies adhere to a coherent human rights framework.

Many would argue that the very basis of the current international economic order is at fault, by placing economic concerns above human concerns.

During the last couple of decades increasing reliance has been placed on the liberalisation of international trade through GATT and now the World Trade Organisation (WTO). With growing restrictions in international capital markets and the contracting net flow of aid, many developing countries have become over-burdened with debts which they are unable to pay.

---

[6] See working papers presented at the Day of General Discussion held by the UN Committee on Economic, Social and Cultural Rights on the role of social safety nets as a means of protecting economic, social and cultural rights, with particular reference to situations involving major structural adjustment and/or transition to a free market economy, 16 May, 1994, Geneva, including paper "*Social Safety Nets and Economic, Social and Cultural Rights*" presented by the Author on behalf of Rights and Humanity.

The WHO Task Force on Health In Development has raised the concern that these policies, which promote the market economy and privatisation, tend to erode some of the fundamental values of equity and public responsibility that have shaped strategies for social welfare and human development. As Lord Frank Judd observed at the Third Meeting of the Task Force this emphasis has tended to promote private affluence at the expense of communal responsibilities. As a result, these international economic policies have had an adverse impact on the enjoyment of such rights as the rights to education and access to health care, particularly for the poorest sectors of society.[7]

HUMAN RIGHTS: THE POST-MODERNIST CHALLENGE

The technological revolution of the industrial age was facilitated by laissez-faire economic policies, and individual liberty. However, the assumption that these were sufficient in themselves to ensure both economic growth and a share for everyone in ever-increasing prosperity and improved quality of life, is being challenged. The increasing materialism of our age, and the focus on economic growth, has led to the assumption that the only "goods" of society are material goods. All too often, individual well-being has been sacrificed in the pursuit of economic gain.

In response to this materialistic world view, new approaches to human development have been promoted based on values of caring and sharing. We live in a post-modern era in which the assumptions of earlier times are being reassessed. The recognition of the need to give greater priority to human development and to the civil, cultural, economic, political and social rights that are the foundation of development, is a part of this post-modernist challenge.

Economists are increasingly recognising that a free market is not the answer to all ills. Checks and balances are necessary to ensure equity and social justice.

A human rights approach is about putting people first

For this Author, a human rights approach to international policy is about putting people first. It is about putting the interests of people above economic and other interests.

It is not about applying some abstract philosophical concept; nor just about taking the moral high ground.

It is about ensuring that the impact of the policies are fully considered, and that they are designed to put the interests of people firmly at the top of the agenda. A human rights approach is about conducting international relations in a way that recognises that improving the quality of life enjoyed by individuals is central to an ethical foreign policy and development agenda.

---

[7] *Report of the Third Meeting of the WHO Task Force on Health in Development,* WHO, 1 - 2 December, 1995.WHO/HPD/96.1 Rev 1.

A human rights approach ensures that
improving the quality of life enjoyed by individuals
is central to international policy and development
co-operation

An effective international human rights policy should, therefore, include debt relief in order to enable less economically developed states to secure the rights and needs of their people. Similarly, it requires a consideration of the human rights impact of trade negotiations.

To take but one example, The Task Force on Health in Development has warned that the application of the Uruguay Round of the GATT negotiations to the pharmaceutical industry has hampered access to essential drugs by poorer nations. There is concern that 90% of the pharmaceutical industry is in the hands of northern trans-national corporations. The impact of WTO's trade liberalisation policies raises issues about the power of this oligopoly, and the need for international policies to ensure equity.[8]

An expert seminar held in preparation of the WSSD expressed the problems inherent in some of the earlier development models as follows:

> "great inequalities, increasing poverty and more violence are some of the extensive list of negative results of the traditional models of development we have witnessed during the last decade. The Communist model had some success in reducing levels of inequality, but its failure had a lot to do with its inability to deal with questions of personal freedom and participation.
>
> The crisis of capitalism, on the other hand, is founded on its inability to permit the development of a society where the results of growth could be more evenly distributed to all its members. A new model is now emerging, where the values of freedom, equality, participation, solidarity and diversity are as important as (or more important than) access to the consumption of goods and services. From the economic point of view, it is clear that in order to survive, private enterprises will have to change from a model based on maximising profit to a model which emphasises social responsibility and accountability to the community."[9]

HUMAN RIGHTS: A BRIDGE LINKING FREEDOM AND EQUITY

Human rights norms provide the bridge between centralised and free market economic models, being concerned both about promoting the freedoms denied under communism, and the equity which is so often missing in an unrestrained free market system.

[8] *Report of the Third Meeting of the WHO Task Force on Health in Development,* WHO, 1-2 December, 1995. WHO/HPD/96.1 Rev 1.
[9] *Report of Expert Seminar on Social Integration,* The Hague, Netherlands, 27 September - 1 October, 1993, paragraphs 55 and 56.

Inclusion of human rights standards
into development theory and practice
should bring with it not only a concern
for physical liberties and freedom of speech
but also for the requirement of
just and equitable access to the resources of society
for all without discrimination

The Universal Declaration of Human Rights recognises the importance of a just international system. Article 28 provides:

> "Everyone is entitled to a social and international order in which the rights and freedoms set forth in this Declaration can be fully realised."

A human rights approach to development should therefore include a concern for overcoming the systemic violations inherent in aspects of the current international order.

The Declaration on the Right to Development confirms the duty of international co-operation to overcome these inequities. Articles 3 and 4 provide *inter alia*:

> "Article 3 (1) States have the primary responsibility for the creation of national and international conditions favourable to the realisation of the right to development.
>
> (3) States have the duty to co-operate with each other in ensuring development and eliminating obstacles to development. States should realise their rights and fulfil their duties in such a manner as to promote a new international economic order based on sovereign equality, interdependence, mutual interest and co-operation among all States, as well as to encourage the observance and realisation of human rights.
>
> Article 4 (1) States have the duty to take steps, individually and collectively, to formulate international development policies with a view to facilitating the full realisation of the right to development.
>
> (2) Sustained action is required to promote more rapid development of developing countries. As a complement to the efforts of developing countries, effective international co-operation is essential in providing these countries with appropriate means and facilities to foster their comprehensive development."

THE NEED FOR HUMAN
RIGHTS IMPACT
ASSESSMENT OF
DEVELOPMENT PROJECTS

It is part of the sorry history of failed development initiatives that some projects have contributed to the denial of human rights. This has been particularly marked in large infrastructural projects, such as the building of dams, which have all too frequently led to the forcible displacement of local communities in circumstances which ignore their historical claims to land rights, deny them access to their traditional livelihood, and undermine their cultures. Other projects may have favoured members of a particular ethnic group over others, or have disadvantaged women by focusing on male participation in the project.

There is a need to develop guidelines
for assessing the human rights impact
of development projects.

A *human rights impact assessment* needs to be integrated into the design and implementation and evaluation of projects in order to ensure that they do not lead to an abuse of human rights and contribute to further impoverishment.

As the impact of economic structural adjustment policies on the most vulnerable sectors of society – particularly women – has taught us, the implementation of some policies required by the international financial institutions has *increased* impoverishment. This has led to calls for *human rights impact assessment at the international* as well as the national level.

As a result of international concern, the World Bank and other aid donors are now paying more attention to the human impact in the design of their projects. Such impact analysis would help to avoid support being given to projects which would have a negative impact on the enjoyment of human rights for society generally or for any particular sector.

*Multi-Sectoral Approach
Required*

The compartmentalisation of development projects could also be seen as a weakness of development efforts. There has been a tendency to establish projects within a single sector, for instance health or education, rather than considering the human person as a whole and responding across the breadth of human need. By being holistic, a human rights approach could help in this regard. A human rights approach to development requires that the human being is the starting point for the planning of development interventions. These will need to be both multi-sectoral and multi-level.

*From Basic Needs to Human
Rights*

For a number of years the UN used the term "basic needs" to cover those essentials for human survival. However, the term fell out of favour, partly as a result of the fact that it failed to recognise that individuals have an inherent right to these essentials. Further, there was a tendency to assume that all that was necessary was to ensure these needs were met at a basic or minimum level.

The aspiration and rights of individuals does
not stop at access to mere survival rations or
the provision of basic services

Human rights require that everyone should live
and be able to develop, in accordance with human dignity

A human rights approach to development does not stop at the eradication of absolute poverty, but supports the continuous improvement in the quality of life and the progressive achievement of the full range of human rights.

7 THE CASE FOR USING A HUMAN RIGHTS APPROACH TO DEVELOPMENT

*"What frightens me is not oppression by the wicked,
it is the indifference of the good."*

Martin Luther King

THE BENEFITS OF USING A HUMAN RIGHTS APPROACH TO DEVELOPMENT

If everyone's rights to a standard of living adequate for health and wellbeing, to education and access to work, and to other rights and freedoms, were to be fully realised without discrimination, the primary goals of human development would be met. Respect for individual rights and liberties, and policies of empowerment and participation, not only sustain the development of the individuals concerned, but also encourage the initiative required for economic and social progress.

There is growing evidence (particularly from parts of Asia) that such progress can itself lead to greater respect for human rights, and thus produce a self-sustaining cycle of progress, nurturing both liberty and other aspects of human development.

The relationship between respect for human rights and development is symbiotic

Whilst respect for human rights is a pre-requisite for development, increased enjoyment of human rights can be an outcome of social and economic progress when the benefits of this process are equitably distributed.

There is considerable advantage in a multi-sectoral approach which brings together the experience and professional knowledge of various disciplines in a joint approach to achieving human development

Box 11
Benefits of a Human Rights Approach to Development

A Human Rights Approach to Development:

Coherent:

Human rights norms have been developed by the world community, and the associated obligations have been voluntarily undertaken by states. Human rights theory and law cover most aspects of human life, and provide a coherent framework for human development and international co-operation.

Contributes vision:

A human rights approach to development adds the vision of what development is striving to achieve. It sets the aim as the realisation by all people of all their human rights recognised under international law. It highlights the gap between what *is* and what *ought to be*. It is closing this gap by *raising up* the quality of people's lives to the standard required by human rights law, that should be the goal and *raison d'etre* of development efforts.

Provides an essential foundation for development:

A human rights approach focuses attention on the inequities, discrimination and systemic violations which are part of the causes of poverty and marginalisation. Its stress on *participation* and respect for individual *autonomy* and *dignity* strengthens development partnerships. Human rights norms provide *benchmarks for measuring progress* in the improvement of the quality of life.

The lens of human rights appraisal can provide insight into the *causes of poverty.*

In so far as poverty results from a denial of human rights, international law helps identify the *solutions,* by setting out the steps to be taken by states to ensure enjoyment of human rights.

Is successful:

There are many examples of successful examples in which human rights have been integrated into development projects. These range from women's rights projects to those designed to empower street children to seek and enjoy their human rights. As the HIV/AIDS pandemic has shown us, *respect for human rights saves lives.*

Empowers, promotes self respect and is sustainable in human terms:

Individuals are *empowered* by learning of their human rights. By seeing the divide between the rights that they should enjoy and their current position, they are encouraged to seek their human rights.

People living in poverty or social isolation are encouraged to think of themselves as Victors rather than Victims (e.g. people living with HIV/AIDS).

Participation in the identification of priorities and in the planning, implementation and evaluation of projects helps poor people to have a sense of *ownership* in the process and outcome of development.

The Time is Right:

The agenda of development and human rights communities have been gradually converging. There is synergy in a joint approach to overcoming the inequities which subject millions of people to poverty.

There is increasing recognition of the need to ensure that the interests and rights of individuals are placed firmly at the centre of international and national policies.

HUMAN RIGHTS
STANDARDS: A COHERENT
FRAMEWORK FOR
DEVELOPMENT

Human rights norms and state obligations concerning such rights as education, health, an adequate standard of living, freedom from hunger, physical security, and freedom of expression, provide a firm foundation for state action at the national and international levels. They provide a framework for action to eliminate poverty and to ensure the progressive improvement in the quality of life.

Human rights standards provide a vision for the world backed by legal obligations

Basing development on international human rights standards is *appropriate*, as it is the world's states that have proclaimed internationally recognised human rights, and that have identified the steps to be taken to ensure their realisation. The obligations to respect, protect, promote and fulfil human rights, and to co-operate internationally to achieve their realisation, have been *voluntarily undertaken* by states.

Internationally recognised human rights have been developed and protected by the world community, including states and representatives of civil society from all over the world. They therefore represent a truly *global agreement on common values and objectives,* reflecting the universal recognition of human dignity, and our common aspiration for freedom and justice.

In addition, by the UN Charter and international human rights conventions, states have accepted a *legal obligation to ensure enjoyment of human rights* in accordance with legal norms and standards recognised by the international community.

Human rights principles and law, therefore, provide a *coherent theoretical* and *legal framework* for national and international development programmes, and for the partnerships necessary for their success.

Human rights standards reflect the moral conscience of the world

Internationally recognised human rights developed by the world community over the last 50 years, and protected by UN and other international conventions:

● reflect the moral conscience of the world and the highest common aspiration that everyone should live free from want and fear with the opportunity to develop in dignity

● represent a global agreement that recognition of the inherent dignity and of the equal and inalienable rights of all members of the human family is the foundation of freedom, justice and peace in the world

● establish defined obligations of states for ensuring the enjoyment of human rights which are the basis for human development

- provide a coherent theoretical and legal framework for practical action at the national and international levels

- establish objective criteria for good governance and the implementation of bi-lateral and multi-lateral development co-operation

- provide a sound basis for participation and partnerships in development.

The contribution of a human rights approach to development is to add ***the vision of what development is striving to achieve.*** A human rights approach highlights the gap between what ***is,*** and what ***ought to be.*** It prompts a comparison to be made between the reality of peoples' lives and the existing entitlements of individuals within national laws and social and cultural settings, on the one hand, with their human rights under international human rights law, on the other. It is closing this gap by ***raising up*** the quality of people's lives to the standards required by human rights law, that should be the goal and *raison d'etre* of development efforts.

An examination of the denial of enjoyment of human rights by poor people and those suffering social marginalisation, can help identify the inequalities, inequities and discrimination that are a major cause of poverty.

The lens of human rights appraisal can provide insight into the causes of poverty

In so far as poverty results from a denial of human rights, international law helps identify the ***solutions,*** by setting out the steps to be taken by states to ensure enjoyment of human rights. Such an approach has the benefit of prior agreement by states as to what these steps should be.

Human rights law and subsequent political commitments undertaken by states under the auspices of UN agencies and at international conferences provide a framework within which national development plans can be formulated. Internationally recognised human rights standards also provide a coherent framework for international development assistance and co-operation.

Finally, the methodology of development assistance would be strengthened by the full integration of such fundamental human rights principles as ***autonomy, equality and participation.*** Admittedly, such principles are already observed in good models of development programmes, but a stress on the human rights foundation for these approaches adds weight and legal strength.

Putting poor people first in policy making and action is not just a moral and - this Author would argue - a legal imperative, but is an essential strategy for human development and economic growth and stability globally. It is clearly in the interests of all states to work for poverty elimination and an improved quality of life for people living in poverty and social isolation.

How can a human rights approach help in this regard? Will a focus of human rights make any difference to the lives of poor people in poor countries? Will it help them to provide for themselves and to enjoy a continuous improvement in their quality of life?

In this Author's view, not only is a human rights approach *effective*, but it is *essential* if any lasting progress is to be made.

Human rights principles and legal standards provide an effective foundation for achieving human development by providing objective global criteria for:

• identification of the causes of poverty and social isolation, and of appropriate solutions

• development of appropriate methodology for the design, implementation, and evaluation of development programmes and for the full participation of intended beneficiaries

• establishment of a focus on the poor and disadvantaged in order to implement equality

• targeting efforts on poverty elimination through implementation of the human rights of women and children, and on the realisation of the rights to education and health, and to an adequate standard of living, including food and housing

• development and use of appropriate benchmarks and indicators for measuring progress in improving the quality of life of poor people in poor countries.

HUMAN RIGHTS APPROACH WORKS!

Policies and projects designed to secure enjoyment by women of their human rights on a basis of equality with men have been shown to be successful in promoting development, and have become an important part of development co-operation. Similar successes have been achieved in promoting the rights of the child.

Particular success has been accomplished in Brazil where groups of street children and organisations concerned with the rights and welfare of children joined forces to seek protection of the rights of the child in the constitution drawn up after the end of military rule in 1986. Following this, in 1990, the Brazilian government promulgated the Children's and Adolescents' Act which protects the rights to health, education, training and other basic services, and provides for special protection and assistance policies for children and adolescents in need.

This has empowered children and adolescents to seek enjoyment of these rights. One example, is the encouragement the Act has given to the Movement of the Republic of Emmaus, an organisation of street children and educators, to intervene when they encounter violence against children, in particular, street children. They carry with them pocket sized versions of the

Children's and Adolescents' Act to show offenders against children's rights that they are contravening the law. Where police officers refuse to observe the law when challenged, children's advocates have sought recourse to the legal process.[1]

Human Rights Approach to HIV/AIDS

The vital importance of a human rights approach has been graphically illustrated by the HIV/AIDS pandemic. There is common agreement that there is a strong public health rationale for ensuring respect for human rights in the context of the public health and social responses to HIV/AIDS. The avoidance of discrimination and respect for such rights as privacy, and other individual rights and freedoms have become cornerstones of global AIDS policies.

Rights and Humanity's work to promote respect for human rights in the context of HIV and AIDS has shown how effective a human rights approach can be. Under the slogan "Respect for Human Rights Saves Lives", Rights and Humanity has promoted the adoption of strategies based on non-discrimination, privacy, and non-coercion.[2] ***The Rights and Humanity Declaration and Charter on HIV and AIDS*** sets out clearly the implications of human rights and legal obligations, and ethical principles in the context of the prevention of HIV transmission, surveillance, health care and social services, research, and in addressing the social consequences of the pandemic.

The Rights and Humanity Declaration and Charter was introduced into the UN Commission on Human Rights by the Gambian government in 1992[3], and has been widely used as a basis for policy and action. It has formed the basis of a series of resolutions in the Commission and the Sub-Commission on the Prevention of Discrimination and Protection of Minorities, and prompted the adoption by the UN of guidelines for states aimed at ensuring respect for human rights in this context. It also provides a useful tool for grass-roots advocates.

The experience reported back to Rights and Humanity is that a human rights approach is globally recognised as being an effective and essential basis for AIDS policies and programmes. For instance, the protection of the right to privacy and coherent strategies to combat discrimination are fundamental to successful programmes.

HUMAN RIGHTS APPROACH EMPOWERS AND PROMOTES SELF RESPECT

The human rights approach to development is not premised on governmental largesse. It is not about discretionary assistance, but about securing enjoyment of human rights which have been recognised by the global community.

In this way it differs from a welfare based model. The latter operates in an essentially comparative manner. Less fortunate people are compared with more fortunate individuals, and measures are taken to achieve a comparatively fairer outcome. This promotes the view that there are no absolute entitlements - only comparative entitlements.

---

[1] For the story of this achievement see Children for Social Change: Education for citizenship of street and working children in Brazil, by Anthony Swift. Further reference is made to this initiative and to this fascinating book in Chapter 8.

[2] See, for example, International Law, Advocacy and Human Rights in the Context of AIDS, plenary Address by Julia Häusermann to the VIII International Conference on AIDS/III STD World Conference, Amsterdam, The Netherlands, 1993.

[3] UN document: E/CN.4/1992/1.

The shift in emphasis inherent in a human rights approach is particularly important for the *self-esteem* of poor people. The experience of using such an approach has shown that beneficiaries feel *empowered*. By contrasting their current situation with what they should experience pursuant to human rights law, they are encouraged to work for change and seek their rights.

As the experience of the women's rights movement has illustrated, individuals are empowered by learning of their human rights.

Similar moves towards empowerment can be witnessed by the increasing number of self-help groups which have adopted a positive approach to securing their rights and needs. People living with AIDS have taken this approach further. They have adopted a number of slogans for conferences and advocacy illustrating this positive approach, for example: "People Living Positively with AIDS", and "From Victim to Victor".

A human rights approach promotes projects in partnership with beneficiaries and ensures that benefits are sustainable

Sustainability

A human rights approach to development promotes respect for individual autonomy and dignity. It therefore prompts development co-operation based on partnerships with the intended beneficiaries. Participation in the identification of priorities and in the planning, implementation and evaluation of projects helps poor people to have a sense of ownership in the process and outcome of development. This in turns adds to the sustainability of the benefits after international support for the project has come to an end.

The International Covenant on Economic, Social and Cultural Rights recognises "the right of everyone to an adequate standard of living for himself and his family ... and to the continuous improvement of living conditions." It has been questioned whether this right to continuous improvement in living conditions is compatible with current priorities concerning sustainable development.

The text of the ICESCR was drafted in the 1960s, before the full implications of the over use of finite resources had been recognised. The term "sustainable development" was yet to be coined.

However, there is no reason why this provision of the Covenant should not be read in conjunction with international commitments concerning sustainability. It is now recognised that sustainability is a pre-requisite for an adequate quality of life. Thus sustainability and the improvement of living conditions are mutually reinforcing, rather than in conflict. What the provision does make clear is that the urgency of ensuring access to the requirements for survival should not mask the fact that human beings are entitled to more than mere subsistence.

As UNDP has recognised in its 1997 Human Development Report, improvement in living conditions should not be seen as being limited to material concerns. A complex variety of quality of life factors make up the parameters of continuous improvement of living conditions. UNDP explains the concept of human development as follows:

> "The process of widening people's choices and the level of well-being they achieve are at the core of the notion of human development. Such choices are neither finite nor static. But regardless of the level of development, the three essential choices for people are to lead a long and healthy life, to acquire knowledge, and to have access to the resources needed for a decent standard of living. Human development does not end there, however. Other choices, highly valued by many people, range from political, economic and social freedom to opportunities for being creative and productive and enjoying self-respect and guaranteed human rights".[4]

The continuous improvement of living conditions in this sense is not, therefore, in conflict with the need to sustain the environment.

Box 12

Human Rights approach to Human Development

A human rights approach to human development is one which:

- stresses *liberty, equality,* and *empowerment*

- puts people first and promotes *human-centred development*

- recognises the *inherent dignity* of every human being without distinction

- recognises and promotes *equality between women and men*

- promotes *equal opportunities and choices* for all so that everyone can develop their own unique potential and have a chance to contribute to development and society

- promotes national and international systems based on *economic equity, equitable access to public resources*, and *social justice*

- promotes *mutual respect* between peoples as a basis for peace, justice and conflict resolution

---

THE TIME IS RIGHT   As chapter 5 illustrated, there has already been a convergence of ideas within the theory and practice of human rights and development. For instance, in the context of development theory and practice, this is confirmed by:

- the move from a primary focus on economic development to a people-centred social/human development model

---

[4] UNDP Human Development Report 1997, page 13.

- the recognition of the importance of a participatory "bottom-up" approach, rather than the trickle down theories of earlier years
- the move from "women in development" to a focus on the implementation of women's human rights, on the basis of equality with men, as a foundation for development
- the attention now being paid to the rights of the child
- the integration into development of a concern for democracy, the rule of law, and respect for civil and political rights through good governance policies

Both OECD in its publication *"Shaping the 21st Century",* and UNDP have emphasised the need for choices, and for promoting women's equal rights. A human rights approach would strengthen the objectives of the new development agenda enunciated by these bodies.

HUMAN RIGHTS APPROACH IS LIKELY TO BE WELCOMED BY PARTNERS

A human rights approach to development of the nature outlined in this Discussion Paper is likely to be welcomed by Southern partners, many of whom have long been advocating for greater attention to be paid to economic, social and cultural rights and to other rights essential for development.

A positive approach to ensuring the realisation of the human rights of poor people will help overcome the perception held by some Southern countries that the West/North is only interested in criticising violations of human rights - particularly civil and political rights. The approach advocated in this Paper could, therefore, play an important role in overcoming the politici-sation of human rights which has separated the world across East/West and North/South divisions.

The experience of the Author in Thailand in April 1991, illustrates how governments can respond to this approach. The Author was invited by Minister Meechai to visit Thailand with a representative of WHO to explain to Privy Councillors and other Ministers the importance of respect for human rights in response to HIV/AIDS. A comparison of AIDS with leprosy had led to the call for a number of AIDS villages to be established in former leper colonies. Furthermore, in an effort to stop the further spread of HIV, the Royal Thai Government had introduced a draft AIDS Bill, which had serious human rights implications across the board.

The Government was, at the time, receiving complaints from local human rights advocates that the Bill violated human rights criteria. But the argument of the Attorney General was that since Thailand had not ratified international human rights legal instruments it was not bound by interna-tional human rights law. He also argued that in any case, controlling the spread of HIV was a justification for restricting the rights of some individuals on the grounds of the protection of public health.

As we have previously seen in this Paper, the protection of the public health does provide a ground for the restriction of individual liberties in specific limited circumstances.

However, the Author was able to explain to the Attorney General and to other Ministers that there was a strong public health rationale for ensuring respect for human rights. The further transmission of HIV could best be prevented by ensuring respect for the rights and dignity of all people, rather than by limiting individual freedoms.

Once the issues had been discussed and understood, the Government reversed its policy, and Thailand is now regarded as having one of the better policies in Asia.

Careful language needs to be used in presenting the human rights approach to development partners. It is important that they do not think it is negative conditionality wrapped up in pretty paper, but rather see it as a genuine partnership effort aimed at promoting sustainable human development for all. In the above example, the Author was able to refer to principles of the Buddhist faith concerning compassion and solidarity in order to set the requirements of respecting the rights of people with HIV/AIDS within the context of local religious and cultural norms.[5]

It is sometimes queried whether such an approach will also be welcomed in Islamic countries. In countries with fundamentalist regimes, the emphasis on women's rights may not be welcomed, but the emphasis on the rights of the poor and children in particular are more likely to be entertained. Furthermore, in the more progressive countries, such as Egypt and Jordan, the full approach is likely to be welcomed. Both countries have well-developed programmes to promote human rights, including women's rights and the rights of the child.

The Need to Stick to Existing Language

In all situations, sensitivity and tact is the key. In discussions with partners it is advisable to stick to the *existing language* of international texts, rather than seeking to be too progressive with language not yet agreed. For instance, a formulation such as "human rights in the context of sexual and reproductive health" would be preferable to the highly controversial term "sex rights" which caused difficulties at the Beijing Women's Conference.

EU and other donor partners are also likely to welcome DFID's new approach. It builds on the priorities identified by the UNDP and the Development Assistance Committee of the OECD.[6] Indeed, the OECD/DAC has already begun to discuss human rights and development. The approach is also likely to be welcomed by Commonwealth partners, particularly since the Harare Communiqué, adopted by the Commonwealth in 1991, lays stress on human rights.

The new approach forms a firm basis for partnerships within civil society, and is likely to be warmly welcomed by NGOs and community-based organisations.

The Need For Sensitivity

The need for sensitivity in promoting a human rights approach to development is critical. This is particularly important when addressing issues of cultural sensitivity, such as female genital mutilation and domestic violence. In human rights terms, both these practices are violations of women's human rights.

---

[5] Fundamental Principles of Human Rights and Ethics Relevant to AIDS Policies and Legislation. Keynote address by Julia Häusermann, Open Forum, Bangkok, 1991.
[6] For an outline of these priorities, see Chapter 8 below.

However, taking an aggressive human rights line may not be the best strategy for seeking change. Rights and Humanity, for example, has developed an approach to addressing domestic violence which links both the health concerns and the need for legal and socio-cultural reform in order to ensure protection of women's rights.[7]   Such an approach is particularly appropriate in Islamic states and other countries with strong patriarchal traditions. In other societies, however, a more direct human rights approach might well be the best way to strengthen efforts to overcome these abuses against women.

COST IMPLICATIONS OF A HUMAN RIGHTS APPROACH

One of the questions frequently asked by people introduced for the first time to a human rights approach to development concerns the cost implications of ensuring the realisation of such rights as the rights to education, housing, and health care.

It is clear that there are cost implications for the implementation of economic, social and cultural rights, just as there are for the fulfilment of civil and political rights - such as the right to vote and freedom of expression. Chapter 2 has examined some of the arguments concerning the cost of implementing state obligations. It was argued there that the protection and fulfilment of *all* human rights has cost implications for states. In this regard, there is nothing unique about economic, social and cultural rights.

There is no such thing as a free right

Some critics of the human rights approach argue that it is pointless to talk in terms of a right to housing or of the universal right of access to primary education when so many states are unable to meet the costs involved. But part of the difficulty arises from a misunderstanding of the obligations of states.

EXAMPLE OF THE RIGHT TO HOUSING

As we have seen in Chapter 3, states are not under an immediate duty to provide housing, rather to take the necessary steps, to the maximum of available resources, towards the progressive achievement of the right of everyone to an adequate standard of living including housing. The obligation of free provision is limited to primary education and, to some extent at least, to social welfare in times of need.

A government is not in breach of its international obligations simply as a result of the existence of people living in abject poverty. It is a failure by states to take the necessary steps towards remedying the position that places them in breach of their international obligations.

---

[7] See for example, Preventing and Redressing Domestic Violence Using a Health and Human rights Approach, by Julia Häusermann, paper presented at Violence, Abuse and Women's Citizenship Conference, Brighton, 10 - 15 November, 1996, and below Chapter 8.

Issues such as these were debated in South Africa in 1995, during the drafting of the new South African Constitution. Concerns were raised that the introduction of economic and social rights into the Bill of Rights contained in the Constitution, might lead the country into bankruptcy. It was considered essential that the rights that were protected by the Constitution should have the full backing of South African law. Did an inclusion of the right to housing give every homeless person the legal grounds to bring a suit against the Government?

In order to air these debates fully the South African Constitutional Assembly held a public hearing on economic and social rights in Cape Town on 1st August, 1995. The Author was invited by the Constitutional Assembly to present the case for inclusion of economic and social rights in the Constitution setting out the international understanding of these rights and the associated state obligations. She argued that States are ***not obliged to provide everyone with free food, clothing and housing, rather to provide the legal, economic and social environment in which individuals might have the opportunity to meet their own needs and that of their families***. In this, protection from discrimination and from such actions as arbitrary eviction is critical.[8] This viewpoint was endorsed by a representative from a squatter organisation. He confirmed that squatters were not demanding free housing. They were demanding an end to the obstacles that denied them equal access to housing and land ownership.

Once this was appreciated, the way was open to include economic and social rights in the Constitution. The wording adopted is interesting as it illustrates clearly the balance between the human rights of individuals and the obligations of states. For instance, the right to housing is expressed as "the right to have access to adequate housing", whilst the "state must take reasonable legislative and other measures, within its available resources, to achieve the progressive realisation of this right."[9]

Box 13
Extracts from the South African Constitution

The right to housing - Article 26

(1)   Everyone has the right to have access to adequate housing.

(2)   The state must take reasonable legislative and other measures, within its available resources, to achieve the progressive realisation of this right.

(3)   No one may be evicted from their home, or have their home demonlished, without an order of court made after considering all the relevant circumstances.

No legislation may permit arbitrary evictions.

The rights to healthcare, food, water and social security - Article 27

(1)   Everyone has the right to have access to:
(a)   health care services, including reproductive health care;
(b)   sufficient food and water; and
(c)   social security including, if they are unable to support themselves and their dependants, appropriate social assistance.

(2)   The state must take reasonable legislative and other measures, within its available resources, to achieve the progressive realisation of each of these rights.

(3)   No one may be refused emergency medical treatment.

---

[8] Häusermann, Julia. 1995. Integrating Economic and Social Rights Into the Bill of Rights Contained in the South Africa Constitution.
[9] Constitution of the Republic of South Africa: adopted 8 May, 1996; amended 11 October, 1996; in force 7 February, 1997.

INCREASED PRIORITY FOR SOCIAL SECTOR IS ESSENTIAL

Ensuring to all access to education, housing, clean water, health services and so forth, is likely to require an increase in budgetary allocations for these essential services. Unfortunately, in a number of countries the percentage of the national budget expended on such services is falling, whilst that set aside for military expenditure and other perceived priorities is increasing. A state which spends a disproportionate amount of its budget on armaments, for example, at the cost of social development, is in breach of its international legal obligations to take steps towards the realisation of economic, social and cultural rights, to the maximum of available resources.

Similarly, if a state fails to develop plans to secure the rights of the poor and vulnerable, it is also failing in its duties. Clearly, a state violates the right to housing if it arbitrarily evicts people from their homes[10]. This has unfortunately been the case in a number of slum clearance programmes in various countries over the last decade involving forced evictions without resettlement.

The UN Committee on Economic, Social and Cultural Rights, which is responsible for monitoring state compliance with the obligations under the ICESCR, has concluded that violations of state obligations also occur when a state fails to take the necessary action to ensure at least minimum essential levels of each of the rights. For example:

> "...a State party in which any significant number of individuals is deprived of essential foodstuffs, of essential primary health care, of basic shelter and housing, or of the most basic forms of education is, prima facie, violating the Covenant."[11]

As we have seen, a denial of economic, social and cultural rights very often stems from inequality of opportunity and discrimination. States are under a duty to protect individuals from such abuse of their equal rights.

SECURING HUMAN RIGHTS: A COST EFFECTIVE INVESTMENT

Whilst there are clearly costs involved in meeting the standards called for by international law, this is a cost effective investment. There is increasing evidence that investment in education and health care, for example, is an effective manner in which to secure both human development and economic growth.

Economic development requires an educated and healthy workforce

[10] See The Maastricht Guidelines on Violations of Economic, Social and Cultural Rights, adopted by an expert meeting in Maastricht, 22-26 January, 1997.
[11] Quoted in the Maastrict Guidelines, ibid, paragraph 9.

Furthermore, as we saw in Chapter 2, there are a number of measures which states can and should take with minimum expenditure. For example, protecting individuals' rights by law reform, and education to combat discrimination, is far cheaper than meeting the welfare costs of people forced into poverty by inequities and social isolation. Protecting women from risk of HIV infection, by ensuring their equality, is cheaper than meeting the economic costs of AIDS.

Impoverished states unable to meet all the costs of securing human rights can, and should, seek international support. The more expensive aspects of the agenda - the building of schools and clinics for example - might in any case have been considered worthy of international support even without the change in policy. In this respect, the difference between a human rights approach and the former policy is less a change of subject matter, than a change of emphasis. For example, the new approach places a greater emphasis on ensuring equal access to resources, and overcoming the obstacles to access experienced by poor people and other marginalised sectors of society.

EXAMPLE OF THE RIGHT TO EDUCATION

Article 13 of the International Covenant on Economic, Social and Cultural Rights recognises the right of everyone to education, and provides that primary education shall be compulsory and available free to all.[12] Article 13 is the only provision in the Covenant that specifically requires states to provide services free of charge. However, the Covenant recognised the difficulty that some developing countries might have in securing, with immediate effect, universal primary education free of charge. Article 14 therefore provides:

> "Each State Party to the present Covenant which, at the time of becoming a Party, has not been able to secure in its metropolitan territory or other territories under its jurisdiction compulsory primary education, free of charge, undertakes, within two years, to work out and adopt a detailed plan of action for the progressive implementation, within a reasonable number of years, to be fixed in the plan, of the principle of compulsory education free of charge for all."

As with other economic, social and cultural rights, some of the steps which states should take to implement their obligations have been clarified in international conferences. For instance, the World Conference on Education for All: Meeting Basic Learning Needs, held in Jomtien, Thailand, in 1990, reconfirmed the commitment of states to securing the realisation of the right to education in the following words:

> **"We, the participants in the World Conference on Education for All, reaffirm the right of all people to education.** This is the foundation of our determination, singly and together, to ensure education for all.

---

[12] See Box 7, Chapter 5 above, for some further provisions of Article 13.

We commit ourselves to act co-operatively through our own spheres of responsibility, taking all necessary steps to achieve the goals of education for all. Together we call on governments, concerned organisations and individuals to join in this urgent undertaking.

The basic learning needs of all can and must be met. ..."[13]

The Conference set out some of the priorities for achieving this goal. Under the heading "Universalising Access and Promoting Equity" the Conference paid special attention to meeting the educational needs of women and of under-served groups. It confirmed, *inter alia*:

"Basic education should be provided to all children, youth and adults. To this end, basic education services of quality should be expanded, and consistent measures must be taken to reduce disparities.

For basic education to be equitable, all children, youth and adults must be given the opportunity to achieve and maintain an acceptable level of learning.

The most urgent priority is to ensure access to, and improve the quality of, education for girls and women, and to remove every obstacle that hampers their active participation. All gender stereotyping in education should be eliminated.

An active commitment must be made to removing educational disparities. Under-served groups - the poor, street and working children; rural and remote populations; nomads, and migrant workers; indigenous peoples; ethnic, racial, and linguistic minorities; refugees; those displaced by war; and people under occupation - should not suffer any discrimination in access to learning opportunities.

The learning needs of the disabled demand special attention. Steps need to be taken to provide equal access to education to every category of disabled persons as an integral part of the education system."[14]

This emphasis on removing disparities forms a fundamental part of the human rights approach. In the context of the rights of minorities, two provisions of the International Covenant on Civil and Political Rights are also relevant. Article 18 (which protect the right to freedom of thought, conscience and religion) includes the following provision:

"The States Parties to the present Covenant undertake to have respect for the liberty of parents and, when applicable, legal guardians to ensure the religious and moral education of their children in conformity with their own convictions."[15]

---

[13] Final statement of the World Declaration on Education for All: Meeting Basic Learning Needs adopted by the Conference. Emphasis in the original.
[14] World Declaration on Education for All: Meeting Basic Learning Needs, Article 3.
[15] Article 18 (4).

Further, Article 27 provides:

> "In those States in which ethnic, religious or linguistic minorities exist, persons belonging to such minorities shall not be denied the right, in community with the other members of their group, to enjoy their own culture, to profess and practise their own religion, or to use their own language."

EDUCATION FOR ALL: A GLOBAL RESPONSIBILITY

The Jomtien World Conference on Education for All also highlighted the need to strengthen international solidarity and co-operation in this regard. Amplifying the obligation of international co-operation, the World Declaration on Education for All adopted by the Conference provides in Article 10:

> "(1) Meeting basic learning needs constitutes a common and universal human responsibility. It requires international solidarity and equitable and fair economic relations in order to redress existing economic disparities. ...
>
> (2) Substantial and long-term increases in resources for basic education will be needed. The world community, including intergovernmental agencies and institutions, has an urgent responsibility to alleviate the constraints that prevent some countries from achieving the goal of education for all. It will mean the adoption of measures that augment the national budgets of the poorest countries or serve to relieve heavy debt burdens. Creditors and debtors must seek innovative and equitable formulae to resolve these burdens, since the capacity of many developing countries to respond effectively to education and other basic needs will be greatly helped by finding solutions to the debt problem."

The Framework for Action, also adopted by the Conference, recognises the need to reduce the "tremendous waste of military resources and shift those resources into socially useful resources, including basic education".[16] It also calls for international co-operation. For example, paragraph 45 provides:

> "Increased international funding is needed to help the less developed countries implement their own autonomous plans of action in line with the expanded vision of basic Education for All. Genuine partnerships characterised by co-operation and joint long-term commitments will accomplish more and provide the basis for a substantial increase in overall funding for this important sub-sector of education."

The Conference recommended indicative phasing of the implementation of the right to education during the decade of the 1990s. This envisaged that each country would determine its own goals and targets, and design a plan of action for achieving them. Similarly, development agencies were called upon to set their own priorities in this regard. Governments, organisations and development agencies were all called upon to undertake mid-term and millennium evaluations of the progress achieved.

---

[16] Framework for Action, paragraph 42.

A concern which is related to the cost implications of a human rights approach is whether it is ethical to promulgate as a *right* a requirement like education or access to health care which a state may not be able to secure immediately, and the full realisation of which remains remote for so many people. However, as we have seen throughout this Discussion Paper, the international community has already recognised as human rights such requirements as education, food, housing and access to health care. States have confirmed these rights in legal instruments by which they have voluntarily undertaken obligations to ensure progressive realisation of the rights. Furthermore, in humanitarian terms the point is rather the inverse.

It is unethical to accept inequality inhumanity, and any other denial of human rights and dignity

There is nothing new in claiming a right that cannot be immediately fulfilled. Slavery was not abolished overnight. Many of us did not expect to see *apartheid* overthrown in our lifetimes. The achievement of human rights is a long-term agenda. For example, the civil rights movement in America, the racial equality agenda in the UK and elsewhere, and the global women's rights movement reflect agendas in progress. But these goals *are achievable*, given the political will.

The enjoyment of human rights and poverty elimination are achievable and affordable

Both the UNDP and the Development Assistance Committee of OECD are convinced that it is possible to halve world poverty by the year 2015. In her speech at the University of Manchester on 30 June 1997, the Secretary of State for International Development adopted this target as DFID's main goal, and continued:

> "The UNDP report gave figures and analysis which showed that the costs are affordable given the political will. And, of course, we shouldn't stop there. If we can halve world poverty by 2015, we can eliminate it in the lifetime of many of us here. And these are not just the words of idealists. It's the hard nosed analysts of the OECD who say we can do it. It is both achievable and affordable. This is the world's major challenge for the new Millennium."

It is therefore incumbent upon us all - states and individuals - to seek the rights of people living in poverty and social isolation. This is the ethical approach.

ECONOMIC BENEFITS OF A
FOCUS ON THE POOR

A further concern which is sometimes raised is that a human rights approach might divert resources from areas where higher returns can be gained.

One approach to economic development requires that resources be invested in those areas and projects that are likely to provide the highest return. This may point to assisting the top levels of the economy, rather than the poorest sectors.

A human rights approach, however, is concerned with **human** development. It requires a concern for **all** people. It therefore supports priority being paid to investing in securing the rights and needs of those people living in poverty and social isolation who are currently denied their fair share of the resources of society.

A human rights approach is complementary to, rather than in conflict with, other development goals. This is evidenced by the increasing recognition that investment in the social sector contributes to economic growth. Conversely, experience from around the world indicates that economic and social inequities, and the failure to resolve in a just manner conflicts over scarce resources, both inhibit development, and can lead to violent conflict.

A human rights approach to development
with its emphasis on social sector investment
and a pro-poor priority
is likely in the longer term to lead
to more sustainable development
- both human and economic -
and to contribute to the prevention of conflict

8 IMPLEMENTING A HUMAN RIGHTS APPROACH: IMPLICATIONS FOR DFID'S POLICIES AND PARTNERSHIPS

"Eradicating absolute poverty in the first decades of the 21st century is feasible, affordable and a moral imperative."

UNDP Human Development Report, 1997

HUMAN RIGHTS APPROACH AND CURRENT DEVELOPMENT PRIORITIES

DFID'S PRIORITIES   At the launch of the 1997 Human Development Report, the Secretary of State confirmed that DFID's priorities reflected those of UNDP and of the Development Assistance Committee of OECD. She stated her aims for DFID's basic principles in the following terms:

- "Girls and women should have opportunities for personal growth, security, realisation of rights; control of fertility and health; literacy and opportunities to participate in political and economic systems. I want them to have more than equal opportunities with men. They are the potential engine for massive human development which will transform and enhance social arrangements for all;

- human development means confronting poverty; ensuring that all men and women have the basic requirements for life - education, basic health care and clean water;

- sustainable human development means enabling people to have opportunities to secure their economic needs through access to assets, markets, and economic institutions which are efficient and properly regulated so that the poor can work and prosper;

- sustainable human development also means strengthening the ability to manage economic, political and administrative authority in support of these aims."[1]

DFID's priorities of poverty elimination, strengthening choices and opportunities for poor people, and ensuring their access to the requirements for life will all be well served by the human rights approach. Human rights law provides a firm foundation for seeking a betterment of the quality of life of people living in poverty and disadvantage, as well as for development co-operation. Enjoyment of human rights facilitates the choices which are so often denied those living in poverty, but which are central to attaining a quality of life commensurate with dignity.

The human rights approach will be of particular benefit in implementing DFID's policy and programmes with regard to promoting security for poor people, in developing partnerships for development, and in ensuring a coherent policy across Whitehall. Adopting the human rights framework also encourages a more empowering manner in which we consider individuals - particularly the most disadvantaged members of our human family.

[1] Speech by the Rt Hon Clare Short MP, Secretary of State for International Development, at the UK Launch of the 1997 Human Development Report at the Overseas Development Institute, 12 June, 1997.

Development should promote respect for
human dignity and autonomy
so that people have the opportunity
to make and implement choices

Human rights principles provide an insight into how we should perceive others. Early on in its work on AIDS, Rights and Humanity was surprised to find that some public health and other government officials tended to view individuals as primarily being in need of coercion and control in order to ensure that they did not behave irresponsibly. Rights and Humanity took a different approach - one based on recognising the inherent dignity and capacity of individuals, and a belief that most people are responsible most of the time.

Rights and Humanity considers the human rights
approach to be founded on the belief that
individuals are capable of rational and
responsible behaviour

Rather than being coerced, individuals should be
encouraged and supported

Such an approach is far less patronising, and more appropriate as a basis for partnership with people living in poverty. Such partnerships, based on participation and respect for individual autonomy, are more likely to be successful than an approach that seeks to "deliver" development from the top down.

Human rights norms and standards
provide a lens through which to view
the position of human beings and
their relationships between one another

The stress on human dignity, justice and equity is an
essential foundation for redressing economic and
social inequities and for achieving equitable
human development

The human rights approach developed in this paper fits well within the priorities, policies and actions proposed by OECD/DAC in its publication *Shaping the 21st Century*. The DAC's strategy is a clear exposition of the new international consensus, which calls for genuine partnerships between developing and industrialised countries. It places an emphasis on achieving results, and sets out a series of goals and targets which have been developed and adopted in recent UN conferences. These form the basis for measuring progress in each of the areas of human development identified. Meeting them will require urgent action to overcome the inequalities, inequities and discrimination, which impede human development.

Similarly, UNDP's Human Development Report for 1997 includes a welcome stress on human rights principles. UNDP explains the concept of human development as follows:

"The process of widening people's choices and the level of well-being they achieve is at the core of the notion of human development. Such choices are neither finite nor static. But regardless of the level of development, the three essential choices for people are to lead a long and healthy life, to acquire knowledge and to have access to the resources needed for a decent standard of living. Human development does not end there, however. Other choices, highly valued by many people, range from political, economic and social freedom to opportunities for being creative and productive and enjoying self-respect and guaranteed human rights."[2]

The stress on opportunities is central to UNDP's approach. As the Human Development Report states *"from a human development perspective, poverty means the denial of choices and opportunities for a tolerable life".*[3]

UNDP points out that, for policy-makers, the poverty of choices and opportunities is often more relevant than the poverty of income, for it focuses on the causes of poverty and leads directly to strategies of empowerment and other actions to enhance opportunities for everyone.

Box 14
UNDP's Poverty Elimination Strategies

1. Everywhere the starting point is to empower women and men – and to ensure their participation in decisions that affect their lives and enable them to build their strengths and assets.

2. Gender equality is essential for empowering women – and for eradicating poverty.

3. Sustained poverty reduction requires pro-poor growth in all countries – and faster growth in the 100 or so developing and transition countries where growth has been failing.

4. Globalization offers great opportunities - but only if it is managed more carefully and with more concern for global equity.

5. In all these areas the state must provide an enabling alliance for pro-poor policies and markets.

6. Special international support is needed for special situations - to reduce the poorest countries' debt faster, to increase their share of aid and to open agricultural markets for their exports.

[2] UNDP Human Development Report, 1997, page 13.
[3] Ibid, page 5.

As UNDP states, in order to achieve poverty elimination:

- Poor people must be politically empowered to organise themselves for collective action and to influence the circumstances and decisions affecting their lives. For their interests to be advanced, they must be visible on the political map.
- Community groups, professional associations, trade unions, private companies, the media, political parties and government institutions need to join in broad-based partnerships for poverty eradication. Such alliances can be built on common interests and brokered compromises.
- Democratic space needs to be maintained by the state to foster peaceful expression of people's demands and to resist pressures from the economically powerful.

These strategies will clearly be strengthened by the human rights approach. Indeed, a human rights theme can be seen to flow throughout UNDP's priorities. The 1997 Human Development Report calls for *pro-poor growth*. This requires:

- restoring full employment as a high priority of economic policy
- lessening inequality and moderating its extremes
- accelerating growth in poor countries.

Key priority actions for the rural poor include:

- creating an enabling environment for small-scale agriculture, micro-enterprises and the informal sector
- reversing environmental decline in marginal regions
- speeding the demographic transition.

UNDP also lists among its priorities:

- education and health for all
- poverty reduction in industrial countries.

Integrating human rights principles and legal standards into policies and programmes designed to achieve these priorities is essential.

In January 1998, the UNDP published a policy document elucidating further how it proposes to integrate human rights into sustainable development.[4] Some of its development strategies which are relevant to human rights are outlined in the following box.

[4] Integrating Human Rights With Sustainable Human Development, a UNDP policy document, January, 1998

Box 15

Some UNDP strategies relevant to the human rights agenda

- Sustainable human development programming with a focus on eliminating poverty.
- Targeting disadvantaged or excluded groups (women, children, minorities, migrant workers, and people with HIV/AIDS), thereby linking social justice, discrimination and development.
- Promoting partnerships with NGOs and civil society organisations (including social and political advocacy groups), thereby encouraging people's participation at all stages of programme initiation, formulation and design, implementation and evaluation.
- Addressing governance issues (such as corruption, the rule of law, participation, democratization and accountability) in which human rights have been integral but, all too often, not explicitly spelled out.
- Strengthening institutions of governance and developing human rights capacity within such institutions.

Source: Integrating Human Rights With Sustainable Human Development, a UNDP policy document, January, 1998

PRACTICAL APPLICATION OF THE HUMAN RIGHTS APPROACH

The integration of human rights into development co-operation can be considered within seven inter-linked categories:

- Using development aid as a carrot and/or stick to promote respect for human rights and overcome abuse, i.e. linking development aid with positive and negative conditionalities.

- Promoting human rights in times of conflict through an integration of a human rights component in peace-making and peace-keeping operations, and in the context of humanitarian assistance.

- Assisting development partner governments to restructure their institutions, laws and policies in order to ensure good governance, the rule of law and respect for human rights at the national level - i.e. good governance projects.

- Providing direct support for what might be called "traditional" human rights projects - e.g. projects aimed at promoting the independence of the judiciary, freedom of the press, police training in human rights and gender sensitivity, support for institutions of civil society concerned with the protection and promotion of human rights, and projects aimed at securing women's rights and the rights of the child.

- Providing technical and financial assistance to partner governments in accordance with the obligation of international co-operation to achieve the progressive realisation of the rights recognised in the International Covenant on Economic, Social and Cultural Rights.

- Addressing the structural, legal, socio-cultural and other systemic inequalities and the various manifestations of discrimination which are part of the root cause of impoverishment and social exclusion.

- Mainstreaming human rights norms and principles into donors' policies, target setting, methodology and the evaluation of development co-operation, and into the manner in which they perceive and conduct partnerships with Governments and civil society institutions in the developing world.

The borders between these various categories are not distinct. Many donors are indeed already engaged to a greater or lesser extent with the first four categories. What is new in this Discussion Paper is the articulation of the remaining three categories.

This Discussion Paper advocates that, whilst negative conditionality may, as a last resort, continue to have its place in the range of options available to donors, this should not provide the focus of a human rights approach to development. Rather, development co-operation should be used for the positive promotion of human rights through projects falling within the remaining categories.

The main thesis of this Paper is that the focus should be on mainstreaming human rights norms and principles throughout the policies and programmes of DFID. The implications of this and other aspects of the human rights approach are considered below, together with some examples of how a human rights approach has been implemented in the past and could be strengthened in the future.

MAINSTREAMING A HUMAN RIGHTS APPROACH

POLICY IMPLICATIONS

Mainstreaming human rights norms and principles throughout DFID's work will require a review of priorities, targets, methodology and evaluation, as well as the manner in which partnerships are perceived and carried out. The Secretary of State has already indicated this shift in her stress on the priorities of women and children and addressing the rights and needs of the poor, as well as in her use of the term "partnerships" for development.

Just like gender before it
a serious commitment to a human rights approach
requires it to be mainstreamed
into all policies and programmes

Pro-poor, Pro-vulnerable

Although human rights norms put stress on equality, it is perfectly legitimate - indeed in this Author's view necessary - for states to take those measures required to overcome inequalities through a focus on the most needy. Thus in terms of priority for development assistance, a human rights approach is **pro-poor** and **pro-vulnerable.** Particular emphasis needs to be given to securing the **realisation by women of their human rights in equality with men**, and of protecting and securing enjoyment by **children** of their rights and needs. Minorities, refugees, people with disability, migrants, people with HIV/AIDS and others suffering ill health, and elderly people all need particular assistance.

A pro-poor emphasis can make an important contribution to ensuring enjoyment of human rights by poor and disadvantaged sectors of society. In some cases it may be possible to introduce positive discrimination in favour of the poor by insisting that they should have priority, for example by preferential or free access to the benefits of a project. This could be considered even in the context of an infrastructure project, such as the development of a water distribution system. Although greater emphasis is now being given to ensuring that women benefit from development, and that projects play a role in overcoming the legal, economic, and social disadvantages faced by women, these efforts could be strengthened.

Bottom-up and Top-down: Simultaneous Agenda

It is only through giving priority to securing the rights and needs of the most needy people that we can hope to eliminate poverty. It is a **bottom-up** approach in contrast to the failed trickle down theories of earlier times.

DFID's pro-poor priority is strengthened by its commitment to securing human rights. Such an approach is holistic, both in terms of the issues and people it addresses, and in terms of the levels at which it needs to be introduced. The pro-poor, bottom-up approach needs to be **supported by legal protection of human rights** at the national level and *the integration of respect for human rights into government policies and actions across all sectors*. It also requires the international community as a whole to meet its collective obligations, both in terms of development co-operation, and in terms of joint action to secure a just and equitable international order.

Need for a Multi-sectoral and Multi-level Approach

To be effective a human rights approach requires a multi-level and multi-sectoral response to poverty elimination and human development. The best planned projects at the grass-roots will be ineffective if state policy and action do not support them, and *vice versa*. What is required is the simultaneous implementation of both bottom-up and top-down strategies.

For instance:

- Rights protected by national law will be meaningless unless the poor and disadvantaged are enabled to seek legal remedies through accessible and affordable processes.

- The formal protection of land rights in national law will be insufficient to protect the rights of an impoverished widow against a more powerful neighbour who grabs her land, if she cannot afford legal process.

- Sectoral projects to support education and health will not assist in eliminating poverty unless measures to ensure equitable access are built into the project.

- The building of schools will not have the desired impact on human development if their classrooms are open only to boys.

- Hospitals catering to elites will not improve the health status of the poorest and most vulnerable.

- A mobile clinic will be of little benefit to women if it visits a village on market day, when the women are selling their produce in the local town.

- The building of a village well will be of little benefit to villagers if an absentee landlord returns and starts charging them for the water.

- Development efforts would be in vain if the outbreak of conflict or the impact of ill-conceived or inequitable international policies were to wipe out their achievements.

GOALS AND TARGETS

Throughout this Paper there has been reference to the obligations undertaken by states under human rights law, and the commitments made at UN Conferences. Read together, these provide a coherent framework of goals and targets for development co-operation. For example, the Secretary of State has already adopted as a target for DFID the OECD target of halving world poverty by 2015. This and other targets are set out in OECD's document *Shaping the 21st Century* and represent a synthesis of the goals and targets adopted at the series of recent world conferences.

METHODOLOGY

Participation: the Key to Sustainable Human Development

A human rights approach to development highlights the principles of **autonomy, equality, and participation**. A human rights approach therefore endorses and adds weight to some of the current development strategies which have sought to put the human person at the centre of development efforts as required by the Declaration on the Right to Development.

The human rights approach takes heed of the rights and needs of **everyone**, of women as well as men, of children as well as adults, of the sick, vulnerable and socially isolated, as well as the more affluent members of society.

A human rights approach to development
is participatory, inclusive and based
on mutual respect

It is increasingly recognised that for development to be sustainable, in **human** as well as environmental terms, development policies and programmes need to be developed and implemented in partnership with the people for whose benefit they are intended. A human rights approach requires that *poor people* also *participate* in the *identification of priorities,* as well as in the *implementation* and *evaluation of projects.*

In this way projects can be targeted to meeting the real needs identified, where possible, by poor people themselves. This creates a sense of *ownership* among the beneficiaries, which will help to ensure the success and sustainability of development efforts.

True participation requires an approach which seeks to hear and understand the concerns of partner governments and beneficiaries, rather than to impose the donor's own perceptions. It is one which respects the views of poor people and those suffering discrimination and isolation. A similar view was expressed by Marigold Best in a paper entitled "Human Rights as if People Mattered". She wrote:

> "Human rights as if people mattered is about people feeling like people who matter and who feel they have some say in what happens to them and to their communities, and that they have the possibility of changing their situation for the better."[5]

An Inclusive Approach Based on Mutual Respect

The human rights approach takes heed of the rights and needs of *everyone*, of women as well as men, of children as well as adults, of the sick and vulnerable and socially isolated, as well as the more affluent members of society. It is an approach calling for mutual respect between individuals, and between governments.

Human Rights Impact Assessment

Mention has already been made (above, Chapter 6) of the advisability of introducing human rights impact assessment criteria into all development policies and projects.

Human rights impact assessment needs to be integrated into the design, implementation and evaluation of projects in order to ensure that they promote human rights rather than lead to an abuse of human rights of particular sectors of society, and/or contribute to further impoverishment.

Similarly, the World Summit for Social Development recognised the need to ensure that structural adjustment policies do not adversely affect the rights and needs of vulnerable people. By Commitment 8, Heads of State and Government stated:

> "We commit ourselves to ensuring that when structural adjustment programmes are agreed to they include social development goals, in particular eradicating poverty, promoting full and productive employment, and enhancing social integration.
>
> To this end, at the national level, we will: ...
>
> (b) Review the impact of structural adjustment programmes on social development, including, where appropriate, by means of gender-sensitive social impact assessments and other relevant

---

[5] Paper circulated at the Quaker Gathering, Swanick, UK, 25-27 March, 1988.

methods, in order to develop policies to reduce their negative effects and improve their positive impact; the co-operation of international financial institutions in the review could be requested by interested countries;

At the international level, we will: ...

(h) Enlist the support and co-operation of regional and international organizations and the United Nations system, in particular the Bretton Woods institutions, in the design, social management and assessment of structural adjustment policies, and in implementing social development goals and integrating them into their policies, programmes and operations."[6]

Use of Human Rights Standards in Evaluation

Human rights standards and the goals and targets established at international conferences provide an appropriate framework for measuring the progress made in human development. An integration of human rights norms and considerations would strengthen the current efforts to develop indicators to measure the quality of life.

PARTNERSHIPS FOR DEVELOPMENT

The use of the term "partnerships" to discuss the relationship between donors and recipients is particularly appropriate. It reflects the fact that in effect "we are all in this together".

Securing the rights of everyone
to the requirements for life, liberty
and development in dignity
is a collective international obligation

It is an obligation that binds more affluent countries as much as those less economically developed. The nature of partnership with developing countries will be particularly important in the re-negotiation of the Lomé Convention (Lomé 5).

Partnerships are Two Way

Partnership is also an appropriate term to reflect the spirit of human rights. Recognition of the equality and autonomy of everyone must lead to relationships based on mutual respect.

In building relations with partners in the South it is as well to appreciate that the benefits of the relationship flow two ways. As we have seen, the human rights approach to development is not founded on government largesse, but on the rights of individuals to have equitable access to the resources of society. Similarly, development co-operation itself should not be perceived simply as benefaction, but as implementation of the legal duties of international co-operation and of overcoming the inequities and discrimination which force so many people into poverty and social isolation.

[6] Copenhagen Declaration and Programme of Action, adopted by the World Summit for Social Development, 1995.

We in the North have as much
to benefit from the partnerships
as our Southern partners

As we face fragmentation in our own societies, we have much to learn from the values of the South, particularly with respect to social cohesion and responsibilities to the community. The importance of this contribution has already been evidenced in the passionate wish for liberty and justice which has fuelled the process of social transformation in South America, primarily through the efforts of the oppressed themselves. As Anthony Swift has noted, the wellspring of such a wish has long existed in poor communities:

> "It was evidenced by a history of people's resistance to their oppression and by the operation in poor communities of besieged social principles deriving from black and Indian cultures. These were the humanitarian principles of co-operation, solidarity, sharing of resources and individual interest identified with that of the community - the antithesis of the prevailing combat culture, in which people pursue personal well-being at the expense and exclusion of others."[7]

As we face the second half-century of international human rights protection we need to re-evaluate our perceptions, and the manner in which we seek to ensure the enjoyment of human rights and human development for all. The values espoused by our development partners will enrich this process.

We need to ensure that the wisdom and knowledge
of all faiths and cultures contribute to
our understanding and progressive development
of human rights law and standards
and the manner in which we seek
to ensure human development for all

Partnerships with UN Agencies

The implementation of the UN Secretary-General's proposal that human rights be integrated into the work of all the UN agencies will considerably strengthen the human rights approach to development. The specialised agencies have the technical knowledge to assist in setting standards, goals and targets for the achievement of the right of everyone to development.

The mainstreaming process will increase the potential for partnerships with a wide range of UN agencies concerned with parts of the human rights and development agenda. These include FAO (on the right to food and freedom from hunger), WHO (health and human rights), UNIFEM (women's rights), UNFPA (rights in the context of sexual and reproductive health), UNICEF (children's rights), ILO (labour rights), HABITAT (right to housing), UNESCO (right to education and cultural rights), and UNHCR (the rights of refugees).

---

[7] *Children for Social Change: Education for citizenship of street and working children in Brazil.* At page 1.

In addition, the UNDP has now integrated human rights into its programmes for sustainable human development. Finally, the UN High Commissioner for Human Rights has the overall UN mandate to ensure a co-ordinated human rights agenda, and to ensure the promotion and protection of the right to development.

Partnerships with these agencies and offices will be particularly important in the context of the follow-up to the various UN conferences, and the evaluation of progress to date.

PROGRESSIVE REALISATION OF ECONOMIC, SOCIAL AND CULTURAL RIGHTS

As we have seen, states are under an individual and collective obligation to promote the realisation of economic, social and cultural rights, such as the rights to education, housing and food, and access to health care. The obligation is for states to take steps, individually and through international assistance and co-operation (especially economic and technical), to the maximum of their available resources.[8]

Since DFID and other donors are already providing support in the education and health sectors, it is sometimes questioned what difference a human rights approach will make in this regard. The answer is that the emphasis and priorities might well be different. A number of examples can be given.

Whereas in the past development assistance might have been targeted at support for the building of a particular school or hospital, the new approach would prompt a focus on the overall strategy of the partner government to attain universal primary education and access to health care for all. In the education field, for example, co-operation might focus on supporting partner states to develop and implement a national strategy for the introduction of universal primary education free of charge as envisaged in the ICESCR and subsequent international conferences. Similarly:

A human rights approach requires that equal access to education is available to the girl-child and women

Such an approach also requires that adequate attention be given to meeting the educational needs of under-served groups as agreed in the Jomtien Declaration.[9]

For example, cultural and linguistic minorities in multi-cultural societies should not be denied the opportunity to educate their children in their own language. In some countries, this will require a review of laws, policies and the social practices that inhibit the full participation of individuals or groups in the cultural life of their choice.[10]

---

[8] International Covenant on Economic, Social and Cultural Rights, Article 2(1) and see Chapter 3 above.

[9] See Chapter 7 above.

[10] *Human Rights and Cultural Policies in a Changing Europe: The Right to Participate in Cultural Life*, Recommendations and Conclusions, Recommendation No. 6, page 77. The Report of the European Round Table, organised by *Rights and Humanity*, CIRCLE, and the Council of Europe, April 30 to May 2, 1993, Helsinki.

In the field of health, whilst earlier projects might have been aimed at the provision of health services for poor people, the new human rights approach requires that attention is also paid to such issues as addressing the socio-cultural norms which condone corporal control over women, deny women freedom of choice over reproductive issues, or lead to son preference.

ADDRESSING STRUCTURAL INEQUALITIES

The need to address the systemic causes of impoverishment has already been considered (Chapter 6, above). As we have seen, urgent attention needs to be given by development partners to ensuring that the policies and actions of non-state actors, including the international financial institutions and trade organisations, do not adversely impact on human rights, particularly on the poor and vulnerable.

In addition, greater attention needs to be paid in national development strategies and international co-operation to overcoming the legal, social and cultural impediments to equality and the discrimination that exacerbate poverty and social isolation. This may require a restructuring of the international economic order, for example, to ensure equitable access by developing countries to trade, investment and markets for their goods and services.

As we have seen, Article 28 of the Universal Declaration recognises that:

> "Everyone is entitled to a social and international order in which the rights and freedoms set forth in this Declaration can be fully realised."

Achieving this right requires action to be taken at the macro level of the global international order, as well as at the micro level to address the impact that structural concerns have on the enjoyment by individuals of their human rights. There are many aspects of reform required, and it is possible to consider only a few of these here.

Rectify Inequalities

At the World Summit for Social Development, Heads of State and Government committed themselves:

> "... to promoting and attaining the goals of universal and equitable access to quality education, the highest attainable standard of physical and mental health and the access of all to primary health care, making particular efforts to rectify inequalities relating to social conditions and without distinction as to race, national origin, gender, age or disability; ..."[11]

More efficient Use of Resources and Debt Relief

Governments also committed themselves to increasing the resources available for social development through, for example, more efficient use of existing resources and debt relief. By Commitment 9 of the Copenhagen Declaration, states committed themselves, at the international level, to:

> "...increase significantly and/or utilize more efficiently the resources allocated to social development in order to achieve the goals of the Summit through national action and regional and international co-operation. ...
>
> Ensure the urgent implementation of existing debt-relief agreements and negotiate further initiatives, in addition to existing ones, to alleviate the debts of the poorest and heavily

---

[11] Copenhagen Declaration and Programme of Action, Commitment 6.

indebted low-income countries at an early date, especially through more favourable terms of debt forgiveness, including application of the terms of debt forgiveness agreed upon in the Paris Club in December 1994, which encompass debt reduction, including cancellation or other debt-relief measures;"

DFID's pro-poor policy encourages support for such initiatives.

Micro-credit Micro-credit schemes to assist poor people have been introduced in a number of regions. However, these projects are not always successful in terms of improving the quality of life of the intended beneficiaries. One reason could be that at the micro level the same assumptions about poverty have been made as those previously made at the macro level. There has too frequently been a focus on "income" alone, rather than on the wider components required for human development.

Recently, however, some progress has been made in the approach to poverty elimination.

Poverty is no longer seen
solely in terms of "income poverty"
but rather in terms of the human poverty
imposed by a lack of opportunities and choices

Similarly, if micro-credit strategies are to be successful, they must not be targeted simply at increasing income, but at reducing human poverty by expanding choices.

For instance, even if a micro-credit project were to be successful in raising income to some extent, what benefit would that be in human development terms if a family were still to be unable to exercise their choice of sending children to school, because there was no access to a school?

A human rights approach to development
is one which will help deliver
the choices and alternatives
which is the basis for human development

In order to achieve human development and secure an improved quality of life it is therefore essential to provide choices and alternatives, by efforts to secure full realisation of human rights across the board. Micro-credit projects therefore need to be linked to the wider agenda. This requires a legal, political, and cultural environment in which human poverty might be decreased by promoting choices, alternatives and full enjoyment of human rights. Clearly, the full enjoyment of all human rights cannot be achieved instantly. But equally, the benefits of grass-roots projects will not be sustainable unless they are complemented by efforts to secure the protection and realisation of the wide range of human rights that make up the complexity of requirements for human autonomy and dignity.

Land and Water Rights

Article 17 of the Universal Declaration of Human Rights recognises that: "(1) Everyone has the right to own property alone as well as in association with others. (2) No one shall be arbitrarily deprived of his property." The right of all people to own property needs to be reinforced, and the ownership by indigenous peoples of their traditional land needs to be protected.

Land reform is an essential foundation for achieving human development for all

Particular attention needs to be paid to securing the position of land-less agricultural workers. As Shimwagi Muntemba reminds us, it is only when policies aimed specifically at the poorest sectors of the economy are implemented that we will begin to make headway in the eradication of hunger; only when the livelihoods of the poor are secure and their children survive infancy does it become rational for the poor to limit their family size; only when resources are sufficiently secured to give the poor a long-term interest in them, will they concern themselves with ecological balance and resource maintenance and enhancement. It is insecure land tenure that prompts quick exploitation, not inherent disregard for ecological balance. Only when there is sustained rural development will poor people stop flooding into the cities in search of an income, swelling the numbers of urban poor.[12]

Land reform is long overdue in many countries. A review of land rights is vital, particularly for indigenous peoples whose tribal lands are the very basis of their culture, survival and society.

This is an area in which international human rights law is weak, and needs strengthening. A focus on land and water rights as part of the approach to poverty elimination is vital.

Human Rights Approach to Promoting Health in Development

For an informed approach to overcoming the inequities which deny to so many people the opportunity of enjoyment of human rights and development, the various disciplines must each play their role. The importance of joint approaches is well illustrated by a human rights approach to promoting health.

In order to achieve enjoyment by everyone of the right to the highest attainable standard of physical and mental health, public policy must address three vital concerns:

- implementation of measures to ensure universal access to affordable health care and services of adequate quality;
- the protection, promotion and realization of a wide range of other human rights, including the right to a standard of living adequate for health and well-being, the right to work and to just and favorable conditions of work, the right to adequate food and housing, the right to education and to access to information, the right to physical security, and liberties and freedoms; as well as the development of multi-sectoral policies for health which protect individuals from known health risks, and promote health and well-being;
- the redress of inequalities and discrimination which lead to disadvantaged health status.

[12] Report on Food Security prepared for the World Commission on Environment and Development, Geneva, 1986.

Only the first point is normally regarded as a health development project. But it is clear that attention to securing universal access to health care services, whilst necessary, is not of itself sufficient to ensure the highest attainable standard of health.

A human rights approach focuses attention on the underlying inequities which impede health

Such an approach is also beneficial in evaluating and monitoring measures to secure access to health care. For instance, in assessing the adequacy of health services, a joint health and human rights analysis could be brought to bear on the development of minimum standards of quality, and guidelines for the progressive improvement of quality.

Furthermore, joint analysis would play an important part in further developing and refining indicators which measure improvements in the *quality* of life. Integrating concern for inequality and discrimination into the collection and analysis of health status data (through, for example, data disaggregated by sex and majority/minority grouping) will make an important contribution to identifying the inequities which are at the root of poverty and the denial of the right to the highest attainable standard of physical and mental health.

Protecting Human Rights in the Context of HIV/AIDS

Reference has already been made to the importance of integrating respect for human rights into the public health and social response to the HIV/AIDS pandemic. States and the international community must address the underlying social and economic dimensions of HIV/AIDS, and should consider action such as:

- combating existing prejudice and inequalities
- combating AIDS related discrimination and social isolation
- addressing the impact of AIDS on families, on orphaned children, and on the community
- ensuring respect for human rights in the public health response to HIV/AIDS including prevention and surveillance strategies, care for the sick, and research
- providing the necessary training in human rights and responsibilities for government officials, health professionals, and project officers
- supporting projects to redress the vulnerability of women to HIV as a result of their disadvantaged legal, economic, and socio-cultural position.

Sexual and Reproductive Health

Many of the needs in the field of sexual and reproductive health are concerned with ensuring for women and men, youth and adolescents, the opportunity of choice and protection from coercion.

A human rights approach prompts the identification of those circumstances in which individuals are denied freedom of choice so that appropriate measures can be introduced to enable individuals to realise their rights

Of particular importance in this regard is the right to privacy. Confidentiality must be strictly protected in all aspects of health care and services.

A human rights approach to sexual and reproductive health also sheds light on which individuals or sectors of society do not have access to adequate information and services. Are any groups being overlooked? Are any deliberately denied access? Is access for youth and adolescents adequate? These are the sort of questions that need to be asked in order to identify inequalities and obstacles to enjoyment of human rights.

A Health and Human Rights Approach to the Prevention and Redress of Violence

Violence is both a public health issue and a serious human rights violation

Violence is fast overtaking infectious diseases as the principal cause of morbidity and mortality worldwide. Interpersonal and group violence also creates great social anxiety, especially among vulnerable populations, such as the elderly[13].

Violence today is the number one reason for premature deaths among young people

At the same time, violence against women has been confirmed as a violation of human rights in a number of significant UN documents and conferences beginning with the World Conference on Human Rights in 1993. The obligations on states to protect individuals from attacks on their physical security requires states to adopt adequate measures to prevent and redress domestic and other forms of violence.

A human rights approach strengthens efforts to overcome violence rape and other forms of coercion

National laws need to be reviewed in order to identify and amend any aspects that tend to condone violence against women - such as the failure to regard rape in marriage as a crime. Similarly, reform of the forensic and criminal process may be necessary in order to ensure sensitivity towards women bringing cases of rape or sexual assault. Training of the police, law officers, and judiciary may be required in order to ensure respect for women's rights and dignity during the investigation and prosecution of allegations of sexual assault, rape, or other crimes of violence.

---

[13] See *Violence and Health*, WHO Task Force on Violence and Health, Geneva, WHO

BOX 16

VIOLENCE AGAINST WOMEN AS A VIOLATION OF
HUMAN RIGHTS STANDARDS

The World Conference on Human Rights (1993), in Vienna, broke new ground by recognising that violence against women is a human rights violation and must be addressed as such. Later that year, the UN adopted the Declaration on the Elimination of Violence Against Women which asserted that violence against women was pervasive in all societies, across lines of income, class and culture, and recognised that violence by private actors is a human rights violation. The Declaration reaffirmed that violence against women is the manifestation of historically unequal power relations between men and women and that it is one of the critical mechanisms by which women are forced into a subordinate status.

Article 1 of the Declaration defined the term "violence against women" to mean:

> "...any act of gender-based violence that results in, or is likely to result in,
> physical, sexual or psychological harm or suffering to women, including
> threats of such acts, coercion or arbitrary deprivations of liberty, whether
> occurring in public or private life."

Among the major international human rights instruments that protect women's physical integrity are:

- The Universal Declaration of Human Rights (1948):

  "...everyone has the right to life, liberty and security of person" (Article 3)
  "No one shall be subjected to torture or to cruel, inhuman, or degrading treatment or punishment" (Article 5).

- The Fourth Geneva Convention (Protecting Civilian Persons in Times of War) (1949):

  "women shall be especially protected against any attack...in particular against rape, enforced prostitution or any form of indecent assault" to counter the use of gender-based sexual and physical assault as a deliberate military strategy (Article 27).

- The Convention on the Elimination of All Forms of Discrimination against Women (1979):

  "States Parties shall take all appropriate measures, including legislation, to suppress all forms of traffic in women and exploitation of prostitution of women." (Article 6)

UN conferences have confirmed the global commitment to protect women against discrimination and violence:

- The International Conference on Population and Development (1994) adopted the Cairo
  Declaration and Programme of Action that confirms the right of women to be free from sexual coercion;

- The Fourth World Conference on Women (1995) adopted the Beijing Declaration and Platform for
  Action that includes combating violence against women as one of its Strategic Objectives for
  coordinated effort.

In 1993, the United Nations General Assembly appointed a Special Rapporteur on Violence Against Women, Mrs. Radhika Coomaraswamy. She has produced three reports as a result of her investigation into the nature and scope of the problem all over the world. Particularly relevant is the Special Rapporteur's framework for model legislation on domestic violence, to serve as a drafting guide to legislatures and lobbying organisations in order to create a comprehensive system, enshrined in law, to combat the phenomenon of domestic violence, and to target prevention efforts. See UN Document: E/CN.4/1996/53/Add.2.

Attempts to solve the problem have consisted mainly in punishing and incarcerating perpetrators of violence. States must be encouraged to adopt a "***zero tolerance***" attitude to violence, and all governments are required to ensure that their national legislation incorporates penal and civil sanctions to condemn all forms of violence. Such laws must provide just, effective, accessible and affordable legal remedies for men and women suffering violence, and adequate punishment of the perpetrators. It is equally important that the investigative and judicial processes respect the rights and dignity of individuals.

However, the criminalisation of violence is not alone sufficient. Governments must also take positive measures to protect individuals by preventing, controlling and reducing the impact of violence. Clearly, it is also a part of state responsibility to provide the necessary physical and mental health services, including counselling, to those affected by violence.

The following box sets out some strategies developed by Rights and Humanity in order to implement a health and human rights approach to the prevention and redress of violence.

Box 17

Strategies to Implement a Health and Human Rights Approach To the Prevention and Redress of Violence against Women

Prevention

1. Public education campaigns to promote zero tolerance and a change in social attitudes need to be introduced, or strengthened and supported. In those countries in which violence against women remains a highly sensitive issue, partnerships could be promoted in order to involve those leaders of society most likely to be sympathetic to the cause (such as health and social work professionals, women parliamentarians and lawyers, and selected religious leaders). In countries where religion plays a major part in shaping social attitudes, consideration could be given to integrating into the wording of public awareness literature, those supportive religious statements that condemn violence against women.

2. Greater involvement in the prevention and redress of violence against women by Ministries of Health and Ministries of Justice needs to be promoted, in recognition that violence is both a major public health concern and a violation of human rights.

3. Additional data collection needs to be promoted, together with guidelines for the protection of medical confidentiality and privacy at all levels of the reporting process.

4. Additional research needs to be conducted into the causes of violence against women, and the steps necessary to protect women from violence. Studies have indicated that relatively simple measures can sometimes be introduced to protect women e.g. changes in refugee camp lay-out can help protect women from rape and other violence; reorganisation of work arrangements can protect women from the risk of rape and other violence during night shifts.

5. Strengthened resources need to be directed towards promoting anger control and the counselling of violent men. Experience has shown that work to prevent domestic violence needs to be targeted at the whole family - men as well as women and children.

6. Law review and reform is required to ensure an appropriate legal environment and response. Review and reform should be undertaken of the laws on murder, manslaughter, actual and grievous bodily harm, rape, sexual abuse, defilement of minors, procurement and traffic in persons, abduction, pornography, sexual harassment and so forth, in order to ensure that they adequately protect women from violence, and provide for appropriate punishment of offenders. Where necessary, law reform should be undertaken to protect women from rape in marriage, rape within prostitution, rape by instrument/anal intercourse/oral sex, and to prevent the punishment of women and girls by male family members for so called "honour crimes". Law review and reform are also necessary to ensure that women are entitled to equal property rights, and to equal rights on divorce. Where not already included, domestic violence should be included as a ground of divorce.

Redress

7. Healthcare workers need training in the recognition of injuries or other ill health caused by domestic violence, and in treating its consequences for mental and physical health. They need to be sensitised to the particular needs of women suffering violence or sexual abuse, and to be informed of counselling and other services available to such women.

8. Guidelines should be developed to ensure that greater involvement by health care professionals in the identification of cases of domestic violence in no way abuses the professional ethic of medical confidentiality.

9. Health services for women suffering violence need to be strengthened. Particular attention needs to be paid to strengthening mental health services in order that they might address the psychological sequelae of violence. Greater recognition needs to be given to the fact that women who suffer long term domestic violence may experience post traumatic stress disorder and other mental health problems.

10. Social services for women suffering violence and their children need to be strengthened. Government support should be made available to shelters and other crisis intervention services, such as help lines, support groups, and material assistance to enable women to leave a situation of domestic violence.

11. Law review and reform are required to ensure that women suffering violence have access to adequate and affordable redress procedures and are entitled to the same compensation as other victims of violence.

12. Training should be provided for police and all those involved in the judicial and penal process in order to ensure that women alleging domestic violence or a sex offence are treated sympathetically. Laws of evidence and procedure should be reviewed with this aim in mind. Consideration should be given to the development of special units within police stations, and, where appropriate, staffed by specially trained women police officers. Special training is required for those carrying out forensic examinations of women alleging sexual offences, in order to ensure that women are not subjected to indignity.

Source: Rights and Humanity: Strategies for Preventing and Redressing Domestic Violence, discussion paper for WHO Global Commission on Women's Health, Working Group on Violence against Women, Geneva, 1996.

A human rights agenda at the national level should include:

- Legal protection of human rights of all people without discrimination within the constitution and other national law.
- The provision of affordable and accessible redress procedures in the case of human rights abuses through, for example, independent human rights commissions, ombudsmen and ombudswomen, complaints tribunals, and the adoption of international protocols granting the right of individual petition to international fora.
- Integration of human rights norms and standards into public policy and action in every sector of government.
- Education and training in human rights and responsibilities for such groups as:

  Public officials, including immigration officials, police and security forces, the judiciary and prison officials;

  Professional groups, including those in the legal and medical fields, social workers and educators;

  Children, both in and out of school, and the wider public, requiring a mass education campaign so that individuals may know and claim their rights, and the public at large may be aware of their responsibility to respect the rights of others, and to promote tolerance and peaceful co-existence.

Good governance requires that there is an opportunity for representatives of civil society to voice their views on political, social and economic priorities, and that there is adequate opportunity for the poor and most vulnerable sectors of society to participate in decisions concerning development priorities and resource allocation.

There are many ways in which governmental and non-governmental capacity could be strengthened through training in human rights and responsibilities. Such projects range from police training in human rights and community policing, to support for local human rights advocacy groups, and legal literacy and legal aid projects.

Development co-operation could support partner governments in meeting these goals and in undertaking any necessary reforms. For instance, partner governments could be assisted in reviewing and amending their legislation and in introducing accessible and affordable redress procedures in the event of an abuse of human rights by a third party or by an organ of state. Strategies such as the introduction of equal opportunity commissions, and the appointment of ombudsmen and ombudswomen could be supported. In addition, efforts to establish independent national human rights commissions that could hear complaints against the state should be supported.

Across the board, there is an urgent need
for education and training
in human rights and responsibilities

For some years, a number of donors have been giving support to groups involved in legal advocacy on the part of people denied full enjoyment of fundamental human rights. Similarly, increasing support is being given to human rights training for those involved in the administration of justice – including legal practitioners and police, prison, and immigration officers. Such support should be continued and strengthened.

Development assistance is also being directed at supporting respect for the rights involved in the democratic process, and most donors have, to a greater or lesser degree, introduced into their policies and programmes a concern for women's equality and gender equity.

WOMEN'S HUMAN RIGHTS AND GENDER EQUITY

Some of the steps which States are obliged to take to ensure protection and enjoyment of human rights by women have been outlined in Chapter 3. Development co-operation could be targeted at assisting states to meet these obligations, as well as at assisting women to realise their human rights. Projects could include those designed to ensure women's equality in law, promote women's participation in the political process, and promote reform in the socio-cultural domain so as to facilitate the realisation of women's equality in practice.

Gender inequality remains a major concern. Securing the realisation of women's human rights on a basis of equality with men is an essential pre-requisite for sustainable development.

Promoting women's rights and gender equity must form a major priority of development policy and programmes

Enjoyment of human rights facilitates the choices which are so often denied women, but which are central to attaining a quality of life commensurate with dignity.

A greater focus on women's human rights, together with the promotion of gender equity, needs to be mainstreamed into all of DFID's work. Throughout this paper, reference has been made to the legal and socio-cultural reforms that are necessary to protect women's rights. There are many reforms necessary. Several examples are given below.

Promoting Women's Participation in the Political Process

Human rights and gender equity require that women participate equally at every level of governance - local and municipal, as well as the national and international levels. Women should participate in all decisions that affect their lives.

Of the many projects which could be cited in this connection, reference can be made to a series of British sponsored projects in Jordan aimed at strengthening the participation of women in the political process. Through the Jordanian National Forum for Women, women at the village and community level are being trained in how to stand for municipal and national elections.

This initiative was supported by a strategy introduced by the Jordanian Government of appointing a number of women to municipal councils. In 1994, 99 women were appointed to municipal and village councils.

As Mai Abu-Samen writes:

> "The appointment experience encouraged women to work within their communities and strengthened their confidence in themselves and the decision making process...[It] had its effect on society and women, which encouraged women to enter the municipal elections in 1995. Nineteen women were nominated and ten won, one of whom was elected Mayor. In the 1997 elections, ten women were nominated and four won membership in the councils."[14]

Integrating Gender Awareness into Sectoral Reform

Gender awareness should be integrated into DFID's partnerships with Ministries. These could promote equal representation of women in civil service, as well as the collection of data disaggregated by sex. Further, these partnerships could be used to promote equality of access for women to public services. The focus on sectoral reform, for instance, provides the ideal opportunity for promoting equality for women, both within the institutional setting, and with regards to service delivery.

Integrating a Gender Perspective into Police Training

DFID's work with police authorities should also contain a gender perspective. The importance of women police officers, particularly to deal with cases of rape and sexual assault, and of gender-awareness training in the context of community policing, should be emphasised.

In effect, every opportunity of contact with governments should be used to promote the realisation of women's equal rights.

A Priority on Women's Rights

It is sometimes asked why DFID should adopt women's rights as a priority area when men's human rights are also violated.

Whilst there is no doubt that men's rights are violated, in most societies of the world, women do not enjoy equal protection of the law, and tend to have less economic, political and other forms of bargaining power. This impedes their development, and that of their societies, and also restricts their ability to call attention to the violation of their rights. Even where there is legal (or *de jure*) equality between men and women, this does not mean that there is equality between men and women in reality (*de facto* equality).

THE RIGHTS OF THE CHILD

For a number of years now, UNICEF has been taking a lead in promoting the rights of the child in development. Promotion of the rights of the child provides an effective entry point for a human rights approach to development. Whereas women's rights cause difficulties in some countries, children's rights have almost universal support. Indeed, the Convention on the Rights of the Child has the largest number of states parties of all international human rights legal texts (191 states parties as of February 1998).

---

[14] Women in Politics: Effecting Change from the Grassroots Up, paper presented at the International Round Table Equal Opportunities for Women: a Question of Rights and Humanity organised by Rights and Humanity in co-operation with the Jordanian National Committee for Women, under the Patronage of HRH Princess Basma bint Talal, 8-10 April, 1997, Amman, Jordan. This Round Table was financed by the former UK Government's Overseas Development Administration, now replaced by the Department for International Development.

There are many ways in which development co-operation can support the protection and promotion of children's rights. Some very innovative projects have been developed in this area and provide useful models, not only for further child's rights projects, but also for other initiatives to support grass roots empowerment.

Children for Social Change

One such project is the work of the Movement of the Republic of Emmaus - the name given to a group of street children and educators working with them in Belém, Brazil. Through the Republic, children living and working on the street were able to play a role in the drafting of the new Brazilian Constitution in 1986, and the Children's and Adolescents' Act a few years later.

The manner in which this was achieved, and the partnerships that were developed, are instructive. These are chronicled in Anthony Swift's book "Children for Social Change: Education for Citizenship of Street and Working Children in Brazil."[15]

As Swift explains, following the end of military rule in 1986, Brazil set about redrafting its constitution. Assisted by UNICEF, the government formed the National Committee of the Child and the Constitution in order to consider how best to incorporate children's rights into the new constitution. Despite widespread publicity about the consultation, the National Committee of the Child and the Constitution did not manage to engage broad popular support as it was felt to be too government-dominated, too "top-down".

Brazilian NGOs then formed the National Forum of Non-governmental Organisations for the Protection of Children and Adolescents (the Forum DCA). It prompted intense mobilisation of the public and media to gather the views of a wide range of civil society on children's rights. As a result of the Forum's work the voices of Brazilian children contributed to the development of the constitutional protection of children's rights. One amendment, for instance, had 1.4 million signatures from children to back it up.

The constitutional provisions to protect children and adolescents include guarantees of the rights to life, adequate food, family life, leisure, education, occupational training, employment rights, culture, dignity, respect, freedom, and social security. Children are to be protected from all forms of negligence, discrimination, exploitation, violence, cruelty and oppression. All children are due special protection as people in a process of development.

In effect, Brazil enacted the essence of the UN Convention on the Rights of the Child even before its adoption by the UN General Assembly. Following this, in 1990, the Brazilian government promulgated the Children's and Adolescent's Act, which protects the rights of the child to health, education, training and other basic services, and provides for special protection and assistance policies for children and adolescents in need. This was a tremendous victory for those advocating on behalf of children.

Swift's study reveals that this Act has been of great significance to children, poor children in particular. One example of this is the authority that the Act has given to educators from the Movement of the Republic of Emmaus to intervene when they encounter violence against children, which has been a

[15] Anthony Swift: "Children for social change: education for citizenship of street and working children in Brazil" Nottingham: Educational Heretics Press 1997

daily occurrence in the lives of street children. The educators carry with them pocket sized versions of the Children's and Adolescent's Act to show offenders against children's rights that they are contravening the law. Where police officers refuse to observe the law when challenged, children's advocates have recourse to the legal process.

Street and working children in programmes such as those run by the Republic of Emmaus are often better versed than other children about their rights. Given their vulnerability to appalling violence, the legislative and constitutional backing provide vital ammunition in the fight by children living and working on the streets to secure their human rights.

Focus on the Disadvantaged

A particular focus should also be paid to supporting initiatives to assist indigenous peoples, minorities, people with disabilities, refugees and displaced persons, people living with HIV/AIDS, and other people marginalised by economic and social pressures. Many projects are already focused on helping to meet the needs of these disadvantaged people. What is required is a shift in emphasis, so that the main thrust is to secure enjoyment of the equal rights which is the foundation of progress, and which is vital to dignity.

It is in such circumstances that the appeal to move on *from charity to rights* becomes so significant.

- If people with disabilities did not face the physical and social obstacles that impede their self-sufficiency, their need for social welfare would be significantly reduced.

- If the human rights, including the cultural rights[16], of indigenous peoples were protected by law, they would not be so vulnerable to the displacement so frequently associated with the activities of logging and mining companies.

- If the dignity and human rights of refugees and displaced persons were respected, and their physical security protected, their ability to rebuild their lives would be enhanced.

- If the human rights of people living with HIV/AIDS - for example, the rights to education, work, housing, access to health care, and to participate in public life - were fully respected, such individuals would have a better opportunity, whilst in good enough health, of providing for themselves and their families, and to contribute to society.

SUPPORT FOR OTHER HUMAN RIGHTS PROJECTS

There are a number of other areas in which development assistance could be given to support the enjoyment of human rights. A list of such projects is potentially very long, but could include projects designed to:

- provide legal assistance to those suffering threat of arbitrary eviction from housing settlements, or eviction without adequate alternatives being made available

[16] It is not possible to go into any detail here, but it must be stressed that protection of the cultural rights of indigenous peoples, which are invariably linked to their tribal lands, is vital for their livelihoods and social cohesion.

- address gender inequalities in access to public services and other resources of society
- promote appropriate legal reforms and positive discrimination measures to ensure enjoyment of equal rights by women (including property rights and custodial and other rights on divorce), as well as by other groups suffering a disadvantaged legal status – such as children, indigenous people, and ethnic or religious minorities
- provide public education to combat prejudice and discrimination in all its forms
- support trade unions
- ensure just and safe working conditions, and other labour rights
- provide education, particularly to disadvantaged groups, on their human rights and their entitlements under national and international law, as well as the process by which they might best secure them
- promote the lifting of existing restrictions in some countries on the freedom of NGOs, so that they might have greater flexibility in their human rights activities
- promote the protection of human rights defenders and advocates.

PROTECTION AND PROMOTION OF HUMAN RIGHTS IN CONFLICT

Recent events are proving that mass violations of human rights seem an inevitable part of conflict. Conflict and abuse provoke massive uprooting and the external and internal displacement of people, at a time when the infrastructure of a society is torn apart. This may be accompanied by a collapse in legitimate government, leaving a political vacuum in which the international community attempts to provide emergency aid and humanitarian assistance.

The lack of a legitimate government in a country causes difficulties for human rights accountability, just as it does for partnerships for development. However, there have been some cases in which non-state actors have been held accountable for their actions. For example, the international community developed the concept of "crimes against humanity" as a part of international humanitarian law during the Nuremberg trials. Similarly, the International Criminal Tribunals for Former Yugoslavia and for Rwanda are bringing prosecutions for war crimes against individuals alleged to have committed atrocities during the recent conflicts in these areas. These developments have been influential in the current drafting of the statute of the planned international criminal court.

The need for information on human rights violations has led to the involvement of human rights monitors in peacekeeping operations. This needs to be complemented and expanded to include the integration of a human rights approach into the delivery of humanitarian assistance itself. For instance:

There is an urgent need to consider how best to deliver food aid to ensure that it reaches the intended beneficiaries

The delivery and distribution of food and other emergency supplies are fraught with difficulties during conflict, and in some circumstances are all but impossible. However, particular attention needs to be given to ensuring that the distribution system does not increase the vulnerability of any individuals or groups by placing them in an inferior position. Women are placed in an extremely vulnerable position when the distribution is solely in the hands of men. There have been numerous reports of women being subjected to sexual harassment in their attempts to obtain emergency supplies.

Impartiality, Equality and Participation

It is also important to consider the long-term impacts of humanitarian assistance, and to ensure that, without in any way compromising humanitarian principles, assistance is directed towards building the foundations for future reconciliation, reconstruction and development. This requires that the principle of impartiality is scrupulously adhered to, and is seen to be respected. It is important that delivery mechanisms promote equality, participation, and mutual respect, in order that they might help to build the culture of human rights necessary for reconciliation and lasting peace.

This is an area in which further analysis is clearly needed, a process which was begun at a recent DFID sponsored conference on the promotion and protection of human rights in acute crises.[17] There are a number of projects currently being developed among NGOs to ensure more ethical and effective relief assistance in times of complex emergencies, and DFID itself is currently engaged in developing ethical guidelines in this respect.

Health as a Bridge for Peace

In considering how best to implement a human rights approach in times of conflict much can be learnt from initiatives to utilise a concern for health as a bridge between factions. Under the banner of "health as a bridge for peace" several projects have been implemented to provide health interventions to prevent the spread of epidemics. For instance, in an example from South America, a cease-fire was implemented to enable inoculation of children on both sides of the conflict. This initiative involved medical personnel from the various sides, which had the added advantage of establishing professional links that could be built on later during the post-war reconciliation and reconstruction.[18]

In designing humanitarian interventions, consideration **must** be given to ensuring respect for human rights and humanitarian principles. In so far as it is possible without compromising these norms, consideration should also be given to the future development of the country, so that interventions may contribute to the prospect of sustainable peace.

---

[17] The Promotion and Protection of Human Rights in Acute Crises, Conference organised by the Department for International Development and the Human Rights Centre, University of Essex, 11-13 February, 1998, London.

[18] Health as a Bridge for Peace, report of a WHO Task Force on Health in Development meeting, 15 May 1996, Geneva.

As UNDP has stated, development co-operation and humanitarian assistance can play an important role in this respect:

> "Any effective development strategy for responding to these emergencies and their aftermath must address their root causes. Development can play a preventive role by addressing the social, economic, cultural and political causes of armed conflicts, which are often manifested by human rights denials and violations. Similarly, a better understanding of the interdependence between the strengthening of democratic governance institutions, respect for human rights, participation in sustainable human development and peace-building can prevent renewed conflict."[19]

COHERENCE OF POLICIES
ACROSS WHITEHALL

As the Secretary of State has recognised, to be effective and credible the new policy to implement a human rights approach to development needs to be supported by inter-departmental policy coherence. There are a number of areas of particular concern, including foreign and domestic policies generally, and the impact of agricultural and trade policies on Southern countries.

As has been argued earlier, it is particularly important that the Foreign Office, in implementing its policy to place human rights at the forefront of foreign policy, give equal weight to **all human rights** - economic, civil, cultural, political, and social - and that the rights of **all people,** including women, children, and minorities, are also given adequate emphasis. These issues are not solely development concerns, but are central to the struggle to secure all human rights for all people.

Inter-departmental co-operation is clearly critical. For instance, DFID has an important contribution to make towards the continued normative development on which the FCO is likely to continue to take a lead. Some of the areas of human rights law which need particular strengthening are the very areas in which DFID might have the most to contribute. As we have seen in Chapter 3, the legal protection of internally displaced persons needs strengthening, as does the protection of minorities, indigenous peoples, people with disabilities, and others suffering inequality and discrimination. Clearly, DFID also has a particular contribution to make in the promotion and protection of the right to development, and the further development of this concept.

The need for a consistent policy relationship between trade policy and human rights also needs to be considered. Although the human rights approach advocated in this Paper calls for a positive approach to the promotion of human rights, there may be circumstances in which negative trade conditionalities are considered to be one of the few remaining options open to governments in their attempts to halt widespread violations. In this regard, as in others, it is essential to ensure that human rights criteria are consistently applied.

The implications of a human rights approach to development will be particularly relevant in the context of the current attempts to strengthen the ILO's protection of children from child labour. For many children engaged in labour their wages are their sole means of livelihood. All too frequently, such children are the breadwinners for other family members.

[19] Integrating Human Rights with Sustainable Human Development, a UNDP Policy Document, January 1998.

Some northern human rights advocates, recognising child labour as a violation of child rights, have focused on trying to stop factories and businesses from utilising child labour. However, such advocates have sometimes failed to consider the implications for child workers of, for example, closing down a garment factory where they work. A prohibition of child labour without other provision for meeting the income needs of children and their families can have the impact of forcing children out of regular employment and into prostitution, crime or starvation. Efforts to protect children from child labour, therefore, need to be matched by social welfare measures combining education and income support measures.

This example illustrates some of the subtleties that are required in implementing a human rights approach. Whilst it is correct to state that child labour is a violation of the rights of the child, and that such practices are prohibited by international labour standards, the approach that is taken to overcoming these practices needs to take into account the considerable complexities involved. It is not that the countries concerned are unaware of the problem. On the contrary, many countries are desperately seeking to resolve this concern. The tendency of some Northern advocates to adopt the "moral high ground" has, on occasions, been perceived by our Southern partners as arrogance, and as an attempt to impose a northern agenda on developing countries.

Considerable care has to be taken to avoid looking as if the North is holding itself out as the sole custodian of human rights and moral values.

The better view would be for development partners to support such governments in their reform efforts, rather than to condemn. Attempts to address the issues surrounding child labour must be carried out in genuine partnerships with the governments and people of the countries most affected. DFID clearly has an important role in ensuring that all government departments concerned with negotiations on child labour are versed in the *human* consequences, as well as in the legal implications.

In this regard, training in human rights norms and principles is critical. DFID has already recognised the need for the training of DFID's staff in human rights and in the implementation of the new policy. Consideration might also be given to the possibility of holding inter-departmental workshops, so that a coherent approach might be developed and implemented by all departments.

There are other areas in which a human rights approach is also relevant, and will become more important as the economic globalisation process continues. These include attempts to prevent corruption and to develop ethical guidelines for transnational companies and codes of conduct to ensure respect for human rights in the implementation of public and private trade and commercial transactions.

Reference has previously been made to the need to match DFID's approach with a similar approach to domestic policy. This will require attention to be paid to overcoming the structural and social inequalities and discrimination that marginalise so many people in our own society.

As UNDP has reminded us, many of the poorest people are kept at the bottom of society by various forms of social exclusion. Redressing the increasing marginalisation of poor and disadvantaged people in industrialised countries cannot, therefore, be regarded solely as an issue of economics. There is also an urgent need to promote social cohesion and solidarity as a basis for the equal enjoyment by all people in the UK of their human rights.

9 CONCLUSION

"Democracy, development and respect for human rights and fundamental freedoms are interdependent and mutually reinforcing ... The promotion and protection of all human rights and fundamental freedoms must be considered as a priority objective of the UN in accordance with its purposes and principles, in particular the purpose of international co-operation."

Vienna Declaration and Programme of Action
Adopted by the World Conference on Human Rights, 1993

If the question is "how do we eliminate poverty and social exclusion?" then the answer must be "through the promotion and realisation of all human rights for all people." The human rights approach to development does not stop at the eradication of absolute poverty, but supports continuous improvement of the quality of the life of poor people and the progressive achievement of the full range of human rights.

Human rights and development are interdependent and mutually reinforcing

The human rights approach to development requires a focus on overcoming the inequities and discrimination that are a root cause of poverty and social exclusion. It focuses on overcoming systemic obstacles to the enjoyment of human rights, and the avoidance of international financial and other policies that have a negative impact on the lives of individuals. It prompts global action to achieve enjoyment of human rights as the foundation of development, democracy and peace.

The human rights approach shapes our relations with partner governments and the intended beneficiaries of development co-operation. These partnerships should be participatory, inclusive and based on mutual respect. The human rights approach will also assist in the setting of goals, targets and standards of achievement and in the measuring of an improved quality of life for poor people.

Such an approach is essential if the goals of the human development agenda are to be met.

OUTCOMES OF THE HUMAN
RIGHTS APPROACH

A Human Rights Approach to Development will:

- provide a firm foundation for sustainable human development

- provide poor people with the opportunities and tools to help themselves, by focusing on securing enjoyment of their human rights

- strengthen their self-esteem, and empower them to seek change and to participate in the wider development of their societies

- focus development efforts on the needs identified by poor people themselves, and encourage their participation at every stage of planning, implementation, monitoring, and evaluation

- prompt the legal reform essential to ensure the protection of human rights at the national level, and the practical implementation of these rights in state policy and action

- prompt the social transformation necessary to overcome cultural causes of inequity – particularly the denial of women's equality with men

- help assure a healthy and educated population able to contribute to the further economic and social development of their societies

- promote human and institutional capacity building based on responsible citizenship, democracy and good governance

- assist partner governments to develop the capacity to take the steps necessary to ensure to all the realisation of economic, social and cultural rights

- raise global awareness of human rights and responsibilities and of the obligations of states in this regard, and prompt a better understanding of human rights and responsibilities among the public - in donor countries as well as in developing countries

- focus on the implementation of the collective international obligations of securing universal respect for human rights, and of international co-operation to ensure the progressive realisation of economic, social and cultural rights

- lead to further clarification of the effective steps which can be taken to ensure realisation by all people of all their human rights, thus providing guidance for the development of both national and international strategies

- help bridge the divide between the aspiration of human rights instruments and the reality of people's lives

- ensure that the concerns and contributions of people living in poverty and social isolation are adequately taken into account in the setting of human rights standards and in other normative development, and

- help build the climate of respect for human rights, which is the foundation of development, democracy and peace.

NEED FOR MULTI-SECTORAL GLOBAL PARTNERSHIPS

A range of questions is likely to emerge as DFID and other development actors implement the human rights approach to development. For instance, development partners will wish to determine how best to measure and evaluate success in achieving the realisation of human rights and human development. This will require clarity as to the starting position. This in turns raises a number of questions: What information will be used to determine the current position in any given country? What indicators will be used? How can these best ensure the reflection of enjoyment of economic, social and cultural rights, as well as civil and political rights, liberties and freedoms? How can we best evaluate respect for the principles of equality, non-discrimination and equitable access to public services? Who will be involved in determining these points? How will progress be measured?

Need for Transparent Criteria
for Development Co-operation

These are some of the very questions with which human rights advocates concerned with economic, social and cultural rights and social justice are currently engaged. There is clearly a case for further joint analysis between human rights and development practitioners in this regard, in order to identify strategies that would both promote human development and secure enjoyment of human rights.

This analysis would be considerably strengthened and given greater credibility if it were carried out jointly with development partners, so that the concerns, priorities and limitations of Southern countries can contribute to strategy development. Such joint analysis will provide the basis for the transparent criteria to shape partnerships that have been called for by the Secretary of State for International Development.

BENEFITS OF JOINT
ANALYSIS

The relationship between the development and human rights agenda is symbiotic - mutually beneficial and reinforcing. This Paper has primarily focused on the benefits that a human rights approach can bring to development theory and practice. However, it is also true to say that the human rights agenda will be considerable strengthened by the insights and concerns raised by the human development agenda.

Set against the considerable progress that has been made in the promotion of democracy and in the protection of human rights in recent decades there is concern that many individuals, particularly people living in poverty and those suffering social marginalisation, are denied full enjoyment of their human rights. They remain excluded from participation in the benefits of development and in the social and economic progress of their countries. This is as much a concern for human rights as it is for development.

A society which excludes any part of its whole membership from participation in its progress is an impoverished society

There is a vast gap between the aspirations of international human rights documents, and the reality of peoples' lives. The failure to realise the aspirations of the Universal Declaration and subsequent legal texts prompts a re-examination of the fundamental assumptions that inspire our common commitment to human rights and dignity. One of these assumptions is that the state can act as the protector of human rights.

The position of the state in global actions is changing. The world is no longer simply a community of nation states, but includes an increasingly complex matrix of international bodies, transnational corporations, international financiers and investment companies, as well as a growing body of international non-governmental organisations, institutions of civil society, and internet users throughout the world. These changes present us with both challenges and opportunities.

However, as the Maastricht Guidelines on Violations of Economic, Social and Cultural Rights confirm, these changes do not relieve states of their legal obligation of guaranteeing human rights.

"Since the end of the Cold War, there has been a trend in all regions of the world to reduce the role of the state and to rely on the market too resolve problems of human welfare, often in response to conditions generated by international and national financial markets and institutions and in an effort to attract investments from the multinational enterprises whose wealth and power exceed that of many states. It is no longer taken for granted that the realization of economic, social and cultural rights depends significantly on action by the state, although, as a matter of international law, the state remains ultimately responsible for guaranteeing the realization of these rights. Whilst the challenge of addressing violations of economic, social and cultural rights is rendered more complicated by these trends, it is more urgent than ever to take these rights seriously and, therefore, to deal with the accountability of governments for failure to meet their obligations in this area."[1]

RESPONSIBILITIES AND ACCOUNTABILITY

There is also an urgent need to find ways of holding international bodies accountable for the human rights impact of their policies and actions. The fact that the Bretton Woods financial institutions[2], the World Trade Organisation, private international financiers and other key players are not part of the UN system increases the complication. However, this obstacle is not insuperable. The move by the World Bank towards a greater emphasis on issues of governance and human rights should assist in this endeavour.

At the same time, developing countries are being forced into ever more competitive markets. It is vital to protect from exploitation those people rendered vulnerable to abuse as a result of poverty or social isolation. As the history of industrialisation in the North has taught us, at a time of economic transition the profit motive is particularly inclined to fuel the greed which leads to exploitation of vulnerable members of our societies. The urgency of protecting the rights of poor and vulnerable people in times of economic transition is great.

An increasing number of people are recognising that human rights can only be fulfilled in daily life by the integration of human rights norms and principles into the process of the development of society itself and its values. This requires the engagement, not only of governments, but also of individuals and the full range of other actors in society.

[1] Adopted by an Expert Meeting, Maastricht, the Netherlands, 22 - 26 January, 1997.

[2] The International Bank for Reconstruction and Development (World Bank) and the International Monetary Fund are generally known as the Bretton Woods institutions, referring to a meeting of international leaders in Bretton Woods, New Hampshire, US, in 1944. The Bretton Woods Conference was held to discuss the reconstruction of the global economic order in the aftermath of World War II.

This is one of the greatest challenges facing human rights. We shall need to give urgent attention to how best to hold non-state actors accountable for the impact of their actions on the enjoyment of human rights. As we have seen, attempts are already underway to develop codes of conduct for trans-national companies, and for overseas investment. Within the context of war crimes tribunals and of the development of an international criminal court, attention is currently being paid to the responsibilities of individuals who commit mass violations of human rights or war crimes.

DEVELOPING A CULTURE OF RESPECT FOR HUMAN RIGHTS

It is not just a question of accountability. What is also required is a deeper appreciation of the role of all individuals and organs of society in securing a just and equitable world in which everyone might enjoy their human rights in dignity.

Urgent attention needs to be given to developing a climate of respect for human rights not only in government policy and action but also in the actions of individuals and communities

The inequities and discrimination that exacerbate poverty and social isolation are not always condoned by the state. Socio-cultural traditions may themselves compound such practices. We need look no further than the traditions that impede women's equality to appreciate this point. Similarly, it is social stigma that all too often imprisons behind the bars of prejudice, people living with HIV/AIDS, their families and associates.

Human rights and development strategies should promote respect for the human rights and dignity of everyone, and seek to build societies based on tolerance, solidarity, compassion and mutual respect. As President Mandela reminds us "...to be free is not merely to cast off one's chains, but to live in a way that respects and enhances the freedom of others."[3]

The importance of this truth for human development is immense. We are all part of the global development agenda. For instance, as consumers we have learnt that we can choose to be part of the problem or a part of the solution. As teachers, or as the children in whose hands the future lies, we have the chance to promote the values of equity, justice and solidarity. As politicians, diplomats, human rights advocates or development workers, we can join forces to seek the betterment of the human condition - not just for a few, but for everyone. We share the responsibility with governments to build a just and equitable world.

[3] *The Long Walk to Freedom: The Autobiography of Nelson Mandela*, p. 751. 1994.

AN ACHIEVABLE VISION
BACKED BY LAW

More than one quarter of our human family lives in poverty, deprived of the basic requirements for life and the opportunities essential for human dignity. Together we have the resources and technical capacity to eliminate poverty worldwide. Our ability to act as a world community is supported by the coherent framework of legal obligations and achievable targets for human development that have been developed and endorsed by the international community.

The human rights approach advocated here
reflects a vision of a just and equitable world
in which all people can live in dignity
and achieve their full potential

It is a vision. But it is a vision with a concrete base. It has its foundation firmly embedded in the provisions of international law and government commitments voluntarily undertaken.

It is a vision
but it is achievable.

ANNEXES

ANNEXES

During the preparation of the White Paper in the summer and autumn of 1997, the Author undertook a number of training seminars and question and answer sessions for members of DFID's staff - particularly from the Social Development, Government and Institutions, Health and Population and Emergency Aid Divisions of DFID, as well as from the Foreign Office.

At the request of DFID, this annex sets out to answer some of the most commonly asked questions about human rights and the human rights approach to development. It also seeks to answer other queries which, although not asked directly, are known to cause difficulties for some people coming to human rights for the first time. In order to keep the annex to a reasonable length, where appropriate readers are referred to the parts of the full text in which the issues are explored in more detail.

GENERAL QUESTIONS
CONCERNING HUMAN RIGHTS

1.   **What are human rights?**

2.   **Who has granted these rights?**

3.   **What is meant by the Universality of human rights?**

4.   **Are human rights merely a Western concept? Are they relevant in other regions of the world?**

5.   **How can we speak of universal human rights norms in a world of cultural diversity?**

6.   **Is it possible to claim that there is universal recognition that women and men are entitled to equal human rights when in so many societies women's rights are curtailed?**

7.   **What is meant by the international protection of human rights? How does it relate to national sovereignty?**

8.   **Who defines human rights?**

9.   **Where can a list of human rights be found?**

10.   **Which human rights are protected by international law?**

11.   **Are some human rights more important than others?**

12.   **What is meant by the indivisibility of human rights?**

13.   **Is the list of human rights fixed for all time?**

14.   **Who bears the duties relating to human rights?**

15.   **What are the obligations of states under international human rights conventions?**

16.   **What are the obligations of states that are NOT party to international human rights conventions?**

17.   **Since states have the primary duty to protect human rights, what are the obligations of individuals, corporations and other social actors?**

18.   **How can the human rights of individuals be balanced with the common good?**

19.   **Liberty rights are easy to understand, but how can we talk in terms of "rights" about basic requirements that need resources for their fulfilment?**

20.   **How can the enjoyment of economic, social and cultural rights be measured? For example, who quantifies the level of nutrition or health care required to fulfil human rights?**

21.   **Is it ethical to promulgate a right which cannot be delivered immediately, and the full realisation of which remains remote for so many people?**

22.   **Since human rights are protected by international law, are they not a legal subject rather than a development issue?**

23.   **How does this new human rights approach differ from earlier aid conditionalities or the welfare model of human development?**

24.   **Is there a risk that a human rights approach will lead to unrealistic expectations and conflict?**

25.   **Is there a "right to development"?**

26.   **Which human rights are essential for development?**

27.   **What difference does it make to speak in terms of rights to housing, access to health care, food and education etc., rather than to call these basic needs?**

28.   **If access to these requirements is a question of rights, who bears the corresponding duties? Do they match?**

29.   **Will a human rights approach to development bankrupt governments?**

30.   **Why should development agencies have a particular emphasis on women's rights, when the rights of men are also violated?**

31.   **What are the controversies over the terms "equity" and "equality"?**

32.   **How can development agencies best work with their partners to implement a gender equity and human rights approach to development?**

33.   **How can the right to a continuous improvement in living conditions be sustainable?**

34.   **Is there a risk that a human rights approach might divert resources from areas where higher returns can be gained?**

35.   **Will a human rights approach be acceptable to DFID's partners?**

36.   **How can a human rights approach to development be applied in the situation of a country without a legitimate government?**

1. WHAT ARE HUMAN RIGHTS?

The term "rights" is being used with increasing frequency in a wide variety of settings. The term may be used to describe a legal right or a moral claim, or merely an aspiration on behalf of an individual or group. DFID staff working in different departments have come across the term "rights" in various settings. For instance, those working in agricultural development are familiar with the term "animal rights" as a claim for humane treatment of animals, and the term "intellectual property rights" in the context of seed development, animal breeding and so forth. These various aspects of rights discourse can be distinguished from *human* rights which have their own history and legal protection, dealt with more fully in chapters 2 and 3 of this Paper. It is for this reason that the Author refers to a "human rights" approach to development rather than a "rights-based" approach.

The term "human rights" is correctly used to refer to all those rights recognised by the international community as being the birthright of every human being. Human rights include all those rights and freedoms necessary for liberty and autonomy, physical integrity, survival, and the development of the full human potential. Many such human rights have now been protected by international legal texts.

Human rights norms are not limited to freedom from torture, or to respect for such rights as freedom of speech, conscience and religion. They cover every aspect of human lives. Human rights include the rights to adequate food, housing, access to health care, and other essentials for life, as well as the rights to enjoy and participate in spiritual, intellectual, cultural and political life.

2. WHO HAS GRANTED THESE RIGHTS?

There have been differing views about the original source of human rights. Some philosophers believe that they derive from human conscience and reason, reflected in the constant striving of the human race for justice and freedom. Moral and religious thinkers of differing faiths have stressed the inherent dignity and equality of humans -whether they regard this as stemming from the dignity of all creation, or from the creation of humans in the image of God.

These various ideas are captured in the founding document of modern day human rights - the Universal Declaration of Human Rights adopted by the United Nations (UN) General Assembly on 10 December 1948. It states in its first preambular paragraph that "recognition of the inherent dignity and of the equal and inalienable rights of all members of the human family is the foundation of freedom, justice and peace in the world". By Article 1, the Universal Declaration proclaims:

> "All human beings are born free and equal in dignity and rights. They are endowed with reason and conscience and should act towards one another in a spirit of brotherhood."

Thus today, an answer to the question "where do human rights come from?" is that they arise from the recognition of their existence by the world community, expressed through numerous UN and other international documents, and adopted by states from every region of the world representing the rich diversity of the world's faiths and cultures.

3. WHAT IS MEANT BY THE UNIVERSALITY OF HUMAN RIGHTS?

Since human rights stem from the inherent dignity of all humans, then they must adhere to every man, woman and child merely by reason of their being human. These rights should be enjoyed irrespective of any distinguishing characteristics such as sex, race, colour, religion, language, political or other opinion, national or social origin, property, birth or other status.

Similarly, human rights belong to *all* human beings, in *every* state, whatever the level of economic development or the political system in place in their country. This is what is meant by the term "the universality of human rights" - a concept of fundamental significance to human rights protection. The universal nature of human rights distinguishes them from the rights which are granted by a state on the basis of citizenship; and from any specific legal rights granted to particular members of society, or arising out of a contractual agreement.

4. ARE HUMAN RIGHTS MERELY A WESTERN CONCEPT? ARE THEY RELEVANT IN OTHER REGIONS OF THE WORLD?

Although historically the political reforms in Europe and North America during the eighteenth and nineteenth century played an important role in shaping modern concepts of human rights and democracy, these have by no means been the only influences. The modern theory of human rights goes far beyond the confines of liberal rights theory associated with the West, and owes much to the influence of philosophies and values from elsewhere in the world, and to notions of equity and social justice.

Securing respect for human rights is one of the aims of the United Nations. All Member States have committed themselves to respect, protect and promote human rights. The Universal Declaration of Human Rights adopted by the UN on 10 December, 1948, was proclaimed as a "common standard of achievement for all peoples and all nations". Further, states from all regions of the world have contributed to the drafting and implementation of international human rights legal texts. International human rights norms therefore provide truly global standards which are binding on all states.

The fact that 171 states took part in the World Conference on Human Rights in Vienna in 1993, and unanimously adopted the Vienna Declaration and Programme of Action, is proof that the human rights regime is now genuinely accepted world-wide. In adopting the Vienna Declaration and Programme of Action the participating states adopted a global human rights agenda for implementation into the next century. As the Vienna Declaration stresses:

> "while the significance of national and regional particularities and various historical, cultural and religious backgrounds must be borne in mine, it is the duty of States, regardless of their political, economic, and social systems, to promote and protect all human rights and fundamental freedoms."

The Vienna Declaration also confirms:

> "Human rights and fundamental freedoms are the birthright of all human beings; their protection and promotion is the first responsibility of all Governments."

5. HOW CAN WE SPEAK OF UNIVERSAL HUMAN RIGHTS NORMS IN A WORLD OF CULTURAL DIVERSITY?

Recognition of the immense cultural diversity in the world leads some to question whether it is possible to talk about the "universal" system of values on which human rights norms are based. Some anthropologists and philosophers use the theory of cultural relativity to question the universal nature of human rights. Anthropologists have observed and documented the very real differences in the values acceptable within different groups of people and which have framed their cultures and traditions. It is a primary principle of anthropology not to import any value judgement from one culture to another.

However, individuals from societies throughout the world do recognise human rights, and the states participating at the World Conference on Human Rights agreed that *"the universal nature of these rights and freedoms is beyond question"*. Thus to hold states accountable for their performance with relation to global human rights standards is not to impose the value system of any one part of the world on another, but to refer to universal values, based on the distilled knowledge and wisdom of all our cultures.

An issue that is frequently raised in this context is that of traditional practices such as female genital mutilation. It has long been recognised that such practices are harmful to the health of women and girls. As a result, the UN and other international agencies have developed strategies to combat these practices. Further, such practices have been recognised as a form of violence against women and condemned in international human rights fora. However, it is sometimes argued that these international initiatives are interfering with the cultures of other societies.

It is not possible here to consider all the implications raised. However, what can be stated is that when an individual donor, such as DFID, assists states to develop appropriate strategies or supports projects designed to overcome such practices, it is not imposing its own domestic values, but is acting in accordance with the global consensus that such practices are harmful to health, and violate the rights of women and girls.

6. IS IT POSSIBLE TO CLAIM THAT THERE IS UNIVERSAL RECOGNITION THAT WOMEN AND MEN ARE ENTITLED TO EQUAL HUMAN RIGHTS WHEN IN SO MANY SOCIETIES WOMEN'S RIGHTS ARE CURTAILED?

The equal rights of women were endorsed by the World Conference on Human Rights in Vienna, 1993, under the slogan *"women's rights are human rights",* and formed the basis of the global agreement at the Fourth World Conference on Women in Beijing, 1995 (in which 189 states participated).

However, during the run up to the Fourth World Conference on Women in Beijing, the concept of the universality of human rights was once again questioned as the implications for women's equality became apparent. Some of the more traditional societies continued to see women's equal rights as a threat to existing power structures, whilst other conservative forces regarded the family responsibilities of women as requiring them to remain in the home.

Nevertheless, the Beijing Declaration and Platform for Action adopted by the Conference confirmed gender equality and contained a full chapter on the protection of women's human rights. This includes agreement to review national laws to ensure the implementation of all human rights treaties, and to ensure equality and non-discrimination both in law and in practice.

7. WHAT IS MEANT BY THE INTERNATIONAL PROTECTION OF HUMAN RIGHTS? HOW DOES IT RELATE TO NATIONAL SOVEREIGNTY?

Until the Second World War, the protection of human rights was left to each state.

The manner in which a state treated its citizens was considered to fall solely within the sovereignty of the state involved. The atrocities committed by the Nazi regime against its own citizens led the post-war world community to determine that no longer could the observance of human rights be left solely to an individual state. Whilst recognising the concept of state sovereignty in other matters, the United Nations set out to ensure that the universal respect for human rights should form one of the primary aims of the new world organisation.

The UN Charter itself provides that the UN shall promote:

> "Universal respect for, and observance of, human rights and fundamental freedoms for all without distinction as to race, sex, language or religion." (Article 55)

By Article 56 of the Charter, the Member States pledge themselves to take joint and separate action in co-operation with the UN for the achievement of this and other aims.

Thus, from its very inception, the UN has recognised that all states have a right, indeed a duty, to be concerned about respect for human rights in other countries. No longer can the claim of state sovereignty be used to deny the legitimacy of international concern for human rights.

The Vienna Declaration adopted by the World Conference on Human Rights in 1993 confirmed this in the following provision:

> "The promotion and protection of all human rights and fundamental freedoms must be considered as a priority objective of the United Nations in accordance with its purposes and principles, in particular the purpose of international co-operation. In the framework of these purposes and principles, the promotion and protection of all human rights is a legitimate concern of the international community."

8. WHO DEFINES HUMAN RIGHTS?

Clearly, if human rights are to be effectively protected it is essential that there is a common understanding of what amounts to a human right. One of the earliest tasks of the United Nations was to compile a list of internationally recognised human rights. It is the international community acting as a whole that drafts international human rights texts, thus giving international recognition to various human rights.

9. WHERE CAN A LIST OF HUMAN RIGHTS BE FOUND?

The global agreement on human rights is contained in international human rights instruments starting with the International Bill of Rights promulgated by the United Nations, through numerous more detailed UN instruments, and regional texts.

INTERNATIONAL BILL OF RIGHTS

The Universal Declaration of Human Rights - adopted by the UN General Assembly on 10 December, 1948. Its provisions were given the force of international law in two covenants:

The International Covenant on Economic, Social and Cultural Rights, and
The International Covenant on Civil and Political Rights - both adopted in 1966 and which came into force between the States Parties in 1976.

These three instruments are referred to together as the International Bill of Rights.[1]

OTHER MAJOR UN TEXTS

The UN has adopted a large number of other international instruments designed to protect human rights in specific circumstances, or to protect the rights of people particularly vulnerable to abuse of their rights. They include:

The Convention on the Elimination of Racial Discrimination (CERD) 1965
The Convention on the Elimination of All Forms of Discrimination Against Women (CEDAW) 1979
The Convention Against Torture and Other Cruel, Inhuman or Degrading Treatment or Punishment (CAT) 1984
The Convention on the Rights of the Child (CRC) 1989.

REGIONAL TEXTS

The Council of Europe, the Organisation of American States, and the Organisation of African Unity have all adopted regional instruments to translate the international texts into additional obligations binding on States Parties within the region.

10. WHICH HUMAN RIGHTS ARE PROTECTED BY INTERNATIONAL LAW?

The list of internationally recognised human rights is long and detailed. It includes, but is not limited to, the following:

- freedom from torture and inhuman and degrading treatment or punishment
- freedom of thought, religion and expression
- freedom of movement and of assembly
- freedom from arbitrary interference with privacy or family life
- rights to life, liberty and security of the person
- right to a standard of living adequate for health and wellbeing, including food and housing
- right to the highest attainable standard of physical and mental health
- right to work, and to just and favourable remuneration and conditions of work
- rights to education, and to seek and impart information
- rights to equality before the law, and to a fair trial and conditions of detention
- rights to participate in political and cultural life, and to share in scientific advancement and its benefits.

The international instruments contain provisions by which States Parties guarantee that the rights enunciated will be exercised without discrimination of any kind as to

[1]See Annex 3 for full texts

race, colour, sex, language, religion, political or other opinion, national or social origin, property, birth or other status. Similarly, States Parties undertake **to ensure the equal rights of men and women to the enjoyment of the rights protected, and to protect the rights of the child**.

11. ARE SOME HUMAN RIGHTS MORE IMPORTANT THAN OTHERS?

There is a tendency to try to list human rights in order of their importance. However, attempts at creating hierarchies of rights are doomed to failure. It is attractive to consider the right to life as the most precious, but without enjoyment of the right to food, the right to life is meaningless.

Each time one attempts to hold up a human right as being the most fundamental, it is possible to find another right that must be enjoyed as a pre-requisite to realisation of the right first identified. Human rights advocates therefore prefer not to get into the game of trying to construct hierarchies. In any case, it would be very difficult to get any real consensus on such a listing. Therefore, human rights advocates prefer to talk of the indivisibility of all human rights which should be given equal priority, rather than trying to identify core rights of primary importance.

12. WHAT IS MEANT BY THE INDIVISIBILITY OF HUMAN RIGHTS?

When the Universal Declaration was first adopted, it was intended that it would be followed by a single legal document. However, the legal drafting was much affected by the ideological differences existing during the Cold War. These were characterised by different interpretations of human rights by the two political blocs. The Western bloc gave priority to civil and political rights - such as freedom of expression, conscience and belief, and democracy rights; whereas the Communist bloc gave priority to economic, social and cultural rights - such as the rights to work, housing, access to health care, and so forth. As a compromise, two Covenants were drafted and adopted.

However, this separation into two branches of law can be misleading. In practice, the two sets of rights are inter-related. A violation of one right invariably impinges on the enjoyment of a wide range of other rights. A person denied the right to education would be disadvantaged in enjoying his or her political rights, for example. Similarly, there is increasing evidence to show that, even in times of food scarcity, widespread famines rarely occur in countries where there is a free press, illustrating that the right to food is inextricably linked to freedom of speech.

Recent international conferences have therefore confirmed that "[a]ll human rights are universal, indivisible, interdependent and interrelated" (Article 5 of Vienna Declaration and Programme of Action adopted by the World Conference on Human Rights on 25 June 1993).

13. IS THE LIST OF HUMAN RIGHTS FIXED FOR ALL TIME?

Although the international human rights community is trying to focus attention on the implementation and enforcement of existing standards, new texts are constantly being developed to address matters of current concern. For instance, a Convention on the Rights of the Child has recently been adopted, and human rights criteria are now beginning to be used to challenge the economic injustice within and between states, and to highlight the human consequences of the imposition of structural adjustment programmes.

Article 28 of the Universal Declaration of Human Rights proclaims that everyone is entitled to a social and international order in which the rights and freedoms set forth in the Declaration can be fully realised. The inequities in access to basic health care, education, clean water, housing and so forth are stark reminders of the failure to establish a just and equitable world society. A number of recent UN Conferences have developed international programmes of action addressed to overcoming these inequities so that all people might live in accordance with their rights and dignity. The programmes for action adopted by the Rio Summit, the Children's Summit, the World Conference on Human Rights, the World Summit for Social Development, the Cairo Conference on Population and Development, and the Beijing Women's Conference, for example, set out global agreements on measures to be adopted.

Whilst not having the force of international law, these political commitments should be read together with the international human rights legal instruments. In such a manner, the scope and understanding of human rights is developing. For instance, at the World Conference on Human Rights it was confirmed that women's rights are human rights, and that violence against women - whether occurring in private or public - is a human rights concern. At Cairo and Beijing the scope and nature of women's rights in the context of sexual and reproductive health were also clarified. In this way, the subject of human rights is both *concrete* - confirmed in international law - and *dynamic* - able to develop in accordance with recognition of the need.

14. WHO BEARS THE DUTIES RELATING TO HUMAN RIGHTS?

The international human rights framework has been developed as a part of public international law. The conventions mentioned above have been adopted by states as a form of contractual obligations towards other states. Thus the primary obligation for the implementation of human rights rests with the States Parties to the various instruments.

This is not to say that individuals have no responsibilities, rather that these duties are governed by a different branch of law. However, states are obliged to protect human rights from abuse by third parties, and should introduce national laws to govern the behaviour of individuals and groups.

15. WHAT ARE THE OBLIGATIONS OF STATES UNDER INTERNATIONAL HUMAN RIGHTS CONVENTIONS?

Once a state has adopted a particular international convention it is obliged to promote and protect the human rights covered by the convention. States are obliged to secure the human rights of all people within its jurisdiction, and not just its own citizens. However, under the International Covenant on Economic, Social and Cultural Rights, developing countries, with due regard to human rights and their national economy, may determine to what extent they would guarantee the economic rights recognised in the Covenant to non-nationals.

The constitutions of most modern states contain at least some provisions to protect human rights, and many states have introduced specific laws to prevent discrimination and protect individuals' human rights, either generally, or in specific circumstances.

The precise obligations of states vary from convention to convention. But in general terms, states can be regarded as being obliged to **respect** the human rights of all people within its jurisdiction, to **protect** individuals from abuse by third parties, to **promote** respect for human rights in its laws, policies and actions, and to take the necessary measures to **ensure realisation** of human rights in practice. For instance, the International Covenant on Civil and Political Rights requires States Parties "to adopt such legislative or other measures as may be necessary to give effect to the rights recognized in the …Covenant".

Recognising that states may not be able to ensure instant realisation of all economic, social and cultural rights, the International Covenant on these rights provides that all States Parties should **take steps, to the maximum of available resources, towards the progressive achievement** of the full realisation of these rights.

There is what is called a *margin of discretion*, which allows a state to choose the manner in which it fulfils its obligations under international human rights law. A state is then able to decide which policies to adopt in order to ensure realisation of the rights within the context of the political, economic, religious, cultural, and other characteristics of the state. For example, if the obligation in question is that of guaranteeing access to health care for all, it is left to the state to decide how medical care is to be provided, i.e. whether through a public health service, private insurance schemes, or a mixture of the two.

Nevertheless, the state remains under a duty to act, and is accountable to the international community for its implementation of this obligation. The margin of discretion does not mean that a state is free to pick and choose which rights to implement, or that it might ignore the rights of a particular section of the community.

The provision concerning "the progressive achievement" of the full realisation of economic, social and cultural rights is very important. The South African Constitution of 1996 provides an excellent example of how these rights and obligations might be incorporated into national law. For example, article 26(1) of the Constitution states that everyone has the right to have access to adequate housing. Article 26(2) requires the state to take reasonable legal and other measures, within its available resources, to achieve the progressive realisation of the right. Article 26(3) provides that no one may be evicted from their home, or have their home demolished, without an order of court made after consideration of all of the relevant circumstances. In addition, no legislation may permit arbitrary evictions.

There is also a duty of international co-operation. The International Covenant on Economic, Social and Cultural Rights also requires States Parties to "take steps, individually and through *international assistance and co-operation*, especially economic and technical, to the maximum of its resources, with a view to achieving progressively the full realisation of the rights recognised in the ...Covenant".

16. WHAT ARE THE OBLIGATIONS OF STATES THAT ARE NOT PARTY TO INTERNATIONAL HUMAN RIGHTS CONVENTIONS?

Some states which violate human rights have sought to push aside international criticism by arguing that they are not bound to respect human rights as they are not party to international human rights conventions.

However, with few exceptions, the majority of states are members of the UN, and as such are bound by the UN Charter. Under the Charter all Member States have undertaken to ensure, jointly and separately "universal respect for, and observance of, human rights and fundamental freedoms for all without distinction as to race, sex, language or religion".

The status of the Universal Declaration of Human Rights is also relevant. Although it does not have the formal status of a legal treaty, it has been globally adopted as the basic international pronouncement of the inalienable rights of all members of the human family. States throughout the world have used it as an authoritative basis for the development of international standards, and for the protection of human rights in their constitutions and other national laws. As a result, international jurists consider that its fundamental provisions now form part of customary international law, binding on every state without exception.

This interpretation is given added weight by the unanimous adoption at the World Conference on Human Rights in 1993 of the Vienna Declaration and Programme of Action which states in its first paragraph:

> "The World Conference on Human Rights reaffirms the solemn commitment of all States to fulfil their obligations to promote universal respect for, and observance and protection of, all human rights and fundamental freedoms for all in accordance with the Charter of the United Nations, other instruments relating to human rights, and international law. The universal nature of these rights and freedoms is beyond question."

17. SINCE STATES HAVE THE PRIMARY DUTY TO PROTECT HUMAN RIGHTS, WHAT ARE THE OBLIGATIONS OF INDIVIDUALS, CORPORATIONS AND OTHER SOCIAL ACTORS?

By international law, it is states that have the primary obligation to ensure the realisation of human rights. As part of their duty, states must protect individuals from abuse of their human rights by third parties. Therefore, states should enact national laws requiring individuals to respect the rights of others.

Attempts are currently being made within the human rights community to find ways of extending individual responsibility to corporations, particularly multi-national companies. The activities of Shell in Ogoniland in Nigeria have shown how devastating the actions of large corporations can be on the lives of people. Clearly, a way must be found to make these bodies accountable for the abuses of rights that they inflict.

Similarly, human rights advocates are striving to hold the international financial institutions accountable for the human rights impact of their policies and programmes. This was prompted by the adverse consequences of the imposition of economic structural adjustment programmes on the poor and vulnerable sectors of society.

18. HOW CAN THE HUMAN RIGHTS OF INDIVIDUALS BE BALANCED WITH THE COMMON GOOD?

Like any law, international human rights law seeks a balance between conflicting interests - between enjoyment of the rights of one, and of the rights of another; between individual rights and the common good. This latter point is important to stress, as critics sometimes fear that a human rights approach means asserting individual liberty at the cost of common welfare; but in fact international human rights law provides for those circumstances in which liberties and freedoms might be curtailed.

Whilst the human rights of individuals are inalienable, they do not imply absolute liberty. Human rights are bounded by the requirement of reasonable behaviour. The limitation in human rights jurisprudence is clear. Individual freedoms can be curtailed, but only in the case of an absolute necessity to preserve public health, public morals, or national security. Furthermore, a state cannot restrict the rights of the individual unless the restriction is *proportional* to the need.

What needs to be emphasised is that an individual does not lose all his or her liberties as a result of a failure to respect the rights of others. A person guilty of harming another is still entitled to the protection of human rights law concerning the fair conduct of criminal proceedings. Further, the right to freedom from torture, and from cruel, inhuman, and degrading treatment or punishment and certain other rights are inalienable. Under international law, there are no circumstances in which torture can be justified.

See chapter 3 for further discussion of these points.

19. LIBERTY RIGHTS ARE EASY TO UNDERSTAND, BUT HOW CAN WE TALK IN TERMS OF "RIGHTS" ABOUT BASIC REQUIREMENTS THAT NEED RESOURCES FOR THEIR FULFILMENT?

There is no such thing as a free right. All human rights, civil and political as much as economic, social and cultural, involve expense. In the past, it has sometimes been argued that civil and political rights are of a different category to economic, social and cultural rights, and that the former is more readily enforced through law (i.e. is justiciable), as it merely imposes negative obligations on the state to abstain from a particular course of action. Economic, social and cultural rights, it is argued, impose positive obligations, and their vagueness prevents them from being justiciable. These are false arguments. ***Each of the two branches of rights impose both negative and positive obligations. All rights are justiciable to a greater or lesser extent.***

For example, protecting civil and political rights involves state expenditure in terms of the provision and training of a police force, the establishment of a criminal process and prison service, and the operation of courts. Even the right to vote involves a state in costs, in terms of administration and the provision of accessible polling stations.

Conversely, the protection of many economic and social rights can be achieved simply by the introduction of appropriate legislation. For instance law can be introduced to prohibit discrimination in the enjoyment of these rights, to protect workers' rights and trade union rights, and the freedoms indispensable for scientific research and creative activity; as well as to prohibit such violations as arbitrary evictions from homes, or other actions which impede livelihood and survival.

Many economic and social rights are indeed already protected by national laws, which, being justiciable, provide redress for those whose rights are infringed. Virtually all states protect some labour rights, and protect tenants from exploitation by landlords, to quote but two examples.

20. HOW CAN THE ENJOYMENT OF ECONOMIC, SOCIAL AND CULTURAL RIGHTS BE MEASURED? FOR EXAMPLE, WHO QUANTIFIES THE LEVEL OF NUTRITION OR HEALTH CARE REQUIRED TO FULFIL HUMAN RIGHTS?

How much food is required for adequate nutrition is a technical matter rather than a legal issue. When the International Bill of Rights was adopted, it was assumed that the specialised agencies would play a role in quantifying what was required for the realisation of economic, social and cultural rights.

UNESCO, UNICEF, UNIFEM, FAO, the ILO and WHO, for example, have all contributed to the international consensus on standards relating to their particular fields. UNDP is also now beginning to address the issue of human rights.

Progress has been made through the series of global conferences held over the last decade. The agreements reached reflect political commitment by states to attaining these standards, and set goals and targets for their achievement.

At the same time, UN human rights bodies have started down the path of developing indicators for measuring the realisation of economic, social and cultural rights. This work is being complemented by the UN Committee on Economic, Social and Cultural Rights, which is developing standards and benchmarks, and is encouraging states to set their own national goals and targets.

21. IS IT ETHICAL TO PROMULGATE A RIGHT WHICH CANNOT BE DELIVERED IMMEDIATELY, AND THE FULL REALISATION OF WHICH REMAINS REMOTE FOR SO MANY PEOPLE?

In humanitarian terms, the point is rather the inverse. It is unethical to accept inequality, inhumanity, and any other denial of human rights and dignity.

There is nothing new in claiming a right that cannot be immediately fulfilled. Slavery was not abolished overnight. Many of us did not expect to see *apartheid* overthrown in our lifetimes. The achievement of human rights is a long-term agenda. For example, both the civil rights movement in America and the women's rights movement reflect agendas in progress.

The UNDP and the Development Assistance Committee of OECD are convinced that it is possible to halve world poverty by the year 2015. In her speech at the University of Manchester on 30 June 1997, the Secretary of State for International Development adopted this target as DFID's main goal, and continued:

> "The UNDP report gave figures and analysis which showed that the costs are affordable given the political will. And, of course, we shouldn't stop there. If we can halve world poverty by 2015, we can eliminate it in the lifetime of many of us here. And these are not just the words of idealists. It's the hard nosed analysts of the OECD who say we can do it. It is both achievable and affordable. This is the world's major challenge for the new Millennium."

It is therefore incumbent upon us all - states and individuals - to seek the rights of people living in poverty and social isolation. This is the ethical approach.

22. SINCE HUMAN RIGHTS ARE PROTECTED BY INTERNATIONAL LAW, ARE THEY NOT A LEGAL SUBJECT RATHER THAN A DEVELOPMENT ISSUE?

Human rights and development theories have emerged from distinct disciplines, resulting in the application of different criteria for establishing the cogency of theoretical models, and for measuring their success. This has sometimes impeded dialogue and comprehension between the two disciplines.

However, for an informed approach to the implementation of human rights, it is necessary for various disciplines to play their part. There is a potential synergy in bringing together the experiences of the human rights and development communities in a joint approach to promoting the achievement of human rights. The international legal standards provide the global framework in which development assistance can be promulgated, whilst development theory and practice provide the technical knowledge and financial assistance that is required to secure human rights in reality.

23. HOW DOES THIS NEW HUMAN RIGHTS APPROACH DIFFER FROM EARLIER AID CONDITIONALITIES OR THE WELFARE MODEL OF HUMAN DEVELOPMENT?

Development assistance and human rights have been linked for some time by donors imposing negative and/or positive human rights conditionalities. The human rights approach advocated in the present paper builds on the promotion of positive conditionalities, but goes further. It promotes the use of development co-operation to assist partners to secure the realisation of all human rights - economic, social and cultural as well as civil and political rights - and articulates a human rights approach to the manner in which aid is delivered. It therefore complements existing good governance policies. At the same time, it is recognised that in extreme circumstances, the cessation of development aid may remain necessary in times of conflict and large-scale human rights violations.

The human rights approach differs from a welfare based model. The latter operates in an essentially comparative manner. Less fortunate people are compared with more fortunate individuals, and measures are taken to achieve a comparatively fairer outcome. This promotes the view that there is no absolute entitlement - only comparative entitlements.

The human rights approach to development is not premised on governmental largesse. It is not about discretionary assistance, but about securing enjoyment of human rights which have been recognised by the global community.

This shift in emphasis is particularly important for the *self-esteem* of poor people. The experience of using such an approach has shown that beneficiaries feel *empowered.* By contrasting their current situation with what they are entitled to pursuant to human rights law, they are encouraged to work for change and seek their rights.

24. IS THERE A RISK THAT A HUMAN RIGHTS APPROACH WILL LEAD TO UNREALISTIC EXPECTATIONS AND CONFLICT?

The daily struggle for survival encourages pragmatism among poor people. They rarely expect overnight miracles from development assistance. However, the manner in which poor people are educated about their rights is very important so as not to create unrealistic expectations. It is equally vital to avoid stirring up the type of resentment over their condition that breeds violent confrontation.

The violations of the rights of the poor in Latin America have taught us that it is the indifference to social and economic injustice, and a government's consistent failure to take steps towards the enjoyment of fundamental human rights by poor people that leads to conflict. Too often poor people claiming their human rights have been subjected to brutal repression by police and security forces.

It is the insecurity of the threatened elite which causes conflict, not the claim of the poor to their human rights. If the opinions of poor people were sought on priorities, if schools were being built and health services provided, if measures were being introduced to protect vulnerable people from police or domestic violence, then there would be no need for the poor to march on capitals in protest. If the repression experienced by poverty-stricken people in Latin America is not to be repeated in other parts of the world, ways must be found to secure enjoyment of human rights by people living in poverty and social isolation.

25. IS THERE A "RIGHT TO DEVELOPMENT"?

The UN General Assembly adopted the Declaration on the Right to Development[2] in 1986. It recognises that development is a human right. Although not yet law, that proclamation was strengthened by the Vienna Declaration adopted by the UN World Conference on Human Rights in 1993, which states that "the right to development is an inalienable human right and an integral part of fundamental human freedoms". This has been further confirmed at recent UN conferences including: the World Summit for Social Development, Copenhagen, 1993; the UN Conference on Population and Development, Cairo, 1994; and the Fourth World Conference on Women, Beijing, 1995.

Article 2 of the Declaration provides:

"1. The human person is the central subject of development and should be the active participant and beneficiary of the right to development.

2. All human beings have a responsibility for development, individually and collectively, taking into account the need for full respect for their human rights and fundamental freedoms as well as their duties to the community, which alone can ensure the free and complete fulfilment of the human being, and they should therefore promote and protect an appropriate political, social and economic order for development.

3. States have the right and the duty to formulate appropriate national development policies that aim at the constant improvement of the well-being of the entire population and of all individuals, on the basis of their active, free and meaningful participation in development and in the fair distribution of the benefits resulting therefrom."

In October 1995, the UN Working Group on the Right to Development stated that:

"the right to development is multidimensional, integrated, dynamic and progressive. Its realization involves the full observance of economic, social, cultural, civil and political rights. It further embraces the different concepts of development of all development sectors, namely sustainable development, human development and the concept of indivisibility, interdependence and universality of all human rights. . . . Realization of the right to development is the responsibility of all actors in development, within the international community, within States at both the national and international levels, within the agencies of the United Nations system."

26. WHICH HUMAN RIGHTS ARE ESSENTIAL FOR DEVELOPMENT?

As this paper has consistently argued, human rights are indivisible. The realisation of *all* human rights is important for development. Denial of one right invariably impacts on the enjoyment of another. The better known civil and political rights are necessary for the creation of the democratic systems within which individuals might freely exercise their human rights and choices, whilst economic, social and

---

[2]See Annex 4 for full texts

cultural rights are essential for life and dignity. Development assistance should therefore support the realisation of all human rights - civil, cultural, economic, political and social.

27. WHAT DIFFERENCE DOES IT MAKE TO SPEAK IN TERMS OF RIGHTS TO HOUSING, ACCESS TO HEALTH CARE, FOOD AND EDUCATION ETC., RATHER THAN TO CALL THESE BASIC NEEDS?

For a number of years the UN used the term "basic needs" to cover those essentials for human survival. However, the term fell out of favour, partly as a result of the fact that it failed to recognise that individuals have an inherent right to these essentials. Further, there was a tendency to assume that all that was necessary was to ensure these needs were met at a basic or minimum level.

However, the aspiration and rights of individuals does not stop at access to mere survival rations or the provision of basic services. Human rights require that everyone should live, and be able to develop, in accordance with human dignity. *A human rights approach to development does not stop at the eradication of absolute poverty, but supports the continuous improvement in the quality of life and the progressive achievement of the full range of human rights.*

28. IF ACCESS TO THESE REQUIREMENTS IS A QUESTION OF "RIGHTS", WHO BEARS THE CORRESPONDING "DUTIES"? DO THEY MATCH?

Some philosophers have argued that there can only be a "right" when there is a corresponding "duty" imposed on an identifiable individual, organisation, or organ of government. This leads some to question what duties are imposed with respect to economic, social and cultural rights, and on whom these duties are placed.

Under international law, the legal duty corresponding to economic, social and cultural rights rests on states. States are obliged to protect these rights through national law and practice. In such a manner, the right of individuals to enjoy economic, social and cultural rights should be protected from third party infringement. In particular, international human rights interpretation within the UN holds that states are under an immediate obligation to protect individuals from discrimination in enjoyment of their economic, social and cultural rights. States should, therefore, penalise discrimination whether practised by organs of the state or private individuals or corporations.

It is generally considered that states are obliged to provide the legal, economic, and social environment in which individuals might have an opportunity to meet their own needs, and that of their families. The International Covenant on Economic, Social and Cultural Rights sets out the obligations of States Parties as being to take measures, to the maximum of available resources, towards the progressive achievement of the rights recognised in the Covenant. (The relevant provision is considered more fully in chapter 3, 5 and 6 of this Paper)

The Covenant does not go as far as saying that states are obliged to provide everyone with free food, clothing and housing. In fact, there is only one provision in the Covenant that expressly calls for state provision. This is Article 13 concerning the right to education, which requires that "primary education shall be compulsory and available free to all". With respect to secondary and higher education, there is a commitment to the progressive introduction of free education.

Further, there is an obligation of international co-operation. States Parties to the covenant undertake to take steps through ***international co-operation and technical assistance*** towards the progressive realisation of the rights protected in the Covenant. Therefore, when an individual country is unable to afford to secure realisation of these rights, it can call upon the international community for assistance. This Author would argue that in times of crisis there is an obligation on the international community as a whole to ensure emergency assistance reaches those in need.

Although not having the force of law, the Declaration on the Right to Development confirms the duty of international co-operation. Articles 3 and 4 provide *inter alia*:

> "Article 3 (1) States have the primary responsibility for the creation of national and international conditions favourable to the realization of the right to development.

> …

> (3) States have the duty to co-operate with each other in ensuring development and eliminating obstacles to development. States should realize their rights and fulfil their duties in such a manner as to promote a new international economic order based on sovereign equality, interdependence, mutual interest and co-operation among all States, as well as to encourage the observance and realization of human rights.

> Article 4 (1) States have the duty to take steps, individually and collectively, to formulate international development policies with a view to facilitating the full realization of the right to development.

> (2) Sustained action is required to promote more rapid development of developing countries. As a complement to the efforts of developing countries, effective international co-operation is essential in providing these countries with appropriate means and facilities to foster their comprehensive development."

29. WILL A HUMAN RIGHTS APPROACH TO DEVELOPMENT BANKRUPT GOVERNMENTS?

It is sometimes feared that the promotion of a human rights approach to development will be very costly for developing countries, as it requires attention to be paid to the realisation of economic, social and cultural rights. It is questioned, for example, whether countries are at risk of legal claims from homeless people.

But as we have seen above, states are not under an immediate duty to provide housing, rather to take the necessary steps, to the maximum of available resources, towards the progressive achievement of the right of everyone to an adequate standard of living including housing. A government is not in breach of its international obligations simply as a result of the existence of people living in abject poverty.

However, if a government spends a disproportionate amount of its budget on armaments, for example, at the cost of social development it will be in breach of its international legal obligations. Similarly, if a state fails to develop plans to secure the rights of the poor and vulnerable, it is also failing in its duties. Clearly, a state violates the right to housing if it arbitrarily evicts people from their homes, as has unfortunately been the case in some slum clearance programmes involving forced evictions without resettlement.

30. WHY SHOULD DEVELOPMENT AGENCIES HAVE A PARTICULAR EMPHASIS ON WOMEN'S RIGHTS, WHEN THE RIGHTS OF MEN ARE ALSO VIOLATED?

Whilst there is no doubt that men's rights are also violated, in most societies of the world, women do not enjoy equal protection of the law, and tend to have less economic, political and other forms of bargaining power. This impedes their development, and that of their societies, and also restricts their ability to call attention to the violation of their rights. Even where there is legal (or *de jure*) equality between men and women, this does not mean that there is equality between men and women in reality, (*de facto* equality).

The control of individuals by the state is reflected in part by the denial of women's rights. In turn, some states anticipate that men will control women, and in many cases, makes it legally possible for them to do so. This can be seen as patriarchy at two levels - a hierarchy where men have few liberties and women even fewer.

31. WHAT ARE THE CONTROVERSIES OVER THE TERMS "EQUITY" AND "EQUALITY"?

During the International Conference on Population and Development in Cairo, 1994, and the Beijing Women's Conference, 1995, considerable controversy arose over the terms "equity" and "equality". Some delegations wished to avoid "equality" as this would, for instance, require recognition that women are entitled to equal property rights. Some Islamic delegations, for example, preferred to use the term "equity", which implied justice rather than equality. They argued that it was equitable for men and women to have differential property rights, as their responsibilities were different.

However, other people (particularly lawyers from the common law tradition) use the term "equity" in a different manner to call for the necessary affirmative action to ensure that women actually enjoy their rights and equality. Thus the word "equity" was being used in different ways by various delegations. For some it was a positive term, whilst others perceived it to be shorthand for something less than equality.

This debate was resolved at Beijing by using both terms together throughout the Beijing Declaration and Platform for Action.

32. HOW CAN DEVELOPMENT AGENCIES BEST WORK WITH THEIR PARTNERS TO IMPLEMENT A GENDER AND HUMAN RIGHTS APPROACH TO DEVELOPMENT?

There are benefits to taking a co-operative approach, one in which both partner governments are reminded of the commitments they have already made pursuant to international law.

There are many potential areas for partnerships which have been proposed throughout this paper, particularly in chapters 7 and 8. It is not necessary to repeat them all here, but one example can be given. In order to ensure gender equity, the opportunity of contacts with a particular government or institution could be used to suggest that records are kept containing disaggregated data on health statistics, education, employment, prison populations, and so forth, to indicate the breakdown between men and women, minorities, and other groups.

33. HOW CAN THE RIGHT TO A CONTINUOUS IMPROVEMENT IN LIVING CONDITIONS BE SUSTAINABLE?

The International Covenant on Economic, Social and Cultural Rights recognises "the right of everyone to an adequate standard of living for himself and his family … and to the continuous improvement of living conditions." This text was drafted in the 1960s, before the full implications of the over use of finite resources had been recognised. The term "sustainable development" was yet to be coined.

However, there is no reason why this provision of the Covenant should not be read in conjunction with international commitments concerning sustainability. It is now recognised that sustainability is a pre-requisite for an adequate quality of life. Thus sustainability and the improvement of living conditions are mutually reinforcing, rather than in conflict. What the provision does make clear is that the urgency of ensuring access to the requirements for survival should not mask the fact that human beings are entitled to more than mere subsistence.

As UNDP has recognised in its 1997 Human Development Report, improvement in living conditions should not be seen as being limited to material concerns. It has long been recognised that a complex variety of quality of life factors make up the parameters of continuous improvement of living conditions. UNDP explains the concept of human development as follows:

> "The process of widening people's choices and the level of well-being they achieve are at the core of the notion of human development. Such choices are neither finite nor static. But regardless of the level of development, the three essential choices for people are to lead a long and healthy life, to acquire knowledge, and to have access to the resources needed for a decent standard of living. Human development does not end there, however. Other choices, highly valued by many people, range from political, economic and social freedom to opportunities for being creative and productive and enjoying self-respect and guaranteed human rights".

The continuous improvement of living conditions in this sense is, therefore, in no way in conflict with the need to sustain the environment.

34. IS THERE A RISK THAT A HUMAN RIGHTS APPROACH MIGHT DIVERT RESOURCES FROM AREAS WHERE HIGHER RETURNS CAN BE GAINED?

One approach to economic development would require that resources be invested in those areas and projects that are likely to provide the highest return. This may point to assisting the top levels of the economy, rather than the poorest sectors.

A human rights approach, however, is concerned with *human* development. It requires concern for *all* people and for overcomiing inequalities and discrimination. It therefore supports priority being paid to investing in securing the rights and needs of those people living in poverty and social isolation who are currently denied their fare share of the resources of society.

However, such an approach is not necessarily in conflict with other development goals. There is increasing evidence that investment in education and health care, for example, is an effective manner in which to secure both human development and economic growth. Experience from around the world indicates that economic and social inequities, and the failure to resolve in a just manner conflicts over scarce resources, both inhibit development, and can lead to violent conflict. Thus a human rights approach to development, with its emphasis on investment in the social sector and a pro-poor priority, is likely in the longer term to lead to more sustainable development, and to contribute to the prevention of conflict.

35. WILL A HUMAN RIGHTS APPROACH BE ACCEPTABLE TO DFID'S PARTNERS?

A human rights approach to development, of the nature outlined in this Paper, is likely to be welcomed by Southern governments, many of which have long been advocating for greater attention to be paid to the realisation of economic, social and cultural rights as an essential pre-requisite for development.

A positive approach to ensuring the realisation of the human rights of poor people will help overcome the perception held by some Southern countries that the West/North is only interested in criticising violations of human rights - particularly civil and political rights. The approach advocated in this Paper could, therefore, play an important role in overcoming the politicisation of human rights, which has separated the world across East/West and North/South divisions. However, careful language needs to be used in presenting the human rights approach to development to recipient partners. It is important that they do not think it is negative conditionality wrapped up in pretty paper, and that they see it as a genuine effort at promoting sustainable human development for all.

It is sometimes queried whether such an approach will also be welcomed in Islamic countries. In countries with fundamentalist regimes the emphasis on women's rights may not be welcomed, but the emphasis on the rights of the poor and children in particular are more likely to be entertained. Furthermore, in the more progressive countries, such as Egypt and Jordan, the full approach is likely to be welcomed. Both countries have well-developed programmes to promote human rights, including women's rights and the rights of the child.

In all situations, sensitivity and tact is the key. For example, in discussions with partners it is advisable to stick to ***existing language*** of international texts, rather than seeking to be too progressive with language not yet agreed. For instance, a formulation such as "human rights in the context of sexual and reproductive health" would be preferable to the highly controversial term "sex rights".

EU and other donor partners are also likely to welcome DFID's new approach. It builds on the priorities identified by the UNDP and OECD/DAC. It is also likely to be welcomed by Commonwealth partners, particularly since the Harare Communiqué adopted by the Commonwealth in 1991 lays stress on human rights.

The new approach forms a firm basis for partnerships within civil society, and is likely to be warmly welcomed by NGOs and community-based organisations.

36. HOW CAN A HUMAN RIGHTS APPROACH TO DEVELOPMENT BE APPLIED IN THE SITUATION OF A COUNTRY WITHOUT A LEGITIMATE GOVERNMENT?

The lack of a legitimate government in a country causes difficulties for human rights accountability, just as it does for partnerships for development. However, there have been some cases in which non-state actors have been held accountable for their actions. For example, the international community developed the concept of "crimes against humanity" as a part of international humanitarian law during the Nuremburg trials. Similarly, the prohibition against rape as a military strategy contained in the Fourth Geneva Convention on the protection of civilians in times of war is currently being used as the basis of prosecution of war criminals from several sides of the Bosnian conflict. These developments also form a basis for the calls for an international criminal court.

CONSULTED SOURCES

Abu-Samen, Mai. (1997) "Women in Politics: Effecting Change from the Grassroots Up." Paper presented at the International Round Table: Equal Opportunities for Women: A Question of Rights and Humanity, organised by Rights and Humanity in cooperation with the Jordanian National Committee for Women, under the Patronage of HRH Princess Basma bint Talal, 8 -10 April, Amman , Jordan.

Armouti, Marzen Dr.,ed. (1996) The Encounter: Islam, the West, and Human Rights. Report of the Round Table on The Universality of Human Rights, December 10-12, 1994. Amman, Jordan, organised by Rights and Humanity in co-operation with The Institute of Diplomacy, Jordan.
Rights and Humanity, UK.

Alston, Philip. (1997) "Making Economic and Social Rights Count: A Strategy for the Future." The Political Quarterly, Vol 68:2, April - June.

Arsenault, Lori Jones, Jennifer Kitts, Janet Hatcher Roberts and Pandu Wijeyaratne, eds. (1993) "Gender Health and Sustainable Development." Report of a Workshop held in Nairobi, Kenya, 5-8 October. Ottawa: International Development Research Centre. ISBN: 0 88936 713 2.

Best, Marigold. (1988). "Human Rights as if People Mattered." Paper presented at the Quaker Gathering, Swanick, UK, 25-27 March.

British Council and the Department for International Development. (1997). "Rights-based Approaches to Poverty Elimination." Report of a workshop, July 18, London.

Cairns, Edmund. (1997) A Safer Future: Reducing the Human Cost of Conflict. Oxford, UK: OXFAM UK. ISBN: 0 85 59838 68.

Clark, Ramsay. (1996) "Report on Civilian Impact of UN Sanctions to the Members of the Security Council." March 1, 1996. Cited in The Children are Dying: The Impact of Sanctions in Iraq. World View Forum.

Commission of the European Communities. (1991) "The Lomé Convention" in The Europe, Asia, Latin America Dialogue. Strasbourg: CEC. ISBN: 92 826 23408.

Commonwealth Secretariat. (1991). The Harare Communiqué, October 1991. Commonwealth Heads of Government Meeting. DTP: London.

. (1995) The Auckland Communiqué, November 1995. Commonwealth Heads of Government Meeting. DTP: London. ISBN: 0 85092 457 X.

Cranston, Maurice. (1973). What are Human Rights? London: The Bodley Head. ISBN: 0 370 10379 3.

Dreze, Jean and Sen, Amartya (1989) Hunger and Public Action. Oxford: Clarendon Press. ISBN: 0 19 828365 2.

The Economist. (1997) "Human Rights and Diplomacy." April 12th edition. ISSN: 830 7000.

Eriksson, John et al. (1996) The International Response to Conflict and Genocide: Lessons from the Rwanda Experience. Joint Evaluation of Emergency Assistance to Rwanda.

Getman, T. and Witte, L. (1995) "A Humanitarian Community Position Paper on Sanctions." World Vision US.

Gibson, Sam. (1997) A Human Rights Approach to Development: Clarification of Issues and Policy Guideline Proposals. Government and Institutions Department, Department for International Development. London: Frontier Consulting.

Gillies, David. (1993). Human Rights, Democracy and "Good Governance": Stretching the World Bank's Policy Frontiers. Ottawa: International Centre for Human Rights and Democratic Development.

Government and Institutions Department. ODA (UK Government) (1993) Technical Note no. 10: Taking Account of Good Government. Department for International Development. London.

Gillies, David. (1996) Between Principle and Practice: Human Rights in North-South Relations. Montreal, Quebec: McGill- Queens' University Press.

Gunatilleke, Dr. Godfrey and Dr. Aleya el Bindari Hammad, eds. (1997). Health: The Courage to Care. A Critical Analysis of the Future of International Health by the Task Force on Health in Development - Health Policy Department, World Health Organisation. Geneva: Office of Publications, WHO. WHO/HPD/97.3.

Häusermann, Julia. (1988). "Myths and Realities Concerning Economic, Social and Cultural Rights." in Human Rights. Peter Davies, ed. London: Routledge. ISBN 0415 02609 1.

Häusermann, Julia. (1989). Effects of the Acquired Immunodeficiency Syndrome on the Advancement of Women. Report on behalf of the Secretary-General to the Commission on the Status of Women, Thirty-third session, Vienna, 29 March - 7 April, 1989. UNDoc./E/CN.6/1989/6/Add.1.

Häusermann, Julia. (1991) "The Realisation and Implementation of Economic, Social and Cultural Rights." in Economic, Social and Cultural Rights-Progress and Achievements. Ralph Beddard and Dilys Hill, eds. London: Macmillan, ISBN 0 333 52196.

Häusermann, Julia and Renée Danziger. (1991). "Women and AIDS: A Human Rights Perspective." Paper presented at the VII International Conference on AIDS, Florence, 16-21 June.

Häusermann, Julia. (1991) "Fundamental Principles of Human Rights and Ethics Relevant to AIDS Policies and Legislation." Keynote address at the Open Forum, chaired by Minister Meechai, The Royal Palace, April, 1991, Bangkok, Thailand. IS/AIDS/Publ. 12/1991.

Häusermann, Julia and Renee Danziger. (1992). The Rights and Humanity Declaration and Charter on HIV/AIDS. Submitted to the forty-eighth session of the UN Commission on Human Rights. Häusermann, J., and Danziger, R., ISBN 1 874680 01 9 (UN Doc. E/CN.4/1992/1).

Häusermann, Julia. (1994). "Good governance and human rights: two sides of the same coin?" in Good Governance: Report of a One World Action Seminar. London: One World Action.

Häusermann, Julia et al. (1994) Human Rights and Cultural Policies in a Changing Europe: The Right to Participate in Cultural Life. Report of European Round Table, organised by Rights and Humanity, CIRCLE and the Council of Europe, 30 April - 2 May, 1993, Helsinki, Finland. Helsinki: Arts Council of Finland.

Häusermann, Julia. (1995). Integrating Economic and Social Rights Into the Bill of Rights Contained in the South African Constitution. Keynote presentation at Public Hearing on Socio-Economic Rights in the Bill of Rights, South African Constitutional Assembly, Theme Committee 4 - Fundamental Rights, National Parliament, Cape Town, 1 August.

Häusermann, Julia (1997) Securing All Human Rights for All People: A Government Obligation Under International Law Background Paper for One World Action Seminar with the Foreign Secretary, Robin Cook, Foreign Policy in the Twenty- First Century, 29 October, 1997

Häusermann, Julia. (1997) "The Right to the Highest Attainable Standard of Physical and Mental Health." Conceptual Working Paper prepared in collaboration with WHO for the Informal Consultation on the Rights to the Highest Attainable Standard of Physical and Mental Health. December 4-5, 1997. Geneva.

The Human Rights Council of Australia Inc. (1995). The Rights Way to Development: A Human Rights Approach to Development Assistance. Sydney, Australia: Breakout Printing. ISBN: 0 646 23559 1.

International Bank for Reconstruction and Development. (1997). World Development Report.

. (1986) "The Limburg Priniciples on the Implementation of the International Covenant on Economic, Social and Cultural Rights." Expert Meeting on the nature and scope of the obligations of States Parties to the International Covenant on Economic, Social and Cultural Rights. University of Limburg, Netherlands, June 2-6.

. (1997) "Maastricht Guidelines on Violations of Economic, Social and Cultural Rights." 1997 Meeting of the Interna tional Commission of Jurists, the Urban Morgan Institute on Human Rights, and the Centre for Human Rights at the Faculty of Law, Maastricht University. 22-26 January, Maastricht, Netherlands.

Mandela, Nelson. (1994) The Long Walk to Freedom: The Autobiography of Nelson Mandela. London: Abacus Books. ISBN: 0 349 10653 3

Muntemba, Shimwagi. (1986) Report on Food Security prepared for the World Commission on Environment and Development, Geneva.

Oakley, Ann. (1997) "A Brief History of Gender." in Who's Afraid of Feminism?:Seeing through the Backlash. Oakley, Ann and Juliet Mitchell, eds. London: Hamish Hamilton. ISBN: 0 241 136 237.

OECD. (1997) Sustainable Development: OECD Policy Approaches for the 21st Century. Paris: OECD Publications. ISBN: 92 64 15487 6.

Rights and Humanity (1993). Concluding statement of the International Round Table "Strengthening Commitment to the Universality of Human Rights" organised by Rights and Humanity, under the patronage of HRH Crown Prince Hassan bin Talal, 5-7 April 1993, Amman, Jordan.

Rights and Humanity. (1998). Report of the International Round Table "Equal Opportunities for Women: a Question of Rights and Humanity" organised by Rights and Humanity in co-operation with the Jordanian National Committee for Women, under the Patronage of HRH Princess Basma bint Talal, 8-10 April, 1997, Amman, Jordan.

Selbervik, Hilde. (1997) Aid as a Tool for Promotion of Human Rights and Democracy: What can Norway Do? Evaluation Report 7.97, Chancellor Michelsen Institute and Norwegian Ministry of Foreign Affairs. Oslo: GCSM AS Printers. ISBN: 82 7177 483 2.

Sen, Amartya. (1981). Poverty and Famine: An Essay on Entitlement and Deprivation. Oxford: Clarendon Press. ISBN: 0 19828 46 32.

South African Constitutional Assembly. (1996) Constitution of the Republic of South Africa Bill. Cape Town: Constitutional Assembly Printers. ISBN: 0 620 20182 7.

Swift, Anthony. (1997). Children for Social Change: Education for Citizenship of Street and Working Children in Brazil. Nottingham, UK: Educational Heretics Press. ISBN: 1 9002 19 09 3.

United Nations

. (1988). Human Rights: A Compilation of International Instruments. New York: United Nations Publications. ISBN: 92 1 154066 6. ISSN: 0251 7035.

. (1993). Report of the Expert Seminar on Social Integration: in Preparation for the World Summit on Social Development. The Hague, Netherlands, 27 September - 1 October.

. (1990) World Declaration on Education For All and Framework for Action to Meet Basic Learning Needs adopted by the World Conference on Education For All: Meeting Basic Learning Needs, Jomtien, Thailand

. (1993) Vienna Declaration and Programme of Action adopted by the World Conference on Human Rights, 25 June

. (1994). Programme of Action of the International Conference on Population and Development, Cairo, 5 - 13 September. New York: United Nations Department of Public Information.

. (1995). Declaration and Programme of Action of the World Summit for Social Development, Copenhagen, 6-12 March. New York: UNDPI.

. (1995). The Beijing Declaration and Platform for Action adopted by the Fourth World Conference on Women, Beijing, 4-15 September. New York: UNDPI.

. (1996). Rome Declaration on World Food Security and World Food Summit Plan of Action, Rome, 13 November.

UNDP. (1997). Human Development Report. New York, Oxford: Oxford University Press. ISBN: 0 19 511996 7.

UNDP. (1998) Integrating Human Rights with Sustainable Human Development New York: UNDPI

WHO. (1988). Social Aspects of AIDS Prevention and Control Programmes. WHO/SPA/GLO/87.2 Geneva: WHO Office of Publications.

WHO. (1994). Health in Development: Prospects for the 21st Century. Report of the first meeting of the Task Force on Health in Development 27-30 June, Geneva. Office of Publications: Geneva. WHO/DGH/94.5.

WHO. (1995). Report of the Second Meeting of the Task Force on Health in Development. Office of Publications: Geneva. WHO/DGH/95.4.

WHO. (1996). Report of the Third Meeting of the Task Force on Health in Development. Office of Publications: Geneva. WHO/HPD/96.1 Rev.1.

WHO. (1996) Report of the Fourth Meeting of the Task Force on Health in Development. Office of Publications: Geneva. WHO/HPD/96.6.

WHO. (1997) Ninth General Programme of Work, Covering the Period 1996-2001. Geneva: Office of WHO Publications.
ISSN: 92 4 180011 9.

World Vision. (1997) Sanctions - Still Stacking Up the Bodies: the Failure of the Concept of Humanitarian Windows.

SUGGESTED FURTHER
READING

Cook, Rebecca. (1994). Women's Health and Human Rights. Geneva: WHO Office of Publications. ISBN: 92 4 156166 1.

Eide, Aisbjorn, Wenche Barth Eide, Susantha Gunnatilake, Joan Gussow, and Omawale, eds. (1984). Food as a Human Right. Tokyo: The United Nations University. ISBN: 92 808 0503 7.

Häusermann, Julia. (1993). The Right to Health. Contribution to the Day of General Discussion, UN Committee on Economic, Social and Cultural Rights, Ninth Session, United Nations, Geneva, 6 IS/ESCR/Publ.12/1993.

. (1993). The case for using a human rights framework to promote women's health. Keynote paper presented at the interagency/interregional meeting on the Global Commission on Women's Health, WHO, Geneva, 8-10 March. IS/Health/Publ.1/1993.

Rights and Humanity. (1994). Analytical report of the intersessional informal consultations in preparation for the World Summit for Social Development. UN headquarters, New York, 24-28 London: IS/Dev/Publ.9/1994.

. (1995). Analysis of the health content of the Declaration and Programme for Action adopted at the World Summit for Social Development. An outline of the drafting history. Copenhagen, March, 1995 London: IS/Dev/Publ.14/1995
. (1995). The right to food and health as a basis for Social Development. Report of a joint briefing by Rights and Humanity and the health caucus with FAO and WHO. UN headquarters, New York, 19 January 1995. London: IS/Dev/Publ.11/1995

Tomasevski, Katarina. (1989) <u>Development Aid and Human Rights.</u> Danish Center for Human Rights. London: Pinter Publishers. ISBN: 0 86187 736 5.

WHO. (1948). Constitution of the World Health Organization. Date of adoption: 22 July 1946. Date of entry into force: 7 April 1948.

. (1986) <u>Intersectoral Action for Health: The Role of Intersectoral Co-operation in National Strategies for Health For All</u>. Geneva: WHO Office of Publications. ISBN: 92 4 156 096 7.

. (1991). <u>Report of the International Forum on Health: A Conditionality for Economic Development - Breaking the Cycle of Poverty and Inequity</u>. Accra, Ghana. (document WHO/DGO/92.1).

. (1992) <u>Health Dimensions of Economic Reform</u>. Geneva: WHO Office of Publications. ISBN: 92 4 156146 7.

. (1995). <u>Health in social development.</u> Position Paper for the World Summit for Social Development, Copenhagen, March. Geneva. Document WHO/DGH/95.1.

. (1995). "Declaration on the Centrality of Health in Social Development." Adopted by the Task Force on Health in Development at the meeting "Health, Development and Poverty" in Paris, 17 February. Geneva: Office of WHO Publications.

. (1996). <u>Report of the Consultation on Health as a Bridge for Peace</u>. Geneva, 15 May 1996. Geneva: Office of WHO Publications. WHO/HPD/96.7/Rev.1.

. (1996). "Partnerships for health in the 21st century". Working paper prepared by the Working Group on Partnerships in the Context of Health-for-All Renewal. Document HPR/96.3, draft No.3. Geneva: Office of WHO Publications.

. (1997). <u>The World Health Report: Conquering Suffering, Enriching Humanity</u>. France: Office of Publications. ISBN: 92 4 156185 8.

WHO Regional Office for South-East Asia. (1997). <u>Poverty and Health: South-East Asia</u>. New Delhi, India.

WHO Task Force on Violence and Health. (1997). <u>Violence and Health Information Pack.</u> Geneva: WHO Office of Publications.

COMPLETE LIST OF RIGHTS AND HUMANITY'S TITLES

HUMAN RIGHTS AND	Hunger - A Human Rights Concern	IS/Dev/Publ.1/1987
DEVELOPMENT	The Right to Development - Legal Briefing	IS/LegBr.2/1987
	People on the Margins of Society - Legal Briefing	IS/LegBr.3/1987
	Statistical Note on Poverty in Europe with particular reference to the UK	IS/GenBr.1/1987
	Economically and Socially Disadvantaged People: Strategies for Action	Afr/Publ.1/1987
	The Jos Declaration on the Rights of the Economically and Socially	
	Disadvantaged People in Africa	Afr/Publ.2/1987
	Human Rights as a Framework for Economic and Social Justice	IS/Dev/Publ.2/1989
	Sudan Update - Reconstruction and Development Newsletter	IS/Dev/Publ.3/1989
	Human Rights as a Framework for Economic and Social Justice	IS/Dev/Publ.4/1990
	Human Rights, Development, and the Relationship between the NGO	
	Community and Government Agencies	IS/Dev/Publ.5/1992
	Good Governance and Human Rights: Two Sides of the Same Coin?	IS/Dev/Publ.7/1994
	A Rights Based Approach to Social Development -	
	What does it have to offer?	IS/Dev/Publ.8/1994
	Analytical Report of the Intersessional Informal Consultations	IS/Dev/Publ.9/1994
	The Right to Food and Health as a Basis for Social Development	IS/Dev/Publ.11/1995
	Analytical Report of the Third Preparatory Committee of the World	
	Summit for Social Development	IS/Dev/Publ.12/1995
	Equity and Social Justice for All. Proposals for Policies and Strategies for Europe	IS/Dev/Publ.13/1995
	Analysis of thc Health Content of the Declaration and Programme of	
	Action adopted at the World Summit for Social Development	IS/Dev/Publ.14/1995
	References to "International Financial Institutions" in the Declaration	
	and Programme of Action of the World Summit for Social Development	IS/Dev/Publ.15/1995
	References to "Rights" in the Declaration and Programme of Action of the	
	World Summit for Social Development	IS/Dev/Publ.16/1995
	References to "Health" in the Declaration and Programme of Action of the	
	World Summit for Social Development	
	IS/Dev/Publ.17/1995	
	References to "Refugees", "Asylum Seekers", "Migrants" and "Displaced	
	Persons" in the Declaration and Programme of Action of the World	
	Summit for Social Development	IS/Dev/Publ.18/1995
	Governments' Commitments for Social Development: Extracts from the	
	Declaration and Programme of Action of the World Summit for Social	
	Development	IS/Dev/Publ.19/1995
	Report of the Human Rights Caucus of the World Summit for Social	
	Development	IS/Dev/Publ.20/1995
	Human Rights and Development	IS/Dev/Publ.21/1995
	Human Rights and Development in South Africa	IS/Dev/Publ.22/1995
	Equity and Social Justice for All - Report of Pan European Round Table	IS/Dev/Publ.23/1995
	Gender and Human Rights	IS/Dev/Publ.24/1997
	Securing All Human Rights for All People: A Government Obligation Under	
	International Law	IS/Dev/Publ.25/1997
ECONOMIC, SOCIAL AND	The International Covenant on Economic, Social and Cultural Rights, and	
CULTURAL RIGHTS	the International Covenant on Civil and Political Rights: An Introduction	
	to their provisions and the procedures for enforcement	IS/LegBr.1/1986
	Overview of the First Session of the UN Committee on Economic, Social	
	and Cultural Rights	IS/ESCR/Publ.1/1987
	The Indivisibility and Interdependence of Human Rights: A Call for Greater	
	Priority to be given to Economic, Social and Cultural Rights	
	IS/ESCR/Publ.2/1988	
	A Turning Point - Report of the Second Session of the UN Committee on	
	Economic, Social and Cultural Rights	IS/ESCR/Publ.3/1988
	Myths and Realities about Economic, Social and Cultural Rights	
	IS/ESCR/Publ.4/1988	
	Analytical Report of the Third Session of the UN Committee on	
	Economic, Social and Cultural Rights	IS/ESCR/Publ.5/1989
	Analytical Report of the Fourth Session of the UN Committee on	
	Economic, Social and Cultural Rights	IS/ESCR/Publ.6/1990
	Analytical Report of the Fifth Session of the UN Committee on	
	Economic, Social and Cultural Rights	IS/ESCR/Publ.7/1990
	The Realisation and Implementation of Economic, Social and Cultural	
	Rights	IS/ESCR/Publ.8/1991
	The Right to Adequate Housing protected under the International Covenant	
	On Economic, Social and Cultural Rights	IS/ESCR/Publ.9/1993
	The Use of Indicators to Measure Realisation of the Right to take part in	
	Cultural Life	IS/ESCR/Publ.10/1993
	Final Statement of the European Round Table "Human Rights and Cultural	
	Policies in a Changing Europe: The Right to Participate in Cultural Life"	
	IS/ESCR/Publ.11/1993	
	The Right to Health Paper presented to a Day of General Discussion	
	Committee on ESCR- UN Committee on Economic, Social and Cultural Rights	
	Ninth Session	IS/ESCR/Publ.12/1993
	Human Rights and Cultural Policies in a Changing Europe: The Right to	
	Participate in Cultural Life. Helsinki: University Press.	
	ISBN: 951 47 98228.	IS/ESCR/Publ.13/1994

	Social Safety Nets - Paper presented to a Day of General Discussion Committee on ESCR a Human Rights Agenda	IS/ESCR/Publ.14/1994
	Human Rights Education - Paper presented to a Day of General Discussion Committee on ESCR UN Committee on Economic, Social and Cultural Rights Eleventh Session	IS/ESCR/Publ.15/1995
	Integrating Economic, Social and Cultural Rights into the Bill of Rights Contained in the South African Constitution	IS/ESCR/Publ.16/1995
	Securing All Human Rights for All People: A Government Obligation Under International Law	IS/Dev/Publ.25/1997
HEALTH AND HUMAN RIGHTS	The Case for Using a Human Rights Framework to Promote Women's Health	IS/Health/Publ.1/1993
	The Right to Health	IS/ESCR/Publ.12/1993
	Report of a Sub Group Meeting of the WHO Task Force on Health in Development Policies IS/Health/Publ.2/1993	
	The Right to Food and Health as a Basis for Social Development	IS/Dev/Publ.11/1995
	Analysis of the Health Content of the Declaration and Programme of Action adopted at the World Summit for Social Development	IS/Dev/Publ.14/1995
	Health in Social Development	IS/Health/Publ.4/1995
	References to "Health" in the Declaration and Programme of Action of the World Summit for Social Development	IS/Dev/Publ.17/1995
	Violence Against Women: A European Study	IS/Health/Publ.5/1995
	Violence Against Women - A Crime Against Humanity	IS/Health/Publ.6/1995
	Preventing and Redressing Domestic Violence Using a Health and Human Rights Approach	IS/Health/Publ.7/1996
	Gender and Human Rights	IS/Dev/Publ.24/1997
	A Health and Human Rights Approach to the Prevention and Redress of Domestic Violence: Some Proposals for a Regional Strategy IS/Health/Publ.8/1997	
	The Right to the Highest Attainable Standard of Physical and Mental Health: Working Paper for the WHO Informal Consultation On Health and Human Rights	IS/Health/Publ.9/1997
HUMAN RIGHTS IN THE CONTEXT OF HIV/AIDS	Human Rights and the International AIDS Crisis	IS/AIDS/Publ.1/1987
	Effects of the Acquired Immunodeficiency Syndrome on the Advancement of Women	IS/AIDS/Publ.2/1989
	AIDS and its effects on the Advancement of Women	IS/AIDS/Publ.3/1989
	AIDS and Human Movement in the Commonwealth	IS/AIDS/Publ.4/1989
	Ethical and Social Aspects of AIDS in Africa	IS/AIDS/Publ.5/1989
	Report of First Sub-Regional Workshop for Countries in East Africa on Ethical and Social Aspects of AIDS in Africa	IS/AIDS/Publ.6/1989
	Survey of Women's Organisations in Britain with AIDS Programmes in the UK or Overseas	IS/AIDS/Publ.7/1989
	Ethical and Social Aspects of AIDS in Africa	IS/AIDS/Publ.8/1990
	Report of Second Sub-Regional Workshop for Countries in West Africa on Ethical and Social Aspects of AIDS in Africa IS/AIDS/Publ.9/1990	
	Ethical and Social Aspects of AIDS in Africa	IS/AIDS/Publ.10/1990
	AIDS: Breaking Down The Barriers (Video)	IS/Video.8/1990
	Women and AIDS: The Social Context IS/AIDS/Publ.11/1990	
	Fundamental Principles of Human Rights and Ethics Relevant to AIDS Policies and Legislation	IS/AIDS/Publ.12/1991
	AIDS: A Question of Rights and Humanity - Background Document for Global Expert Meeting, the Hague	IS/AIDS/Publ.13/1991
	AIDS: A Question of Rights and Humanity - Opening Statement for Global Expert Meeting, the Hague IS/AIDS/Publ.14/1991	
	Discrimination against People Infected with HIV or People with AIDS	IS/AIDS/Publ.15/1991
	Women and AIDS: A Human Rights Perspective	IS/AIDS/Publ.16/1991
	HIV and AIDS in the Context of Human Rights: Towards Strategies for Promoting Respect for Individual Rights and Dignity	IS/AIDS/Publ.17/1991
	Promoting Respect for Human Rights in the Context of AIDS: Priorities For Funders	IS/AIDS/Publ.19/1991
	The Human Rights Dimensions of HIV/AIDS	IS/AIDS/Publ.20/1992
	Report of the Pan-European Consultation on HIV/AIDS in the Context of Public Health and Human Rights	IS/AIDS/Publ.21/1992
	The Rights and Humanity Declaration and Charter on HIV/AIDS IS/AIDS/Publ.22/1992	
	International Law, Advocacy and Human Rights in the Context of AIDS	IS/AIDS/Publ.23/1992
	Discrimination against People Infected with HIV or People with AIDS	IS/AIDS/Publ.24/1992
	Briefing on AIDS and Discrimination for UN Sub-Commission on Prevention of Discrimination and Protection of Minorities IS/AIDS/Publ.25/1992	
	Protecting Human Rights in the Context of HIV/AIDS	IS/AIDS/Publ.26/1993

The Impact of AIDS on the Rights of the Child	IS/AIDS/Publ.27/1994
Human Rights and HIV/AIDS	IS/AIDS/Publ.28/1994
Discrimination in the Context of HIV or AIDS	IS/AIDS/Publ.29/1994
Promoting Respect for Human Rights in the Context of HIV/AIDS:	
A Church and Community Response	IS/AIDS/Publ.30/1995
Briefing Note on Resolutions of the Commission on Human Rights and	
the Sub-Commission on the Prevention of Discrimination and the	
Protection of Minorities on Human Rights in the Context of HIV/AIDS	IS/AIDS/Publ.31/1995
Strategies to Ensure Respect for Human Rights and Ethics in the Context	
Of the HIV/AIDS Pandemic: A Global Survey	IS/AIDS/Publ.32/1996

THE UNIVERSALITY OF HUMAN RIGHTS AND RESPONSIBILITIES

Human Rights: A Universal Responsibility	IS/Uni/Publ.1/1988
Rights, Responsibilities, and the Universality of Human Rights - Article in World	
Goodwill's Newsletter 1989 (No. 2)	
IS/Uni/Publ.2/1989	
Strengthening the Commitment to the Universality of Human Rights	
- Presentation By HRH Crown Prince El Hassan Bin Talal,	
at Rights and Humanity Round Table, Amman, Jordan, 5-7 April 1993	IS/Uni/Publ.3/1993
Strengthening the Commitment to the Universality of Human Rights	
Report of the Rights and Humanity Round Table,	
Amman, Jordan, 5-7 April 1993	IS/Uni/Publ.4/1993
Promoting a Global Ethic of Human Responsibility	
IS/Uni/Publ.6/1993	
Strengthening the Commitment to the Universality of Human Rights	IS/Uni/Publ.7/1994
Universality of Human Rights and the Equal Rights of Women	IS/Uni/Publ.8/1995

Many of these items are available at cost price. Please quote the right hand reference number when making enquiries to:

Rights and Humanity
65A Swinton Street
London WC1X 9NT

Tel: (+44) 171 837 4188
Fax: (+44) 171 278 4576

e-mail: rights.humanity@pop3.poptel.org.uk

The Universal Declaration of Human Rights
Adopted and proclaimed by General Assembly resolution 217 A (III) of
10 December 1948

PREAMBLE

Whereas recognition of the inherent dignity and of the equal and inalienable rights of all members of the human family is the foundation of freedom, justice and peace in the world,

Whereas disregard and contempt for human rights have resulted in barbarous acts which have outraged the conscience of mankind, and the advent of a world in which human beings shall enjoy freedom of speech and belief and freedom from fear and want has been proclaimed as the highest aspiration of the common people,

Whereas it is essential, if man is not to be compelled to have recourse, as a last resort, to rebellion against tyranny and oppression, that human rights should be protected by the rule of law,

Whereas it is essential to promote the development of friendly relations between nations,

Whereas the peoples of the United Nations have in the Charter reaffirmed their faith in fundamental human rights, in the dignity and worth of the human person and in the equal rights of men and women and have determined to promote social progress and better standards of life in larger freedom,

Whereas Member States have pledged themselves to achieve, in cooperation with the United Nations, the promotion of universal respect for and observance of human rights and fundamental freedoms,

Whereas a common understanding of these rights and freedoms is of the greatest importance for the full realization of this pledge,

Now, therefore,

The General Assembly,

Proclaims this Universal Declaration of Human Rights as a common standard of achievement for all peoples and all nations, to the end that every individual and every organ of society, keeping this Declaration constantly in mind, shall strive by teaching and education to promote respect for these rights and freedoms and by progressive measures, national and international, to secure their universal and effective recognition and observance, both among the peoples of Member States themselves and among the peoples of territories under their jurisdiction.

Article I
All human beings are born free and equal in dignity and rights. They are endowed with reason and conscience and should act towards one another in a spirit of brotherhood.

Article 2
Everyone is entitled to all the rights and freedoms set forth in this Declaration, without distinction of any kind, such as race, colour, sex, language, religion, political or other opinion, national or social origin, property, birth or other status.

Furthermore, no distinction shall be made on the basis of the political, jurisdictional or international status of the country or territory to which a person belongs, whether it be independent, trust, non-self-governing or under any other limitation of sovereignty.

Article 3
Everyone has the right to life, liberty and security of person.

Article 4
No one shall be held in slavery or servitude; slavery and the slave trade shall be prohibited in all their forms.

Article 5
No one shall be subjected to torture or to cruel, inhuman or degrading treatment or punishment.

Article 6
Everyone has the right to recognition everywhere as a person before the law.

Article 7
All are equal before the law and are entitled without any discrimination to equal protection of the law. All are entitled to equal protection against any discrimination in violation of this

Declaration and against any incitement to such discrimination.
Article 8

Everyone has the right to an effective remedy by the competent national tribunals for acts violating the fundamental
rights granted him by the constitution or by law.

Article 9
No one shall be subjected to arbitrary arrest, detention or exile.

Article 10
Everyone is entitled in full equality to a fair and public hearing by an independent and impartial tribunal, in the determination of his rights and obligations and of any criminal charge against him.

Article 11
1. Everyone charged with a penal offence has the right to be presumed innocent until proved guilty according to law in a public trial at which he has had all the guarantees necessary for his defence.
2. No one shall be held guilty of any penal offence on account of any act or omission which did not constitute a penal offence, under national or international law, at the time when it was committed. Nor shall a heavier penalty be imposed than the one that was applicable at the time the penal offence was committed.

Article 12
No one shall be subjected to arbitrary interference with his privacy, family, home or correspondence, nor to attacks upon his honour and reputation. Everyone has the right to the protection of the law against such interference or attacks.

Article 13
1. Everyone has the right to freedom of movement and residence within the borders of each State.
2. Everyone has the right to leave any country, including his own, and to return to his country.

Article 14
1. Everyone has the right to seek and to enjoy in other countries asylum from persecution.
2. This right may not be invoked in the case of prosecutions genuinely arising from non-political crimes or from acts contrary to the purposes and principles of the United Nations.

Article 15
1. Everyone has the right to a nationality.
2. No one shall be arbitrarily deprived of his nationality nor denied the right to change his nationality.

Article 16
1. Men and women of full age, without any limitation due to race, nationality or religion, have the right to marry and to found a family. They are entitled to equal rights as to marriage, during marriage and at its dissolution.
2. Marriage shall be entered into only with the free and full consent of the intending spouses.
3. The family is the natural and fundamental group unit of society and is entitled to protection by society and the State.

Article 17
1. Everyone has the right to own property alone as well as in association with others.
2. No one shall be arbitrarily deprived of his property.

Article 18
Everyone has the right to freedom of thought, conscience and religion; this right includes freedom to change his religion or belief, and freedom, either alone or in community with others and in public or private, to manifest his religion or belief in teaching, practice, worship and observance.

Article 19
Everyone has the right to freedom of opinion and expression; this right includes freedom to hold opinions without interference and to seek, receive and impart information and ideas through any media and regardless of frontiers.

Article 20
1. Everyone has the right to freedom of peaceful assembly and association.
2. No one may be compelled to belong to an association.

Article 21
1. Everyone has the right to take part in the government of his country, directly or through freely chosen representatives.
2. Everyone has the right to equal access to public service in his country.
3. The will of the people shall be the basis of the authority of government; this will shall be expressed in periodic and genuine elections which shall be by universal and equal suffrage and shall be held by secret vote or by equivalent free voting procedures.

Article 22
Everyone, as a member of society, has the right to social security and is entitled to realization, through national effort and international co-operation and in accordance with the organization and resources of each State, of the economic, social and cultural rights indispensable for his dignity and the free development of his personality.

Article 23
1. Everyone has the right to work, to free choice of employment, to just and favourable conditions of work and to protection against unemployment.
2. Everyone, without any discrimination, has the right to equal pay for equal work.
3. Everyone who works has the right to just and favourable remuneration ensuring for himself and his family an existence worthy of human dignity, and supplemented, if necessary, by other means of social protection.
4. Everyone has the right to form and to join trade unions for the protection of his interests.

Article 24
Everyone has the right to rest and leisure, including reasonable limitation of working hours and periodic holidays with pay.

Article 25
1. Everyone has the right to a standard of living adequate for the health and well-being of himself and of his family, including food, clothing, housing and medical care and necessary social services, and the right to security in the event of unemployment, sickness, disability, widowhood, old age or other lack of livelihood in circumstances beyond his control.
2. Motherhood and childhood are entitled to special care and assistance. All children, whether born in or out of wedlock, shall enjoy the same social protection.

Article 26
1. Everyone has the right to education. Education shall be free, at least in the elementary and fundamental stages. Elementary education shall be compulsory. Technical and professional education shall be made generally available and higher education shall be equally accessible to all on the basis of merit.
2. Education shall be directed to the full development of the human personality and to the strengthening of respect for human rights and fundamental freedoms. It shall promote understanding, tolerance and friendship among all nations, racial or religious groups, and shall further the activities of the United Nations for the maintenance of peace.
3. Parents have a prior right to choose the kind of education that shall be given to their children.

Article 27
1. Everyone has the right freely to participate in the cultural life of the community, to enjoy the arts and to share in scientific advancement and its benefits.
2. Everyone has the right to the protection of the moral and material interests resulting from any scientific, literary or artistic production of which he is the author.

Article 28
Everyone is entitled to a social and international order in which the rights and freedoms set forth in this Declaration can be fully realized.

Article 29
1. Everyone has duties to the community in which alone the free and full development of his personality is possible.
2. In the exercise of his rights and freedoms, everyone shall be subject only to such limitations as are determined by law solely for the purpose of securing due recognition and respect for the rights and freedoms of others and of meeting the just requirements of morality, public order and the general welfare in a democratic society.
3. These rights and freedoms may in no case be exercised contrary to the purposes and principles of the United Nations.

Article 30
Nothing in this Declaration may be interpreted as implying for any State, group or person any right to engage in any activity or to perform any act aimed at the destruction of any of the rights and freedoms set forth herein.

International Covenant on Economic, Social and Cultural Rights

Adopted and opened for signature, ratification and accession by General Assembly resolution 2200A (XXI) of 16 December 1966

ENTRY INTO FORCE: 3 January 1976, in accordance with article 27

PREAMBLE

The States Parties to the present Covenant,

Considering that, in accordance with the principles proclaimed in the Charter of the United Nations, recognition of the inherent dignity and of the equal and inalienable rights of all members of the human family is the foundation of freedom, justice and peace in the world,

Recognizing that these rights derive from the inherent dignity of the human person,

Recognizing that, in accordance with the Universal Declaration of Human Rights, the ideal of free human beings enjoying freedom from fear and want can only be achieved if conditions are created whereby everyone may enjoy his economic, social and cultural rights, as well as his civil and political rights,

Considering the obligation of States under the Charter of the United Nations to promote universal respect for, and observance of, human rights and freedoms,

Realizing that the individual, having duties to other individuals and to the community to which he belongs, is under a responsibility to strive for the promotion and observance of the rights recognized in the present Covenant,

Agree upon the following articles:

PART I

Article 1
1. All peoples have the right of self-determination. By virtue of that right they freely determine their political status and freely pursue their economic, social and cultural development.
2. All peoples may, for their own ends, freely dispose of their natural wealth and resources without prejudice to any obligations arising out of international economic co-operation, based upon the principle of mutual benefit, and international law. In no case may a people be deprived of its own means of subsistence.
3. The States Parties to the present Covenant, including those having responsibility for the administration of Non-Self-Governing and Trust Territories, shall promote the realization of the right of self-determination, and shall respect that right, in conformity with the provisions of the Charter of the United Nations.

PART II

Article 2
1. Each State Party to the present Covenant undertakes to take steps, individually and through international assistance and co-operation, especially economic and technical, to the maximum of its available resources, with a view to achieving progressively the full realization of the rights recognized in the present Covenant by all appropriate means, including particularly the adoption of legislative measures.
2. The States Parties to the present Covenant undertake to guarantee that the rights enunciated in the present Covenant will be exercised without discrimination of any kind as to race, colour, sex, language, religion, political or other opinion, national or social origin, property, birth or other status.
3. Developing countries, with due regard to human rights and their national economy, may determine to what extent they would guarantee the economic rights recognized in the present Covenant to non-nationals.

Article 3
The States Parties to the present Covenant undertake to ensure the equal right of men and women to the enjoyment of all economic, social and cultural rights set forth in the present Covenant.

Article 4
The States Parties to the present Covenant recognize that, in the enjoyment of those rights provided by the State in conformity with the present Covenant, the State may subject such rights only to such limitations as are determined by law only in so far as this may be compatible with the nature of these rights and solely for the purpose of promoting the general welfare in a democratic society.

Article 5

1. Nothing in the present Covenant may be interpreted as implying for any State, group or person any right to engage in any activity or to perform any act aimed at the destruction of any of the rights or freedoms recognized herein, or at their limitation to a greater extent than is provided for in the present Covenant.

2. No restriction upon or derogation from any of the fundamental human rights recognized or existing in any country in virtue of law, conventions, regulations or custom shall be admitted on the pretext that the present Covenant does not recognize such rights or that it recognizes them to a lesser extent.

PART III

Article 6

1. The States Parties to the present Covenant recognize the right to work, which includes the right of everyone to the opportunity to gain his living by work which he freely chooses or accepts, and will take appropriate steps to safeguard this right.

2. The steps to be taken by a State Party to the present Covenant to achieve the full realization of this right shall include technical and vocational guidance and training programmes, policies and techniques to achieve steady economic, social and cultural development and full and productive employment under conditions safeguarding fundamental political and economic freedoms to the individual.

Article 7

The States Parties to the present Covenant recognize the right of everyone to the enjoyment of just and favourable conditions of work which ensure, in particular:

(*a*) Remuneration which provides all workers, as a minimum, with:

(i) Fair wages and equal remuneration for work of equal value without distinction of any kind, in particular women being guaranteed conditions of work not inferior to those enjoyed by men, with equal pay for equal work;

(ii) A decent living for themselves and their families in accordance with the provisions of the present Covenant;

(*b*) Safe and healthy working conditions;

(*c*) Equal opportunity for everyone to be promoted in his employment to an appropriate higher level, subject to no considerations other than those of seniority and competence;

(d) Rest, leisure and reasonable limitation of working hours and periodic holidays with pay, as well as remuneration for public holidays

Article 8

1. The States Parties to the present Covenant undertake to ensure:

(*a*) The right of everyone to form trade unions and join the trade union of his choice, subject only to the rules of the organization concerned, for the promotion and protection of his economic and social interests. No restrictions may be placed on the exercise of this right other than those prescribed by law and which are necessary in a democratic society in the interests of national security or public order or for the protection of the rights and freedoms of others;

(*b*) The right of trade unions to establish national federations or confederations and the right of the latter to form or join international trade-union organizations;

(*c*) The right of trade unions to function freely subject to no limitations other than those prescribed by law and which are necessary in a democratic society in the interests of national security or public order or for the protection of the rights and freedoms of others;

(*d*) The right to strike, provided that it is exercised in conformity with the laws of the particular country.

2. This article shall not prevent the imposition of lawful restrictions on the exercise of these rights by members of the armed forces or of the police or of the administration of the State.

3. Nothing in this article shall authorize States Parties to the International Labour Organisation Convention of 1948 concerning Freedom of Association and Protection of the Right to Organize to take legislative measures which would prejudice, or apply the law in such a manner as would prejudice, the guarantees provided for in that Convention.

Article 9

The States Parties to the present Covenant recognize the right of everyone to social security, including social insurance.

Article 10

The States Parties to the present Covenant recognize that:

1. The widest possible protection and assistance should be accorded to the family, which is the natural and fundamental group unit of society, particularly for its establishment and while it is responsible for the care and education of dependent children. Marriage must be entered into with the free consent of the intending spouses.

2. Special protection should be accorded to mothers during a reasonable period before and after childbirth. During such period working mothers should be accorded paid leave or leave with adequate social security benefits.

3. Special measures of protection and assistance should be taken on behalf of all children and young persons without any discrimination for reasons of parentage or other conditions. Children and young persons should be protected from economic and social exploitation. Their employment in work harmful to their morals or health or dangerous to life or likely to hamper their normal development should be punishable by law. States should also set age limits below which the paid employment of child

labour should be prohibited and punishable by law.

Article 11

1. The States Parties to the present Covenant recognize the right of everyone to an adequate standard of living for himself and his family, including adequate food, clothing and housing, and to the continuous improvement of living conditions. The States Parties will take appropriate steps to ensure the realization of this right, recognizing to this effect the essential importance of international co-operation based on free consent.

2. The States Parties to the present Covenant, recognizing the fundamental right of everyone to be free from hunger, shall take, individually and through international co-operation, the measures, including specific programmes, which are needed:

(*a*) To improve methods of production, conservation and distribution of food by making full use of technical and scientific knowledge, by disseminating knowledge of the principles of nutrition and by developing or reforming agrarian systems in such a way as to achieve the most efficient development and utilization of natural resources;

(*b*) Taking into account the problems of both food-importing and food-exporting countries, to ensure an equitable distribution of world food supplies in relation to need.

Article 12

1. The States Parties to the present Covenant recognize the right of everyone to the enjoyment of the highest attainable standard of physical and mental health.

2. The steps to be taken by the States Parties to the present Covenant to achieve the full realization of this right shall include those necessary for:

(*a*) The provision for the reduction of the stillbirth-rate and of infant mortality and for the healthy development of the child;

(*b*) The improvement of all aspects of environmental and industrial hygiene;

(*c*) The prevention, treatment and control of epidemic, endemic, occupational and other diseases;

(*d*) The creation of conditions which would assure to all medical service and medical attention in the event of sickness.

Article 13

1. The States Parties to the present Covenant recognize the right of everyone to education. They agree that education shall be directed to the full development of the human personality and the sense of its dignity, and shall strengthen the respect for human rights and fundamental freedoms. They further agree that education shall enable all persons to participate effectively in a free society, promote understanding, tolerance and friendship among all nations and all racial, ethnic or religious groups, and further the activities of the United Nations for the maintenance of peace.

2. The States Parties to the present Covenant recognize that, with a view to achieving the full realization of this right:

(*a*) Primary education shall be compulsory and available free to all;

(*b*) Secondary education in its different forms, including technical and vocational secondary education, shall be made generally available and accessible to all by every appropriate means, and in particular by the progressive introduction of free education;

(*c*) Higher education shall be made equally accessible to all, on the basis of capacity, by every appropriate means, and in particular by the progressive introduction of free education;

(*d*) Fundamental education shall be encouraged or intensified as far as possible for those persons who have not received or completed the whole period of their primary education;

(*e*) The development of a system of schools at all levels shall be actively pursued, an adequate fellowship system shall be established, and the material conditions of teaching staff shall be continuously improved.

3. The States Parties to the present Covenant undertake to have respect for the liberty of parents and, when applicable, legal guardians to choose for their children schools, other than those established by the public authorities, which conform to such minimum educational standards as may be laid down or approved by the State and to ensure the religious and moral education of their children in conformity with their own convictions.

4. No part of this article shall be construed so as to interfere with the liberty of individuals and bodies to establish and direct educational institutions, subject always to the observance of the principles set forth in paragraph I of this article and to the requirement that the education given in such institutions shall conform to such minimum standards as may be laid down by the State.

Article 14

Each State Party to the present Covenant which, at the time of becoming a Party, has not been able to secure in its metropolitan territory or other territories under its jurisdiction compulsory primary education, free of charge, undertakes, within two years, to work out and adopt a detailed plan of action for the progressive implementation, within a reasonable number of years, to be fixed in the plan, of the principle of compulsory education free of charge for all.

Article 15

1. The States Parties to the present Covenant recognize the right of everyone:

(*a*) To take part in cultural life;

(*b*) To enjoy the benefits of scientific progress and its applications;

(*c*) To benefit from the protection of the moral and material interests resulting from any scientific, literary or artistic production of which he is the author.

2. The steps to be taken by the States Parties to the present Covenant to achieve the full realization of this right shall include those necessary for the conservation, the development and the diffusion of science and culture.

3. The States Parties to the present Covenant undertake to respect the freedom indispensable for scientific research and creative activity.

4. The States Parties to the present Covenant recognize the benefits to be derived from the encouragement and development of international contacts and co-operation in the scientific and cultural fields.

PART IV

Article 16

1. The States Parties to the present Covenant undertake to submit in conformity with this part of the Covenant reports on the measures which they have adopted and the progress made in achieving the observance of the rights recognized herein.

2. (*a*) All reports shall be submitted to the Secretary-General of the United Nations, who shall transmit copies to the Economic and Social Council for consideration in accordance with the provisions of the present Covenant;

(*b*) The Secretary-General of the United Nations shall also transmit to the specialized agencies copies of the reports, or any relevant parts therefrom, from States Parties to the present Covenant which are also members of these specialized agencies in so far as these reports, or parts therefrom, relate to any matters which fall within the responsibilities of the said agencies in accordance with their constitutional instruments.

Article 17

1. The States Parties to the present Covenant shall furnish their reports in stages, in accordance with a programme to be established by the Economic and Social Council within one year of the entry into force of the present Covenant after consultation with the States Parties and the specialized agencies concerned.

2. Reports may indicate factors and difficulties affecting the degree of fulfilment of obligations under the present Covenant.

3. Where relevant information has previously been furnished to the United Nations or to any specialized agency by any State Party to the present Covenant, it will not be necessary to reproduce that information, but a precise reference to the information so furnished will suffice.

Article 18

Pursuant to its responsibilities under the Charter of the United Nations in the field of human rights and fundamental freedoms, the Economic and Social Council may make arrangements with the specialized agencies in respect of their reporting to it on the progress made in achieving the observance of the provisions of the present Covenant falling within the scope of their activities. These reports may include particulars of decisions and recommendations on such implementation adopted by their competent organs.

Article 19

The Economic and Social Council may transmit to the Commission on Human Rights for study and general recommendation or, as appropriate, for information the reports concerning human rights submitted by States in accordance with articles 16 and 17, and those concerning human rights submitted by the specialized agencies in accordance with article 18.

Article 20

The States Parties to the present Covenant and the specialized agencies concerned may submit comments to the Economic and Social Council on any general recommendation under article 19 or reference to such general recommendation in any report of the Commission on Human Rights or any documentation referred to therein.

Article 21

The Economic and Social Council may submit from time to time to the General Assembly reports with recommendations of a general nature and a summary of the information received from the States Parties to the present Covenant and the specialized agencies on the measures taken and the progress made in achieving general observance of the rights recognized in the present Covenant.

Article 22

The Economic and Social Council may bring to the attention of other organs of the United Nations, their subsidiary organs and specialized agencies concerned with furnishing technical assistance any matters arising out of the reports referred to in this part of the present Covenant which may assist such bodies in deciding, each within its field of competence, on the advisability of international measures likely to contribute to the effective progressive implementation of the present Covenant.

Article 23

The States Parties to the present Covenant agree that international action for the achievement of the rights recognized in the present Covenant includes such methods as the conclusion of conventions, the adoption of recommendations, the furnishing of technical assistance and the holding of regional meetings and technical meetings for the purpose of consultation and study organized in conjunction with the Governments concerned.

Article 24

Nothing in the present Covenant shall be interpreted as impairing the provisions of the Charter of the United Nations and of the constitutions of the specialized agencies which define the respective responsibilities of the various organs of the United Nations and of the specialized agencies in regard to the matters dealt with in the present Covenant.

Article 25

Nothing in the present Covenant shall be interpreted as impairing the inherent right of all peoples to enjoy and utilize fully and freely their natural wealth and resources.

PART V

Article 26

1. The present Covenant is open for signature by any State Member of the United Nations or member of any of its specialized agencies, by any State Party to the Statute of the International Court of Justice, and by any other State which has been invited by the General Assembly of the United Nations to become a party to the present Covenant.

2. The present Covenant is subject to ratification. Instruments of ratification shall be deposited with the Secretary-General of the United Nations.

3. The present Covenant shall be open to accession by any State referred to in paragraph 1 of this article.

4. Accession shall be effected by the deposit of an instrument of accession with the Secretary-General of the United Nations.

5. The Secretary-General of the United Nations shall inform all States which have signed the present Covenant or acceded to it of the deposit of each instrument of ratification or accession.

Article 27

1. The present Covenant shall enter into force three months after the date of the deposit with the Secretary-General of the United Nations of the thirty-fifth instrument of ratification or instrument of accession.

2. For each State ratifying the present Covenant or acceding to it after the deposit of the thirty-fifth instrument of ratification or instrument of accession, the present Covenant shall enter into force three months after the date of the deposit of its own instrument of ratification or instrument of accession.

Article 28

The provisions of the present Covenant shall extend to all parts of federal States without any limitations or exceptions.

Article 29

1. Any State Party to the present Covenant may propose an amendment and file it with the Secretary-General of the United Nations. The Secretary-General shall thereupon communicate any proposed amendments to the States Parties to the present Covenant with a request that they notify him whether they favour a conference of States Parties for the purpose of considering and voting upon the proposals. In the event that at least one third of the States Parties favours such a conference, the Secretary-General shall convene the conference under the auspices of the United Nations. Any amendment adopted by a majority of the States Parties present and voting at the conference shall be submitted to the General Assembly of the United Nations for approval.

2. Amendments shall come into force when they have been approved by the General Assembly of the United Nations and accepted by a two-thirds majority of the States Parties to the present Covenant in accordance with their respective constitutional processes.

3. When amendments come into force they shall be binding on those States Parties which have accepted them, other States Parties still being bound by the provisions of the present Covenant and any earlier amendment which they have accepted.

Article 30

Irrespective of the notifications made under article 26, paragraph 5, the Secretary-General of the United Nations shall inform all States referred to in paragraph 1 of the same article of the following particulars:

(*a*) Signatures, ratifications and accessions under article 26;

(*b*) The date of the entry into force of the present Covenant under article 27 and the date of the entry into force of any amendments under article 29.

Article 31

1. The present Covenant, of which the Chinese, English, French, Russian and Spanish texts are equally authentic, shall be deposited in the archives of the United Nations.

2. The Secretary-General of the United Nations shall transmit certified copies of the present Covenant to all States referred to in article 26.

International Covenant on Civil and Political Rights
Adopted and opened for signature, ratification and accession by General Assembly resolution 2200A (XXI) of 16 December 1966

ENTRY INTO FORCE: 23 March 1976, in accordance with Article 49

PREAMBLE

The States Parties to the present Covenant,

Considering that, in accordance with the principles proclaimed in the Charter of the United Nations, recognition of the inherent dignity and of the equal and inalienable rights of all members of the human family is the foundation of freedom, justice and peace in the world,

Recognizing that these rights derive from the inherent dignity of the human person,

Recognizing that, in accordance with the Universal Declaration of Human Rights, the ideal of free human beings enjoying civil and political freedom and freedom from fear and want can only be achieved if conditions are created whereby everyone may enjoy his civil and political rights, as well as his economic, social and cultural rights,

Considering the obligation of States under the Charter of the United Nations to promote universal respect for, and observance of, human rights and freedoms,

Realizing that the individual, having duties to other individuals and to the community to which he belongs, is under a responsibility to strive for the promotion and observance of the rights recognized in the present Covenant,

Agree upon the following articles:

PART I

Article 1

1. All peoples have the right of self-determination. By virtue of that right they freely determine their political status and freely pursue their economic, social and cultural development.

2. All peoples may, for their own ends, freely dispose of their natural wealth and resources without prejudice to any obligations arising out of international economic co-operation, based upon the principle of mutual benefit, and international law. In no case may a people be deprived of its own means of subsistence.

3. The States Parties to the present Covenant, including those having responsibility for the administration of Non-Self-Governing and Trust Territories, shall promote the realization of the right of self-determination, and shall respect that right, in conformity with the provisions of the Charter of the United Nations.

PART II

Article 2

1. Each State Party to the present Covenant undertakes to respect and to ensure to all individuals within its territory and subject to its jurisdiction the rights recognized in the present Covenant, without distinction of any kind, such as race, colour, sex, language, religion, political or other opinion, national or social origin, property, birth or other status.

2. Where not already provided for by existing legislative or other measures, each State Party to the present Covenant undertakes to take the necessary steps, in accordance with its constitutional processes and with the provisions of the present Covenant, to adopt such legislative or other measures as may be necessary to give effect to the rights recognized in the present Covenant.

3. Each State Party to the present Covenant undertakes:

(*a*) To ensure that any person whose rights or freedoms as herein recognized are violated shall have an effective remedy, notwithstanding that the violation has been committed by persons acting in an official capacity;

(*b*) To ensure that any person claiming such a remedy shall have his right thereto determined by competent judicial, administrative or legislative authorities, or by any other competent authority provided for by the legal system of the State, and to develop the possibilities of judicial remedy;

(*c*) To ensure that the competent authorities shall enforce such remedies when granted.

Article 3

The States Parties to the present Covenant undertake to ensure the equal right of men and women to the enjoyment of all civil and political rights set forth in the present Covenant.

Article 4

1 . In time of public emergency which threatens the life of the nation and the existence of which is officially proclaimed, the States Parties to the present Covenant may take measures derogating from their obligations under the present Covenant to the extent strictly required by the exigencies of the situation, provided that such measures are not inconsistent with their other obligations under international law and do not involve discrimination solely on the ground of race, colour, sex, language, religion or social origin.

2. No derogation from articles 6, 7, 8 (paragraphs 1 and 2), 11, 15, 16 and 18 may be made under this provision.

3. Any State Party to the present Covenant availing itself of the right of derogation shall immediately inform the other States Parties to the present Covenant, through the intermediary of the Secretary-General of the United Nations, of the provisions from which it has derogated and of the reasons by which it was actuated. A further communication shall be made, through the same intermediary, on the date on which it terminates such derogation.

Article 5

1. Nothing in the present Covenant may be interpreted as implying for any State, group or person any right to engage in any activity or perform any act aimed at the destruction of any of the rights and freedoms recognized herein or at their limitation to a greater extent than is provided for in the present Covenant.

2. There shall be no restriction upon or derogation from any of the fundamental human rights recognized or existing in any State Party to the present Covenant pursuant to law, conventions, regulations or custom on the pretext that the present Covenant does not recognize such rights or that it recognizes them to a lesser extent.

PART III

Article 6

1. Every human being has the inherent right to life. This right shall be protected by law. No one shall be arbitrarily deprived of his life.

2. In countries which have not abolished the death penalty, sentence of death may be imposed only for the most serious crimes in accordance with the law in force at the time of the commission of the crime and not contrary to the provisions of the present Covenant and to the Convention on the Prevention and Punishment of the Crime of Genocide. This penalty can only be carried out pursuant to a final judgement rendered by a competent court.

3. When deprivation of life constitutes the crime of genocide, it is understood that nothing in this article shall authorize any State Party to the present Covenant to derogate in any way from any obligation assumed under the provisions of the Convention on the Prevention and Punishment of the Crime of Genocide.

4. Anyone sentenced to death shall have the right to seek pardon or commutation of the sentence. Amnesty, pardon or commutation of the sentence of death may be granted in all cases.

5. Sentence of death shall not be imposed for crimes committed by persons below eighteen years of age and shall not be carried out on pregnant women.

6. Nothing in this article shall be invoked to delay or to prevent the abolition of capital punishment by any State Party to the present Covenant.

Article 7

No one shall be subjected to torture or to cruel, inhuman or degrading treatment or punishment. In particular, no one shall be subjected without his free consent to medical or scientific experimentation.

Article 8

1. No one shall be held in slavery; slavery and the slave-trade in all their forms shall be prohibited.

2. No one shall be held in servitude.

3. (*a*) No one shall be required to perform forced or compulsory labour;

(*b*) Paragraph 3 (*a*) shall not be held to preclude, in countries where imprisonment with hard labour may be imposed as a punishment for a crime, the performance of hard labour in pursuance of a sentence to such punishment by a competent court;

(*c*) For the purpose of this paragraph the term "forced or compulsory labour" shall not include:

(i) Any work or service, not referred to in subparagraph (*b*), normally required of a person who is under detention in consequence of a lawful order of a court, or of a person during conditional release from such detention;

(ii) Any service of a military character and, in countries where conscientious objection is recognized, any national service required by law of conscientious objectors;

(iii) Any service exacted in cases of emergency or calamity threatening the life or well-being of the community;

(iv) Any work or service which forms part of normal civil obligations.

Article 9

1. Everyone has the right to liberty and security of person. No one shall be subjected to arbitrary arrest or detention. No one shall be deprived of his liberty except on such grounds and in accordance with such procedure as are established by law.

2. Anyone who is arrested shall be informed, at the time of arrest, of the reasons for his arrest and shall be promptly informed of any charges against him.

3. Anyone arrested or detained on a criminal charge shall be brought promptly before a judge or other officer authorized by law to exercise judicial power and shall be entitled to trial within a reasonable time or to release. It shall not be the general rule that persons awaiting trial shall be detained in custody, but release may be subject to guarantees to appear for trial, at any other stage of the judicial proceedings, and, should occasion arise, for execution of the judgement.

4. Anyone who is deprived of his liberty by arrest or detention shall be entitled to take proceedings before a court, in order that that court may decide without delay on the lawfulness of his detention and order his release if the detention is not lawful.

5. Anyone who has been the victim of unlawful arrest or detention shall have an enforceable right to compensation.

Article 10

1. All persons deprived of their liberty shall be treated with humanity and with respect for the inherent dignity of the human person.

2. (*a*) Accused persons shall, save in exceptional circumstances, be segregated from convicted persons and shall be subject to separate treatment appropriate to their status as unconvicted persons;

(*b*) Accused juvenile persons shall be separated from adults and brought as speedily as possible for adjudication.

3. The penitentiary system shall comprise treatment of prisoners the essential aim of which shall be their reformation and social rehabilitation. Juvenile offenders shall be segregated from adults and be accorded treatment appropriate to their age and legal status.

Article 11

No one shall be imprisoned merely on the ground of inability to fulfil a contractual obligation.

Article 12

1. Everyone lawfully within the territory of a State shall, within that territory, have the right to liberty of movement and freedom to choose his residence.

2. Everyone shall be free to leave any country, including his own.

3. The above-mentioned rights shall not be subject to any restrictions except those which are provided by law, are necessary to protect national security, public order (*ordre public*), public health or morals or the rights and freedoms of others, and are consistent with the other rights recognized in the present Covenant.

4. No one shall be arbitrarily deprived of the right to enter his own country.

Article 13

An alien lawfully in the territory of a State Party to the present Covenant may be expelled therefrom only in pursuance of a decision reached in accordance with law and shall, except where compelling reasons of national security otherwise require, be allowed to submit the reasons against his expulsion and to have his case reviewed by, and be represented for the purpose before, the competent authority or a person or persons especially designated by the competent authority.

Article 14

1. All persons shall be equal before the courts and tribunals. In the determination of any criminal charge against him, or of his rights and obligations in a suit at law, everyone shall be entitled to a fair and public hearing by a competent, independent and impartial tribunal established by law. The press and the public may be excluded from all or part of a trial for reasons of morals, public order (*ordre public*) or national security in a democratic society, or when the interest of the private lives of the parties so requires, or to the extent strictly necessary in the opinion of the court in special circumstances where publicity would prejudice the interests of justice; but any judgement rendered in a criminal case or in a suit at law shall be made public except where the interest of juvenile persons otherwise requires or the proceedings concern matrimonial disputes or the guardianship of children.

2. Everyone charged with a criminal offence shall have the right to be presumed innocent until proved guilty according to law.

3. In the determination of any criminal charge against him, everyone shall be entitled to the following minimum guarantees, in full equality:

(*a*) To be informed promptly and in detail in a language which he understands of the nature and cause of the charge against him;

(*b*) To have adequate time and facilities for the preparation of his defence and to communicate with counsel of his own choosing;

(*c*) To be tried without undue delay;

(*d*) To be tried in his presence, and to defend himself in person or through legal assistance of his own choosing; to be informed, if he does not have legal assistance, of this right; and to have legal assistance assigned to him, in any case where the interests of justice so require, and without payment by him in any such case if he does not have sufficient means to pay for it;

(*e*) To examine, or have examined, the witnesses against him and to obtain the attendance and examination of witnesses on his behalf under the same conditions as witnesses against him;

(*f*) To have the free assistance of an interpreter if he cannot understand or speak the language used in court;

(*g*) Not to be compelled to testify against himself or to confess guilt.

4. In the case of juvenile persons, the procedure shall be such as will take account of their age and the desirability of promoting their rehabilitation.

5. Everyone convicted of a crime shall have the right to his conviction and sentence being reviewed by a higher tribunal according to law.

6. When a person has by a final decision been convicted of a criminal offence and when subsequently his conviction has been reversed or he has been pardoned on the ground that a new or newly discovered fact shows conclusively that there has been a miscarriage of justice, the person who has suffered punishment as a result of such conviction shall be compensated according to law, unless it is proved that the non-disclosure of the unknown fact in time is wholly or partly attributable to him.

7. No one shall be liable to be tried or punished again for an offence for which he has already been finally convicted or acquitted in accordance with the law and penal procedure of each country.

Article 15

1. No one shall be held guilty of any criminal offence on account of any act or omission which did not constitute a criminal offence, under national or international law, at the time when it was committed. Nor shall a heavier penalty be imposed than the one that was applicable at the time when the criminal offence was committed. If, subsequent to the commission of the offence, provision is made by law for the imposition of the lighter penalty, the offender shall benefit thereby.

2. Nothing in this article shall prejudice the trial and punishment of any person for any act or omission which, at the time when it was committed, was criminal according to the general principles of law recognized by the community of nations.

Article 16

Everyone shall have the right to recognition everywhere as a person before the law.

Article 17

1. No one shall be subjected to arbitrary or unlawful interference with his privacy, family, home or correspondence, nor to unlawful attacks on his honour and reputation.

2. Everyone has the right to the protection of the law against such interference or attacks.

Article 18

1. Everyone shall have the right to freedom of thought, conscience and religion. This right shall include freedom to have or to adopt a religion or belief of his choice, and freedom, either individually or in community with others and in public or private, to manifest his religion or belief in worship, observance, practice and teaching.

2. No one shall be subject to coercion which would impair his freedom to have or to adopt a religion or belief of his choice.

3. Freedom to manifest one's religion or beliefs may be subject only to such limitations as are prescribed by law and are necessary to protect public safety, order, health, or morals or the fundamental rights and freedoms of others.

4. The States Parties to the present Covenant undertake to have respect for the liberty of parents and, when applicable, legal guardians to ensure the religious and moral education of their children in conformity with their own convictions.

Article 19

1. Everyone shall have the right to hold opinions without interference.

2. Everyone shall have the right to freedom of expression; this right shall include freedom to seek, receive and impart information and ideas of all kinds, regardless of frontiers, either orally, in writing or in print, in the form of art, or through any other media of his choice.

3. The exercise of the rights provided for in paragraph 2 of this article carries with it special duties and responsibilities. It may therefore be subject to certain restrictions, but these shall only be such as are provided by law and are necessary:

(*a*) For respect of the rights or reputations of others;

(*b*) For the protection of national security or of public order (*ordre public*), or of public health or morals.

Article 20

1. Any propaganda for war shall be prohibited by law.

2. Any advocacy of national, racial or religious hatred that constitutes incitement to discrimination, hostility or violence shall be prohibited by law.

Article 21

The right of peaceful assembly shall be recognized. No restrictions may be placed on the exercise of this right other than those imposed in conformity with the law and which are necessary in a democratic society in the interests of national security or public safety, public order (*ordre public*), the protection of public health or morals or the protection of the rights and freedoms of others.

Article 22

1. Everyone shall have the right to freedom of association with others, including the right to form and join trade unions for the protection of his interests.

2. No restrictions may be placed on the exercise of this right other than those which are prescribed by law and which are necessary in a democratic society in the interests of national security or public safety, public order (*ordre public*), the protection of public health or morals or the protection of the rights and freedoms of others. This article shall not prevent the imposition of lawful restrictions on members of the armed forces and of the police in their exercise of this right.

3. Nothing in this article shall authorize States Parties to the International Labour Organisation Convention of 1948 concerning Freedom of Association and Protection of the Right to Organize to take legislative measures which would prejudice, or to apply the law in such a manner as to prejudice the guarantees provided for in that Convention.

Article 23

1. The family is the natural and fundamental group unit of society and is entitled to protection by society and the State.
2. The right of men and women of marriageable age to marry and to found a family shall be recognized.
3. No marriage shall be entered into without the free and full consent of the intending spouses.
4. States Parties to the present Covenant shall take appropriate steps to ensure equality of rights and responsibilities of spouses as to marriage, during marriage and at its dissolution. In the case of dissolution, provision shall be made for the necessary protection of any children.

Article 24

1. Every child shall have, without any discrimination as to race, colour, sex, language, religion, national or social origin, property or birth, the right to such measures of protection as are required by his status as a minor, on the part of his family, society and the State.
2. Every child shall be registered immediately after birth and shall have a name.
3. Every child has the right to acquire a nationality.

Article 25

Every citizen shall have the right and the opportunity, without any of the distinctions mentioned in article 2 and without unreasonable restrictions:
(*a*) To take part in the conduct of public affairs, directly or through freely chosen representatives;
(*b*) To vote and to be elected at genuine periodic elections which shall be by universal and equal suffrage and shall be held by secret ballot, guaranteeing the free expression of the will of the electors;
(*c*) To have access, on general terms of equality, to public service in his country.

Article 26

All persons are equal before the law and are entitled without any discrimination to the equal protection of the law. In this respect, the law shall prohibit any discrimination and guarantee to all persons equal and effective protection against discrimination on any ground such as race, colour, sex, language, religion, political or other opinion, national or social origin, property, birth or other status.

Article 27

In those States in which ethnic, religious or linguistic minorities exist, persons belonging to such minorities shall not be denied the right, in community with the other members of their group, to enjoy their own culture, to profess and practise their own religion, or to use their own language.

PART IV

Article 28

1. There shall be established a Human Rights Committee (hereafter referred to in the present Covenant as the Committee). It shall consist of eighteen members and shall carry out the functions hereinafter provided.
2. The Committee shall be composed of nationals of the States Parties to the present Covenant who shall be persons of high moral character and recognized competence in the field of human rights, consideration being given to the usefulness of the participation of some persons having legal experience.
3. The members of the Committee shall be elected and shall serve in their personal capacity.

Article 29

1. The members of the Committee shall be elected by secret ballot from a list of persons possessing the qualifications prescribed in article 28 and nominated for the purpose by the States Parties to the present Covenant.
2. Each State Party to the present Covenant may nominate not more than two persons. These persons shall be nationals of the nominating State.
3. A person shall be eligible for renomination.

Article 30

The iinitial election shall be held no later than six months after the date of the entry into force of the present Covenant.
2. At least four months before the date of each election to the Committee, other than an election to fill a vacancy declared in accordance with article 34, the Secretary-General of the United Nations shall address a written invitation to the States Parties to the present Covenant to submit their nominations for membership of the Committee within three months.
3. The Secretary-General of the United Nations shall prepare a list in alphabetical order of all the persons thus nominated, with an indication of the States Parties which have nominated them, and shall submit it to the States Parties to the present Covenant no later than one month before the date of each election.
4. Elections of the members of the Committee shall be held at a meeting of the States Parties to the present Covenant convened by the Secretary General of the United Nations at the Headquarters of the United Nations. At that meeting, for which two thirds of the States Parties to the present Covenant shall constitute a quorum, the persons elected to the Committee shall be those nominees who obtain the largest number of votes and an absolute majority of the votes of the representatives of States Parties present and voting.

Article 31

1. The Committee may not include more than one national of the same State.
2. In the election of the Committee, consideration shall be given to equitable geographical distribution of membership and to the representation of the different forms of civilization and of the principal legal systems.

Article 32

1. The members of the Committee shall be elected for a term of four years. They shall be eligible for re-election if renominated. However, the terms of nine of the members elected at the first election shall expire at the end of two years; immediately after the first election, the names of these nine members shall be chosen by lot by the Chairman of the meeting referred to in article 30, paragraph 4.
2. Elections at the expiry of office shall be held in accordance with the preceding articles of this part of the present Covenant.

Article 33

1. If, in the unanimous opinion of the other members, a member of the Committee has ceased to carry out his functions for any cause other than absence of a temporary character, the Chairman of the Committee shall notify the Secretary-General of the United Nations, who shall then declare the seat of that member to be vacant.
2. In the event of the death or the resignation of a member of the Committee, the Chairman shall immediately notify the Secretary-General of the United Nations, who shall declare the seat vacant from the date of death or the date on which the resignation takes effect.

Article 34

1. When a vacancy is declared in accordance with article 33 and if the term of office of the member to be replaced does not expire within six months of the declaration of the vacancy, the Secretary-General of the United Nations shall notify each of the States Parties to the present Covenant, which may within two months submit nominations in accordance with article 29 for the purpose of filling the vacancy.
2. The Secretary-General of the United Nations shall prepare a list in alphabetical order of the persons thus nominated and shall submit it to the States Parties to the present Covenant. The election to fill the vacancy shall then take place in accordance with the relevant provisions of this part of the present Covenant.
3. A member of the Committee elected to fill a vacancy declared in accordance with article 33 shall hold office for the remainder of the term of the member who vacated the seat on the Committee under the provisions of that article.

Article 35

The members of the Committee shall, with the approval of the General Assembly of the United Nations, receive emoluments from United Nations resources on such terms and conditions as the General Assembly may decide, having regard to the importance of the Committee's responsibilities.

Article 36

The Secretary-General of the United Nations shall provide the necessary staff and facilities for the effective performance of the functions of the Committee under the present Covenant.

Article 37

1. The Secretary-General of the United Nations shall convene the initial meeting of the Committee at the Headquarters of the United Nations.
2. After its initial meeting, the Committee shall meet at such times as shall be provided in its rules of procedure.
3. The Committee shall normally meet at the Headquarters of the United Nations or at the United Nations Office at Geneva.

Article 38

Every member of the Committee shall, before taking up his duties, make a solemn declaration in open committee that he will perform his functions impartially and conscientiously.

Article 39

1. The Committee shall elect its officers for a term of two years. They may be re-elected.
2. The Committee shall establish its own rules of procedure, but these rules shall provide, *inter alia*, that:
(*a*) Twelve members shall constitute a quorum;
(*b*) Decisions of the Committee shall be made by a majority vote of the members present.

Article 40

1. The States Parties to the present Covenant undertake to submit reports on the measures they have adopted which give effect to the rights recognized herein and on the progress made in the enjoyment of those rights:
(*a*) Within one year of the entry into force of the present Covenant for the States Parties concerned;
(*b*) Thereafter whenever the Committee so requests.
2. All reports shall be submitted to the Secretary-General of the United Nations, who shall transmit them to the Committee for consideration. Reports shall indicate the factors and difficulties, if any, affecting the implementation of the present Covenant.

3. The Secretary-General of the United Nations may, after consultation with the Committee, transmit to the specialized agencies concerned copies of such parts of the reports as may fall within their field of competence.

4. The Committee shall study the reports submitted by the States Parties to the present Covenant. It shall transmit its reports, and such general comments as it may consider appropriate, to the States Parties. The Committee may also transmit to the Economic and Social Council these comments along with the copies of the reports it has received from States Parties to the present Covenant.

5. The States Parties to the present Covenant may submit to the Committee observations on any comments that may be made in accordance with paragraph 4 of this article.

Article 41

1. A State Party to the present Covenant may at any time declare under this article that it recognizes the competence of the Committee to receive and consider communications to the effect that a State Party claims that another State Party is not fulfilling its obligations under the present Covenant. Communications under this article may be received and considered only if submitted by a State Party which has made a declaration recognizing in regard to itself the competence of the Committee. No communication shall be received by the Committee if it concerns a State Party which has not made such a declaration. Communications received under this article shall be dealt with in accordance with the following procedure:

(*a*) If a State Party to the present Covenant considers that another State Party is not giving effect to the provisions of the present Covenant, it may, by written communication, bring the matter to the attention of that State Party. Within three months after the receipt of the communication the receiving State shall afford the State which sent the communication an explanation, or any other statement in writing clarifying the matter which should include, to the extent possible and pertinent, reference to domestic procedures and remedies taken, pending, or available in the matter;

(*b*) If the matter is not adjusted to the satisfaction of both States Parties concerned within six months after the receipt by the receiving State of the initial communication, either State shall have the right to refer the matter to the Committee, by notice given to the Committee and to the other State;

(*c*) The Committee shall deal with a matter referred to it only after it has ascertained that all available domestic remedies have been invoked and exhausted in the matter, in conformity with the generally recognized principles of international law. This shall not be the rule where the application of the remedies is unreasonably prolonged;

(*d*) The Committee shall hold closed meetings when examining communications under this article;

(*e*) Subject to the provisions of subparagraph (*c*), the Committee shall make available its good offices to the States Parties concerned with a view to a friendly solution of the matter on the basis of respect for human rights and fundamental freedoms as recognized in the present Covenant;

(*f*) In any matter referred to it, the Committee may call upon the States Parties concerned, referred to in subparagraph (*b*), to supply any relevant information;

(*g*) The States Parties concerned, referred to in subparagraph (*b*), shall have the right to be represented when the matter is being considered in the Committee and to make submissions orally and/or in writing;

(*h*) The Committee shall, within twelve months after the date of receipt of notice under subparagraph (*b*), submit a report:

(i) If a solution within the terms of subparagraph (*e*) is reached, the Committee shall confine its report to a brief statement of the facts and of the solution reached;

(ii) If a solution within the terms of subparagraph (*e*) is not reached, the Committee shall confine its report to a brief statement of the facts; the written submissions and record of the oral submissions made by the States Parties concerned shall be attached to the report. In every matter, the report shall be communicated to the States Parties concerned.

2. The provisions of this article shall come into force when ten States Parties to the present Covenant have made declarations under paragraph I of this article. Such declarations shall be deposited by the States Parties with the Secretary-General of the United Nations, who shall transmit copies thereof to the other States Parties. A declaration may be withdrawn at any time by notification to the Secretary-General. Such a withdrawal shall not prejudice the consideration of any matter which is the subject of a communication already transmitted under this article; no further communication by any State Party shall be received after the notification of withdrawal of the declaration has been received by the Secretary-General, unless the State Party concerned has made a new declaration.

Article 42

1. (*a*) If a matter referred to the Committee in accordance with article 41 is not resolved to the satisfaction of the States Parties concerned, the Committee may, with the prior consent of the States Parties concerned, appoint an *ad hoc* Conciliation Commission (hereinafter referred to as the Commission). The good offices of the Commission shall be made available to the States Parties concerned with a view to an amicable solution of the matter on the basis of respect for the present Covenant;

(*b*) The Commission shall consist of five persons acceptable to the States Parties concerned. If the States Parties concerned fail to reach agreement within three months on all or part of the composition of the Commission, the members of the Commission concerning whom no agreement has been reached shall be elected by secret ballot by a two-thirds majority vote of the Committee from among its members.

2. The members of the Commission shall serve in their personal capacity. They shall not be nationals of the States Parties concerned, or of a State not Party to the present Covenant, or of a State Party which has not made a declaration under article 41.

3. The Commission shall elect its own Chairman and adopt its own rules of procedure.

4. The meetings of the Commission shall normally be held at the Headquarters of the United Nations or at the United Nations Office at Geneva. However, they may be held at such other convenient places as the Commission may determine in consultation with the Secretary-General of the United Nations and the States Parties concerned.

5. The secretariat provided in accordance with article 36 shall also service the commissions appointed under this article.

6. The information received and collated by the Committee shall be made available to the Commission and the Commission may call upon the States Parties concerned to supply any other relevant information.

7. When the Commission has fully considered the matter, but in any event not later than twelve months after having been seized of the matter, it shall submit to the Chairman of the Committee a report for communication to the States Parties concerned:

(*a*) If the Commission is unable to complete its consideration of the matter within twelve months, it shall confine its report to a brief statement of the status of its consideration of the matter;

(*b*) If an amicable solution to the matter on the basis of respect for human rights as recognized in the present Covenant is reached, the Commission shall confine its report to a brief statement of the facts and of the solution reached;

(*c*) If a solution within the terms of subparagraph (*b*) is not reached, the Commission's report shall embody its findings on all questions of fact relevant to the issues between the States Parties concerned, and its views on the possibilities of an amicable solution of the matter. This report shall also contain the written submissions and a record of the oral submissions made by the States Parties concerned;

(*d*) If the Commission's report is submitted under subparagraph (*c*), the States Parties concerned shall, within three months of the receipt of the report, notify the Chairman of the Committee whether or not they accept the contents of the report of the Commission.

8. The provisions of this article are without prejudice to the responsibilities of the Committee under article 41.

9. The States Parties concerned shall share equally all the expenses of the members of the Commission in accordance with estimates to be provided by the Secretary-General of the United Nations.

10. The Secretary-General of the United Nations shall be empowered to pay the expenses of the members of the Commission, if necessary, before reimbursement by the States Parties concerned, in accordance with paragraph 9 of this article.

Article 43

The members of the Committee, and of the *ad hoc* conciliation commissions which may be appointed under article 42, shall be entitled to the facilities, privileges and immunities of experts on mission for the United Nations as laid down in the relevant sections of the Convention on the Privileges and Immunities of the United Nations.

Article 44

The provisions for the implementation of the present Covenant shall apply without prejudice to the procedures prescribed in the field of human rights by or under the constituent instruments and the conventions of the United Nations and of the specialized agencies and shall not prevent the States Parties to the present Covenant from having recourse to other procedures for settling a dispute in accordance with general or special international agreements in force between them.

Article 45

The Committee shall submit to the General Assembly of the United Nations, through the Economic and Social Council, an annual report on its activities.

PART V

Article 46 .

Nothing in the present Covenant shall be interpreted as impairing the provisions of the Charter of the United Nations and of the constitutions of the specialized agencies which define the respective responsibilities of the various organs of the United Nations and of the specialized agencies in regard to the matters dealt with in the present Covenant.

Article 47

Nothing in the present Covenant shall be interpreted as impairing the inherent right of all peoples to enjoy and utilize fully and freely their natural wealth and resources.

PART VI

Article 48

1. The present Covenant is open for signature by any State Member of the United Nations or member of any of its specialized agencies, by any State Party to the Statute of the International Court of Justice, and by any other State which has been invited by the General Assembly of the United Nations to become a Party to the present Covenant.

2. The present Covenant is subject to ratification. Instruments of ratification shall be deposited with the Secretary-General of the United Nations.

3. The present Covenant shall be open to accession by any State referred to in paragraph 1 of this article.

4. Accession shall be effected by the deposit of an instrument of accession with the Secretary-General of the United Nations.

5. The Secretary-General of the United Nations shall inform all States which have signed this Covenant or acceded to it of the deposit of each instrument of ratification or accession.

Article 49

1. The present Covenant shall enter into force three months after the date of the deposit with the Secretary-General of the United Nations of the thirty-fifth instrument of ratification or instrument of accession.

2. For each State ratifying the present Covenant or acceding to it after the deposit of the thirty-fifth instrument of ratification or instrument of accession, the present Covenant shall enter into force three months after the date of the deposit of its own instrument of ratification or instrument of accession.

Article 50

The provisions of the present Covenant shall extend to all parts of federal States without any limitations or exceptions.

Article 51

1. Any State Party to the present Covenant may propose an amendment and file it with the Secretary-General of the United Nations. The Secretary-General of the United Nations shall thereupon communicate any proposed amendments to the States Parties to the present Covenant with a request that they notify him whether they favour a conference of States Parties for the purpose of considering and voting upon the proposals. In the event that at least one third of the States Parties favours such a conference, the Secretary-General shall convene the conference under the auspices of the United Nations. Any amendment adopted by a majority of the States Parties present and voting at the conference shall be submitted to the General Assembly of the United Nations for approval.

2. Amendments shall come into force when they have been approved by the General Assembly of the United Nations and accepted by a two-thirds majority of the States Parties to the present Covenant in accordance with their respective constitutional processes.

3. When amendments come into force, they shall be binding on those States Parties which have accepted them, other States Parties still being bound by the provisions of the present Covenant and any earlier amendment which they have accepted.

Article 52

Irrespective of the notifications made under article 48, paragraph 5, the Secretary-General of the United Nations shall inform all States referred to in paragraph 1 of the same article of the following particulars:

(*a*) Signatures, ratifications and accessions under article 48;

(*b*) The date of the entry into force of the present Covenant under article 49 and the date of the entry into force of any amendments under article 51.

Article 53

1. The present Covenant, of which the Chinese, English, French, Russian and Spanish texts are equally authentic, shall be deposited in the archives of the United Nations.

2. The Secretary-General of the United Nations shall transmit certified copies of the present Covenant to all States referred to in article 48.

ANNEX 4: SOME RELEVANT UN DECLARATIONS

Declaration on Social Progress and Development
Proclaimed by General Assembly resolution 2542 (XXIV) of 11 December
1969

The General Assembly,

Mindful of the pledge of Members of the United Nations under the Charter to take joint and separate action in co-operation with the Organization to promote higher standards of living, full employment and conditions of economic and social progress and development,

Reaffirming faith in human rights and fundamental freedoms and in the principles of peace, of the dignity and worth of the human person, and of social justice proclaimed in the Charter,

Recalling the principles of the Universal Declaration of Human Rights, the International Covenants on Human Rights, the Declaration of the Rights of the Child, the Declaration on the Granting of Independence to Colonial Countries and Peoples, the International Convention on the Elimination of All Forms of Racial Discrimination, the United Nations Declaration on the Elimination of All Forms of Racial Discrimination, the Declaration on the Promotion among Youth of the Ideals of Peace, Mutual Respect and Understanding between Peoples, the Declaration on the Elimination of Discrimination against Women and of resolutions of the United Nations,

Bearing in mind the standards already set for social progress in the constitutions, conventions, recommendations and resolutions of the International Labour Organisation, the Food and Agriculture Organization of the United Nations, the United Nations Educational, Scientific and Cultural Organization, the World Health Organization, the United Nations Children's Fund and of other organizations concerned,

Convinced that man can achieve complete fulfilment of his aspirations only within a just social order and that it is consequently of cardinal importance to accelerate social and economic progress everywhere, thus contributing to international peace and solidarity,

Convinced that international peace and security on the one hand, and social progress and economic development on the other, are closely interdependent and influence each other,

Persuaded that social development can be promoted by peaceful coexistence, friendly relations and co-operation among States with different social, economic or political systems,

Emphasizing the interdependence of economic and social development in the wider process of growth and change, as well as the importance of a strategy of integrated development which takes full account at all stages of its social aspects,

Regretting the inadequate progress achieved in the world social situation despite the efforts of States and the international community,

Recognizing that the primary responsibility for the development of the developing countries rests on those countries themselves and acknowledging the pressing need to narrow and eventually close the gap in the standards of living between economically more advanced and developing countries and, to that end, that Member States shall have the responsibility to pursue internal and external policies designed to promote social development throughout the world, and in particular to assist developing countries to accelerate their economic growth,

Recognizing the urgency of devoting to works of peace and social progress resources being expended on armaments and wasted on conflict and destruction,

Conscious of the contribution that science and technology can render towards meeting the needs common to all humanity,

Believing that the primary task of all States and international organizations is to eliminate from the life of society all evils and obstacles to social progress, particularly such evils as inequality, exploitation, war, colonialism and racism,

Desirous of promoting the progress of all mankind towards these goals and of overcoming all obstacles to their realization,

Solemnly proclaims this Declaration on Social Progress and Development and calls for national and international action for its use as a common basis for social development policies:

PART I

PRINCIPLES

Article 1
All peoples and all human beings, without distinction as to race, colour, sex, language, religion, nationality, ethnic origin, family or social status, or political or other conviction, shall have the right to live in dignity and freedom and to enjoy the fruits of social progress and should, on their part, contribute to it.

Article 2
Social progress and development shall be founded on respect for the dignity and value of the human person and shall ensure the promotion of human rights and social justice, which requires:
(*a*) The immediate and final elimination of all forms of inequality, exploitation of peoples and individuals, colonialism and racism, including nazism and *apartheid*, and all other policies and ideologies opposed to the purposes and principles of the United Nations;
(*b*) The recognition and effective implementation of civil and political rights as well as of economic, social and cultural rights without any discrimination.

Article 3
The following are considered primary conditions of social progress and development:
(*a*) National independence based on the right of peoples to self- determination;
(*b*) The principle of non-interference in the internal affairs of States;
(*c*) Respect for the sovereignty and territorial integrity of States;
(*d*) Permanent sovereignty of each nation over its natural wealth and resources;
(*e*) The right and responsibility of each State and, as far as they are concerned, each nation and people to determine freely its own objectives of social development, to set its own priorities and to decide in conformity with the principles of the Charter of the United Nations the means and methods of their achievement without any external interference;
(*f*) Peaceful coexistence, peace, friendly relations and co-operation among States irrespective of differences in their social, economic or political systems.

Article 4
The family as a basic unit of society and the natural environment for the growth and well-being of all its members, particularly children and youth, should be assisted and protected so that it may fully assume its responsibilities within the community. Parents have the exclusive right to determine freely and responsibly the number and spacing of their children.

Article 5
Social progress and development require the full utilization of human resources, including, in particular:
(*a*) The encouragement of creative initiative under conditions of enlightened public opinion;
(*b*) The dissemination of national and international information for the purpose of making individuals aware of changes occurring in society as a whole;
(*c*) The active participation of all elements of society, individually or through associations, in defining and in achieving the common goals of development with full respect for the fundamental freedoms embodied in the Universal Declaration of Human Rights;
(*d*) The assurance to disadvantaged or marginal sectors of the population of equal opportunities for social and economic advancement in order to achieve an effectively integrated society.

Article 6
Social development requires the assurance to everyone of the right to work and the free choice of employment. Social progress and development require the participation of all members of society in productive and socially useful labour and the establishment, in conformity with human rights and fundamental freedoms and with the principles of justice and the social function of property, of forms of ownership of land and of the means of production which preclude any kind of exploitation of man, ensure equal rights to property for all and create conditions leading to genuine equality among people.

Article 7
The rapid expansion of national income and wealth and their equitable distribution among all members of society are fundamental to all social progress, and they should therefore be in the forefront of the preoccupations of every State and

Government. The improvement in the position of the developing countries in international trade resulting among other things from the achievement of favourable terms of trade and of equitable and remunerative prices at which developing countries market their products is necessary in order to make it possible to increase national income and in order to advance social development.

Article 8

Each Government has the primary role and ultimate responsibility of ensuring the social progress and well-being of its people, of planning social development measures as part of comprehensive development plans, of encouraging and co-ordinating or integrating all national efforts towards this end and of introducing necessary changes in the social structure. In planning social development measures, the diversity of the needs of developing and developed areas, and of urban and rural areas, within each country, shall be taken into due account.

Article 9

Social progress and development are the common concerns of the international community, which shall supplement, by concerted international action, national efforts to raise the living standards of peoples.

Social progress and economic growth require recognition of the common interest of all nations in the exploration, conservation, use and exploitation, exclusively for peaceful purposes and in the interests of all mankind, of those areas of the environment such as outer space and the sea-bed and ocean floor and the subsoil thereof, beyond the limits of national jurisdiction, in accordance with the purposes and principles of the Charter of the United Nations.

PART II

OBJECTIVES

Social progress and development shall aim at the continuous raising of the material and spiritual standards of living of all members of society, with respect for and in compliance with human rights and fundamental freedoms, through the attainment of the following main goals:

Article 10

(*a*) The assurance at all levels of the right to work and the right of everyone to form trade unions and workers' associations and to bargain collectively; promotion of full productive employment and elimination of unemployment and under-employment; establishment of equitable and favourable conditions of work for all, including the improvement of health and safety conditions; assurance of just remuneration for labour without any discrimination as well as a sufficiently high minimum wage to ensure a decent standard of living; the protection of the consumer;

(*b*) The elimination of hunger and malnutrition and the guarantee of the right to proper nutrition;

(*c*) The elimination of poverty; the assurance of a steady improvement in levels of living and of a just and equitable distribution of income;

(*d*) The achievement of the highest standards of health and the provision of health protection for the entire population, if possible free of charge;

(*e*) The eradication of illiteracy and the assurance of the right to universal access to culture, to free compulsory education at the elementary level and to free education at all levels; the raising of the general level of life-long education;

(*f*) The provision for all, particularly persons in low income groups and large families, of adequate housing and community services.

Social progress and development shall aim equally at the progressive attainment of the following main goals:

Article 11

(*a*) The provision of comprehensive social security schemes and social welfare services; the establishment and improvement of social security and insurance schemes for all persons who, because of illness, disability or old age, are temporarily or permanently unable to earn a living, with a view to ensuring a proper standard of living for such persons and for their families and dependants;

(*b*) The protection of the rights of the mother and child; concern for the upbringing and health of children; the provision of measures to safeguard the health and welfare of women and particularly of working mothers during pregnancy and the infancy of their children, as well as of mothers whose earnings are the sole source of livelihood for the family; the granting to women of pregnancy and maternity leave and allowances without loss of employment or wages;

(*c*) The protection of the rights and the assuring of the welfare of children, the aged and the disabled; the provision of protection for the physically or mentally disadvantaged;

(*d*) The education of youth in, and promotion among them of, the ideals of justice and peace, mutual respect and understanding among peoples; the promotion of full participation of youth in the process of national development;

(*e*) The provision of social defence measures and the elimination of conditions leading to crime and delinquency especially juvenile delinquency;

(*f*) The guarantee that all individuals, without discrimination of any kind, are made aware of their rights and obligations and receive the necessary aid in the exercise and safeguarding of their rights.

Social progress and development shall further aim at achieving the following main objectives:

Article 12

(*a*) The creation of conditions for rapid and sustained social and economic development, particularly in the developing countries; change in international economic relations; new and effective methods of international co-operation in which equality of opportunity should be as much a prerogative of nations as of individuals within a nation;

(*b*) The elimination of all forms of discrimination and exploitation and all other practices and ideologies contrary to the purposes and principles of the Charter of the United Nations;

(*c*) The elimination of all forms of foreign economic exploitation, particularly that practised by international monopolies, in order to enable the people of every country to enjoy in full the benefits of their national resources.

Social progress and development shall finally aim at the attainment of the following main goals:

Article 13

(*a*) Equitable sharing of scientific and technological advances by developed and developing countries, and a steady increase in the use of science and technology for the benefit of the social development of society;

(*b*) The establishment of a harmonious balance between scientific, technological and material progress and the intellectual, spiritual, cultural and moral advancement of humanity;

(*c*) The protection and improvement of the human environment.

PART III

MEANS AND METHODS

On the basis of the principles set forth in this Declaration, the achievement of the objectives of social progress and development requires the mobilization of the necessary resources by national and international action, with particular attention to such means and methods as:

Article 14

(*a*) Planning for social progress and development as an integrated part of balanced overall development planning;

(*b*) The establishment, where necessary, of national systems for framing and carrying out social policies and programmes, and the promotion by the countries concerned of planned regional development, taking into account differing regional conditions and needs, particularly the development of regions which are less favoured or under-developed by comparison with the rest of the country;

(*c*) The promotion of basic and applied social research, particularly comparative international research applied to the planning and execution of social development programmes.

Article 15

(*a*) The adoption of measures, to ensure the effective participation, as appropriate, of all the elements of society in the preparation and execution of national plans and programmes of economic and social development;

(*b*) The adoption of measures for an increasing rate of popular participation in the economic, social, cultural and political life of countries through national govern-mental bodies, non-governmental organizations, co-operatives, rural associations, workers' and employers' organizations and women's and youth organizations, by such methods as national and regional plans for social and economic progress and community development, with a view to achieving a fully integrated national society, accelerating the process of social mobility and consolidating the democratic system;

(*c*) Mobilization of public opinion, at both national and international levels, in support of the principles and objectives of social progress and development;

(*d*) The dissemination of social information, at the national and the international level, to make people aware of changing circumstances in society as a whole, and to educate the consumer.

Article 16

(*a*) Maximum mobilization of all national resources and their rational and efficient utilization; promotion of increased and accelerated productive investment in social and economic fields and of employment; orientation of society towards the development process;

(*b*) Progressively increasing provision of the necessary budgetary and other resources required for financing the social aspects of development;

c) Achievement of equitable distribution of national income, utilizing, *inter alia*, the fiscal system and government spending as an instrument for the equitable distribution and redistribution of income in order to promote social progress;

(*d*) The adoption of measures aimed at prevention of such an outflow of capital from developing countries as would be detrimental to their economic and social development.

Article 17

(*a*) The adoption of measures to accelerate the process of industrialization, especially in developing countries, with due regard for its social aspects, in the interests of the entire population; development of an adequate organization and legal framework conducive to an uninterrupted and diversified growth of the industrial sector; measures to overcome the adverse social effects which may result from urban development and industrialization, including automation; maintenance of a proper balance between rural and urban development, and in particular, measures designed to ensure healthier living conditions, especially in large industrial centres;

(*b*) Integrated planning to meet the problems of urbanization and urban development;

(*c*) Comprehensive rural development schemes to raise the levels of living of the rural populations and to facilitate such urban-rural relationships and population distribution as will promote balanced national development and social progress;

(*d*) Measures for appropriate supervision of the utilization of land in the interests of society. The achievement of the objectives of social progress and development equally requires the implementation of the following means and methods:

Article 18

(*a*) The adoption of appropriate legislative, administrative and other measures ensuring to everyone not only political and civil rights, but also the full realization of economic, social and cultural rights without any discrimination;

(*b*) The promotion of democratically based social and institutional reforms and motivation for change basic to the elimination of all forms of discrimination and exploitation and conducive to high rates of economic and social progress, to include land reform, in which the ownership and use of land will be made to serve best the objectives of social justice and economic development;

(*c*) The adoption of measures to boost and diversify agricultural production through, *inter alia*, the implementation of democratic agrarian reforms, to ensure an adequate and well-balanced supply of food, its equitable distribution among the whole population and the improvement of nutritional standards;

(*d*) The adoption of measures to introduce, with the participation of the Government, low-cost housing programmes in both rural and urban areas;

(*e*) Development and expansion of the system of transportation and communications, particularly in developing countries.

Article 19

(*a*) The provision of free health services to the whole population and of adequate preventive and curative facilities and welfare medical services accessible to all;

(*b*) The enactment and establishment of legislative measures and administrative regulations with a view to the implementation of comprehensive programmes of social security schemes and social welfare services and to the improvement and co-ordination of existing services;

(*c*) The adoption of measures and the provision of social welfare services to migrant workers and their families, in conformity with the provisions of Convention No. 97 of the International Labour Organisation and other international instruments relating to migrant workers;

(*d*) The institution of appropriate measures for the rehabilitation of mentally or physically disabled persons, especially children and youth, so as to enable them to the fullest possible extent to be useful members of society- these measures shall include the provision of treatment and technical appliances, education, vocational and social guidance, training and selective placement, and other assistance required-and the creation of social conditions in which the handicapped are not discriminated against because of their disabilities.

Article 20

(*a*) The provision of full democratic freedoms to trade unions; freedom of association for all workers, including the right to bargain collectively and to strike; recognition of the right to form other organizations of working people; the provision for the growing participation of trade unions in economic and social development; effective participation of all members in trade unions in the deciding of economic and social issues which affect their interests;

(*b*) The improvement of health and safety conditions for workers, by means of appropriate technological and legislative measures and the provision of the material prerequisites for the implementation of those measures, including the limitation of working hours;

(*c*) The adoption of appropriate measures for the development of harmonious industrial relations.

Article 21

(*a*) The training of national personnel and cadres, including administrative, executive, professional and technical personnel needed for social development and for overall development plans and policies;

(*b*) The adoption of measures to accelerate the extension and improvement of general, vocational and technical education and of training and retraining, which should be provided free at all levels;

(*c*) Raising the general level of education; development and expansion of national information media, and their rational and full use towards continuing education of the whole population and towards encouraging its participation in social development activities; the constructive use of leisure, particularly that of children and adolescents;

(*d*) The formulation of national and international policies and measures to avoid

the "brain drain" and obviate its adverse effects.

Article 22

(*a*) The development and co-ordination of policies and measures designed to strengthen the essential functions of the family as a basic unit of society;

(*b*) The formulation and establishment, as needed, of programmes in the field of population, within the framework of national demographic policies and as part of the welfare medical services, including education, training of personnel and the provision to families of the knowledge and means necessary to enable them to exercise their right to determine freely and responsibly the number and spacing of their children;

(*c*) The establishment of appropriate child-care facilities in the interest of children and working parents. The achievement of the objectives of social progress and development finally requires the implementation of the following means and methods:

Article 23

(*a*) The laying down of economic growth rate targets for the developing countries within the United Nations policy for development, high enough to lead to a substantial acceleration of their rates of growth;

(*b*) The provision of greater assistance on better terms; the implementation of the aid volume target of a minimum of I per cent of the gross national product at market prices of economically advanced countries; the general easing of the terms of lending to the developing countries through low interest rates on loans and long grace periods for the repayment of loans, and the assurance that the allocation of such loans will be based strictly on socioeconomic criteria free of any political considerations;

(*c*) The provision of technical, financial and material assistance, both bilateral and multilateral, to the fullest possible extent and on favourable terms, and improved co-ordination of international assistance for the achievement of the social objectives of national development plans;

(*d*) The provision to the developing countries of technical, financial and material assistance and of favourable conditions to facilitate the direct exploitation of their national resources and natural wealth by those countries with a view to enabling the peoples of those countries to benefit fully from their national resources;

(*e*) The expansion of international trade based on principles of equality and non-discrimination, the rectification of the position of developing countries in international trade by equitable terms of trade, a general nonreciprocal and non-discriminatory system of preferences for the exports of developing countries to the developed countries, the establishment and implementation of general and comprehensive commodity agreements, and the financing of reasonable buffer stocks by international institutions.

Article 24

(*a*) Intensification of international co-operation with a view to ensuring the international exchange of information, knowledge and experience concerning social progress and development;

(*b*) The broadest possible international technical, scientific and cultural co-operation and reciprocal utilization of the experience of countries with different economic and social systems and different levels of development, on the basis of mutual advantage and strict observance of and respect for national sovereignty;

(*c*) Increased utilization of science and technology for social and economic development; arrangements for the transfer and exchange of technology, including know-how and patents, to the developing countries.

Article 25

(*a*) The establishment of legal and administrative measures for the protection and improvement of the human environment, at both national and international level;

(*b*) The use and exploitation, in accordance with the appropriate international regimes, of the resources of areas of the environment such as outer space and the sea-bed and ocean floor and the subsoil thereof, beyond the limits of national jurisdiction, in order to supplement national resources available for the achievement of economic and social progress and development in every country, irrespective of its geographical location, special consideration being given to the interests and needs of the developing countries.

Article 26

Compensation for damages, be they social or economic in nature- including restitution and reparations-caused as a result of aggression and of illegal occupation of territory by the aggressor.

Article 27

(*a*) The achievement of general and complete disarmament and the channelling of the progressively released resources to be used for economic and social progress for the welfare of people everywhere and, in particular, for the benefit of developing countries;

(*b*) The adoption of measures contributing to disarmament, including, *inter alia*, the complete prohibition of tests of nuclear weapons, the prohibition of the development, production and stockpiling of chemical and bacteriological (biological) weapons and the prevention of the pollution of oceans and inland waters by nuclear wastes.

Declaration on the Right to Development
Adopted by General Assembly resolution 41/128 of 4 December 1986

The General Assembly,

Bearing in mind the purposes and principles of the Charter of the United Nations relating to the achievement of international co-operation in solving international problems of an economic, social, cultural or humanitarian nature, and in promoting and encouraging respect for human rights and fundamental freedoms for all without distinction as to race, sex, language or religion,

Recognizing that development is a comprehensive economic, social, cultural and political process, which aims at the constant improvement of the well-being of the entire population and of all individuals on the basis of their active, free and meaningful participation in development and in the fair distribution of benefits resulting therefrom,

Considering that under the provisions of the Universal Declaration of Human Rights everyone is entitled to a social and international order in which the rights and freedoms set forth in that Declaration can be fully realized,

Recalling the provisions of the International Covenant on Economic, Social and Cultural Rights and of the International Covenant on Civil and Political Rights,

Recalling further the relevant agreements, conventions, resolutions, recommendations and other instruments of the United Nations and its specialized agencies concerning the integral development of the human being, economic and social progress and development of all peoples, including those instruments concerning decolonization, the prevention of discrimination, respect for and observance of, human rights and fundamental freedoms, the maintenance of international peace and security and the further promotion of friendly relations and co-operation among States in accordance with the Charter,

Recalling the right of peoples to self-determination, by virtue of which they have the right freely to determine their political status and to pursue their economic, social and cultural development,

Recalling also the right of peoples to exercise, subject to the relevant provisions of both International Covenants on Human Rights, full and complete sovereignty over all their natural wealth and resources,

Mindful of the obligation of States under the Charter to promote universal respect for and observance of human rights and fundamental freedoms for all without distinction of any kind such as race, colour, sex, language, religion, political or other opinion, national or social origin, property, birth or other status,

Considering that the elimination of the massive and flagrant violations of the human rights of the peoples and individuals affected by situations such as those resulting from colonialism, neo-colonialism, apartheid, all forms of racism and racial discrimination, foreign domination and occupation, aggression and threats against national sovereignty, national unity and territorial integrity and threats of war would contribute to the establishment of circumstances propitious to the development of a great part of mankind,

Concerned at the existence of serious obstacles to development, as well as to the complete fulfilment of human beings and of peoples, constituted, inter alia, by the denial of civil, political, economic, social and cultural rights, and considering that all human rights and fundamental freedoms are indivisible and interdependent and that, in order to promote development, equal attention and urgent consideration should be given to the implementation, promotion and protection of civil, political, economic, social and cultural rights and that, accordingly, the promotion of, respect for and enjoyment of certain human rights and fundamental freedoms cannot justify the denial of other human rights and fundamental freedoms,

Considering that international peace and security are essential elements for the realization of the right to development,

Reaffirming that there is a close relationship between disarmament and development and that progress in the field of disarmament would considerably promote progress in the field of development and that resources released through disarmament measures should be devoted to the economic and social development and well-being of all peoples and, in particular, those of the developing countries,

Recognizing that the human person is the central subject of the development process and that development policy should therefore make the human being the main participant and beneficiary of development,

Recognizing that the creation of conditions favourable to the development of peoples and individuals is the primary responsibility of their States,

Aware that efforts at the international level to promote and protect human rights should be accompanied by efforts to establish a new international economic order,

Confirming that the right to development is an inalienable human right and that equality of opportunity for development is a prerogative both of nations and of individuals who make up nations,

Proclaims the following Declaration on the Right to Development:

Article 1
1. The right to development is an inalienable human right by virtue of which every human person and all peoples are entitled to participate in, contribute to, and enjoy economic, social, cultural and political development, in which all human rights and fundamental freedoms can be fully realized.
2. The human right to development also implies the full realization of the right of peoples to self-determination, which includes, subject to the relevant provisions of both International Covenants on Human Rights, the exercise of their inalienable right to full sovereignty over all their natural wealth and resources.

Article 2
1. The human person is the central subject of development and should be the active participant and beneficiary of the right to development.
2. All human beings have a responsibility for development, individually and collectively, taking into account the need for full respect for their human rights and fundamental freedoms as well as their duties to the community, which alone can ensure the free and complete fulfilment of the human being, and they should therefore promote and protect an appropriate political, social and economic order for development.
3. States have the right and the duty to formulate appropriate national development policies that aim at the constant improvement of the well-being of the entire population and of all individuals, on the basis of their active, free and meaningful participation in development and in the fair distribution of the benefits resulting therefrom.

Article 3
1. States have the primary responsibility for the creation of national and international conditions favourable to the realization of the right to development.
2. The realization of the right to development requires full respect for the principles of international law concerning friendly relations and co-operation among States in accordance with the Charter of the United Nations.
3. States have the duty to co-operate with each other in ensuring development and eliminating obstacles to development. States should realize their rights and fulfil their duties in such a manner as to promote a new international economic order based on sovereign equality, interdependence, mutual interest and co-operation among all States, as well as to encourage the observance and realization of human rights.

Article 4
1. States have the duty to take steps, individually and collectively, to formulate international development policies with a view to facilitating the full realization of the right to development.
2. Sustained action is required to promote more rapid development of developing countries. As a complement to the efforts of developing countries, effective international co-operation is essential in providing these countries with appropriate means and facilities to foster their comprehensive development.

Article 5
States shall take resolute steps to eliminate the massive and flagrant violations of the human rights of peoples and human beings affected by situations such as those resulting from *apartheid*, all forms of racism and racial discrimination, colonialism, foreign domination and occupation, aggression, foreign interference and threats against national sovereignty, national unity and territorial integrity, threats of war and refusal to recognize the fundamental right of peoples to self-determination.

Article 6
1. All States should co-operate with a view to promoting, encouraging and strengthening universal respect for and observance of all human rights and fundamental freedoms for all without any distinction as to race, sex, language or religion.
2. All human rights and fundamental freedoms are indivisible and interdependent; equal attention and urgent consideration should be given to the implementation, promotion and protection of civil, political, economic, social and cultural rights.
3. States should take steps to eliminate obstacles to development resulting from failure to observe civil and political rights, as well as economic social and cultural rights.

Article 7
All States should promote the establishment, maintenance and strengthening of international peace and security and, to that end, should do their utmost to achieve general and complete disarmament under effective international control, as well as to ensure that the resources released by effective disarmament measures are used for comprehensive development, in particular that of the developing countries.

Article 8

1. States should undertake, at the national level, all necessary measures for the realization of the right to development and shall ensure, *inter alia*, equality of opportunity for all in their access to basic resources, education, health services, food, housing, employment and the fair distribution of income. Effective measures should be undertaken to ensure that women have an active role in the development process. Appropriate economic and social reforms should be carried out with a view to eradicating all social injustices.

2. States should encourage popular participation in all spheres as an important factor in development and in the full realization of all human rights.

Article 9

1. All the aspects of the right to development set forth in the present Declaration are indivisible and interdependent and each of them should be considered in the context of the whole.

2. Nothing in the present Declaration shall be construed as being contrary to the purposes and principles of the United Nations, or as implying that any State, group or person has a right to engage in any activity or to perform any act aimed at the violation of the rights set forth in the Universal Declaration of Human Rights and in the International Covenants on Human Rights.

Article 10

Steps should be taken to ensure the full exercise and progressive enhancement of the right to development, including the formulation, adoption and implementation of policy, legislative and other measures at the national and international levels.

ANNEX 5: ABOUT RIGHTS AND HUMANITY

Rights and Humanity
The International Movement for the Promotion and
Realisation of Human Rights and Responsibilities

MISSION STATEMENT

Rights and Humanity promotes economic and social justice and human development for all, through respect for human rights and the observance of responsibilities at all levels of international and national governance and society; so that all people can live in dignity and achieve their full potential in a just and compassionate world.

FROM VISION TO REALITY

Rights and Humanity was established in 1986 in response to the suffering of those living in poverty and social isolation, and in the belief that human rights law and the principles of humanity provide an essential framework for appropriate remedial action at the international, national and community levels.

Strategies for Prevention

This required a new approach to human rights work. Rights and Humanity set out to complement the work of existing organisations by focusing its main attention on developing effective strategies for the *prevention* of violations, including the integration of human rights norms and principles into policy-making, education in human rights and responsibilities, and the empowerment of individuals so that they might live in accordance with their rights and dignity.

In so doing, it has developed a new holistic approach to human rights which recognises the links between human rights and development, social welfare and public policy. It considers the human person as a whole, recognising that the full dignity of people demands that both their material and spiritual needs be met, and that their rights – economic, social and cultural as well as civil and political – be fully respected and implemented. In protecting the full worth and dignity of people these rights are non-negotiable, universal and indivisible.

Human Rights:
A Universal Responsibility

Human rights law deals primarily with state responsibility, but equally important is the responsibility shared by all individuals and organs of society.

Whilst providing an essential foundation for action, human rights law is not sufficient in itself to ensure the full enjoyment of rights or respect for human dignity. It may provide the parameters of legitimate state action, but frequently it cannot offer clear guidance on appropriate strategies. For this it is necessary to consider the ethics of public policy-making. Rights and Humanity therefore uses as its basis, not only the standards and norms enshrined in the international human rights legal instruments, but also ethical principles, and those principles of humanity – mutual respect, compassion and solidarity – which act as a common bond between all peoples. By focusing on the elements common to various philosophies, faiths and cultures, Rights and Humanity encourages a truly global approach to respect for human rights and dignity.

Rights and Humanity was started by a group of African and European human rights lawyers and development workers. Today, this international humanitarian movement links people from many faiths and walks of life, united in the desire to ensure the full protection and realisation of human rights and dignity, and sharing a commitment to humanitarian principles. The global multi-faith character of Rights and Humanity is reflected in its Patrons, who are **Dom Helder Camara**, Emeritus Archbishop of Olinda and Recife, Brazil, **HRH El Hassan bin Talal**, Crown Prince of Jordan, **Sir Sigmund Sternberg**, Order of St John KCSG JP, and Nobel Laureates **His Holiness the Dalai Lama** and **Archbishop Desmund Tutu**.

Rights and Humanity was established as a non-profit making association under Swiss Law. The UK Association of Rights and Humanity is registered as a charity (charity registration number 1001555). Together with an international network of supporters in nearly sixty countries, these bodies make up the International Movement for Rights and Humanity.

In the eleven years since its establishment, Rights and Humanity has pioneered a proactive, solution-orientated approach to human rights, which has involved extensive work with policy-makers to develop strategies to promote respect for human rights and dignity in action and policy at all levels, as a foundation for development, equality, and justice.

Of particular success has been the Movement's approach to consensus-building, by which it encourages dialogue between representatives of different faith groups, professions and policy-makers, together with those suffering social isolation, poverty, or other denial of their rights. In this way, rather than identifying the lowest common denominator between conflicting views, Rights and Humanity strikes out towards a new vision of respect for human rights and dignity – a vision directed towards concrete improvements in living and working conditions commensurate with human development in dignity. It is an inclusive approach, encouraging the participation of those denied full enjoyment of their rights, as well as drawing on the wisdom and experience of different faiths, and professional and social groupings.

Rights and Humanity promotes the legal, economic, political, social, and cultural environment necessary for the realisation of human rights by all people. It promotes action to overcome the inequalities, inequities and discrimination which compound poverty, social isolation and conflict. As a result of its concern for people living in poverty it has a particular focus on women. Its concern for social isolation has taken it into new areas of discrimination, such as that suffered by people living with HIV/AIDS.

1987- 1997   A DECADE OF PROGRESS

During its first decade, Rights and Humanity has developed strategies for the practical implementation of human rights in law, policy, and action at every level of governance and society. It has focused on several key areas of public policy in order to demonstrate that the realisation of human rights is an essential pre-requisite for human development, justice and peace.

Its programme areas include:

- Promoting the protection of human rights in international and national laws
- Strengthening commitment to the universality of human rights
- Promoting a multi-faith and multi-cultural consensus on human rights and responsibilities
- Promoting a just international economic order and a human rights approach to international relations
- Promoting a human rights approach to development
- Promoting a human rights approach to health, and developing strategies and projects to implement a joint approach
- Protecting the rights of women
- Promoting respect for human rights in the context of the HIV/AIDS pandemic
- Promoting recognition of the right to cultural identity and other cultural rights
- Education and training in human rights and responsibilities

SOME KEY ACHIEVEMENTS **During its first decade, Rights and Humanity has:**

- *Raised awareness of Economic, Social and Cultural Rights, and clarified the nature and content of these rights and associated state obligations*

- *Advised the South African Constitutional Assembly in 1996 on the integration of economic and social rights into the Bill of Rights in the New Constitution*

- *Articulated and promoted the human rights framework for human development and development co-operation*

- *Secured commitment at the World Summit for Social Development, Copenhagen, 1995, to realising human rights as a pre-requisite for social development*

- *Secured commitment to a human rights approach to health within the policies and programmes of the World Health Organisation, and the Renewed Health for All Strategy*

- *Developed a coherent response to the human rights implications of the HIV/AIDS pandemic, and developed global consensus on securing respect for human rights and the principles of ethics and humanity at all levels of governance and society*

- *Established the Human Rights and Development Forum in 1992 to promote dialogue between human rights NGOs, development groups and governmental agencies*

- *Developed strategies to prevent and redress domestic violence using a health and human rights approach*

- *Secured consensus on controversial issues concerning human rights and responsibilities in the context of sexual and reproductive health at the Fourth World Conference on Women, Beijing, 1995*

- *Developed consensus in 1997 on strategies for the implementation of women's human rights in Islamic and comparable societies*

- *Developed a multi-faith, multi-cultural consensus concerning the universality of human rights in preparation of the World Conference on Human Rights, Vienna, 1993*

- *Focused international attention on cultural rights, and prompted the Council of Europe to strengthen the legal protection of cultural rights*

- Provided para-legal training for people living in poor rural and urban communities in Nigeria, and established a legal aid clinic for people living in the slums of Lagos

- *Produced and broadcast via the European Space Agency's "Olympus" Satellite, distance learning programmes on international humanitarian concerns for a Pan-European audience*

- *Provided education and training on human rights and responsibilities, tolerance and mutual respect, for students from throughout Eastern Europe, 1991 - 3*

- *Facilitated the establishment of the Jagiellonian University Centre for Education and Training in Human Rights, Krakow, Poland in 1992*

- Developed curricula and training courses in human rights and respon-sibilities for teachers, lawyers, social workers, health professionals, the police, and development workers

- *Established and taught a multi-disciplinary master's degree course on economic, social and cultural rights at Essex University, UK, in 1992*

FOR FURTHER INFORMATION PLEASE CONTACT

Rights and Humanity

65A Swinton Street,
London WC1X 9NT
Tel (44) 171 837 4188 Fax (44) 171 278 4576
e-mail: rights.humanity@pop3.poptel.org.uk